Learn To Read English With Directions In Korean
Homework
Color Edition

ISBN 978-1-945738-70-8
© 2022 – Wendy A. Charles & Alexander J. Charles
All Rights Reserved
Baldwin, New York
www.intellastic.com

All rights reserved. No portion of this book may be reproduced, stored in a retrieval system, or transmitted in any form or by any means – electronic, mechanical, photocopy, recording, video presentation, private instruction, scanning or other – except for brief quotations in critical reviews or articles, without the prior written permission of the writers.

All Rights Reserved. Printed in the USA.

Table of Contents

Unit A

Lesson 1.1	Reading Words with the Letter A/a	1
Lesson 1.2	Reading Words with the Short Vowel "a" Sound	2
Lesson 1.2	Reading & Writing Words with the Short Vowel "a" Sound	3
Lesson 1.3	Reading Words with the Long Vowel "a" Sound	4
Lesson 1.3	Reading & Writing Words with the Long Vowel "a" Sound	5
Lessons 1.2 & 1.3	Reading Short Vowel and Long Vowel Words	6
Lesson 1.4	Reading Words with the "age" Letter Combination	7
Lesson 1.5	Reading Words with the "ai" Vowel Pair	8
Lesson 1.6	Reading Letter "a" Words with the Schwa Sound	9
Lesson 1.7	Reading Words with the "ar" Letter Combination	10
Lesson 1.7	Reading Words with the "ar" Letter Combination	11
Lesson 1.8	Reading Words with a Silent Letter "a"	12
Unit Review	Reading Words with Vowel "a" Sounds: /ă/,/ā/,/ə/ & Silent	13
Lesson 1.9	Reading Multisyllable Words	14
Lesson 1.9	Reading Multisyllable Words	15
Lesson 1.10	Proper and Common Nouns and Adjectives	16

Unit B

Lesson 2.1	Reading Words with the Letter B/b	17
Lesson 2.2	Reading Words with the "br" Letter Combination	18
Lesson 2.3	Reading Words with the "bl" Letter Combination	19
Lesson 2.3	Reading Words with the "ble" Letter Combination	20
Lesson 2.4	Reading Words with the "mb" Letter Combination	21
Lesson 2.4	Reading Words with the "bt" Letter Combination	22
Lesson 2.5	Reading Words with a Silent Letter "b"	23
Lesson 2.6	Reading Multisyllable Words	24
Lesson 2.6	Reading Multisyllable Words	25
Lesson 2.7	Proper and Common Nouns and Adjectives	26

Unit C

Lesson 3.1	Reading Words with the Letter C/c	27
Lesson 3.1	Reading Words with the Hard Letter "c"	28
Lesson 3.2	Reading Words with the Soft Letter "c"	29
Lessons 3.1 & 3.2	Reading Hard Letter "c" and Soft Letter "c" Words	30
Lesson 3.3	Reading Words with the "cr" Letter Combination	31
Lesson 3.4	Reading Words with the "cl" Letter Combination	32
Lesson 3.4	Reading Words with the "cle" Letter Combination	33
Lesson 3.5	Reading Words with the "ct" Letter Combination	34
Lesson 3.6	Reading Soft Letter "c" Words	35
Lesson 3.6	Reading Soft Letter "c" Words	36
Lesson 3.7	Reading Words with the "ch" Letter Combination	37
Lesson 3.8	Reading Words with the "cc" Letter Combination	38
Lesson 3.9	Reading Words with a Silent Letter "c"	39
Lesson 3.10	Reading Multisyllable Words	40
Lesson 3.10	Reading Multisyllable Words	41
Lesson 3.11	Proper and Common Nouns and Adjectives	42

Unit D

Lesson 4.1	Reading Words with the Letter D/d	43
Lesson 4.2	Reading Letter "d" Words with the /d/ Sound & /j/ Sound	44
Lesson 4.2	Reading Words with the "dr" Letter Combination	45
Lesson 4.3	Reading Words with the "ed" Suffix/ Past Tense Verbs	46
Lesson 4.4	Reading Words with a Silent Letter "d"	47
Lesson 4.5	Reading Multisyllable Words	48
Lesson 4.5	Reading Multisyllable Words	49
Lesson 4.6	Proper and Common Nouns and Adjectives	50

Unit E

Lesson 5.1	Reading Words with the Letter E/e	51
Lesson 5.2	Reading Words with the Short Vowel "e" Sound	52
Lesson 5.2	Reading & Writing Words with the Short Vowel "e" Sound	53

Lesson 5.3	Reading Words with the Long Vowel "e" Sound	54
Lesson 5.3	Reading & Writing Words with the Long Vowel "e" Sound	55
Lessons 5.2 & 5.3	Reading Short Vowel and Long Vowel Words	56
Lesson 5.4	Reading Words with Letter "e" Vowel Pairs	57
Lesson 5.5	Reading Words with the Final Letter "e"	58
Lesson 5.6	Reading Letter "e" Words with the Schwa Vowel Sound	59
Lesson 5.7	Reading Words with the "er" Letter Combination	60
Lesson 5.8	Reading Words with the "eu" and "ew" Letter Combinations	61
Lesson 5.9	Reading Words with the "ey" Letter Combination	62
Lesson 5.10	Reading Words with a Silent Letter "e"	63
Unit Review	Reading Words with Vowel "e" Sounds: /ĕ/, /ē/, /ə/ & Silent	64
Lesson 5.11	Reading Multisyllable Words	65
Lesson 5.11	Reading Multisyllable Words	66
Lesson 5.12	Proper and Common Nouns and Adjectives	67

Unit F

Lesson 6.1	Reading Words with the Letter F/f	68
Lesson 6.2	Reading Words with the "fr" Letter Combination	69
Lesson 6.3	Reading Words with the "fl" Letter Combination	70
Lesson 6.3	Reading Words with the "fle" Letter Combination	71
Lesson 6.4	Reading Words with the "ft," "lf" and "ff" Letter Combinations	72
Lesson 6.5	Reading Words with a Silent Letter "f"	73
Lesson 6.6	Reading Singular and Plural forms of Words Ending in "-f" & "-fe"	74
Lesson 6.7	Reading Multisyllable Words	75
Lesson 6.7	Reading Multisyllable Words	76
Lesson 6.8	Proper and Common Nouns and Adjectives	77

Unit G

Lesson 7.1	Reading Words with the Letter G/g	78
Lesson 7.1	Reading Words with the Hard Letter "g"	79
Lesson 7.2	Reading Words with the Soft Letter G/g	80
Lessons 7.1 & 7.2	Reading Hard Letter "g" and Soft Letter "g" Words	81

Lessons 7.1 & 7.2	Reading Hard Letter "g" and Soft Letter "g" Words	82
Lesson 7.3	Reading Words with the "gr" Letter Combination	83
Lesson 7.4	Reading Words with the "gl" Letter Combination	84
Lesson 7.4	Reading Words with the "gle" Letter Combination	85
Lesson 7.5	Reading Words with the "gh" Letter Combination	86
Lesson 7.6	Reading Words with the "gn" Letter Combination	87
Lesson 7.7	Reading Words with a Silent Letter "g"	88
Lesson 7.8	Reading Multisyllable Words	89
Lesson 7.8	Reading Multisyllable Words	90
Lesson 7.9	Proper and Common Nouns and Adjectives	91

Unit H

Lesson 8.1	Reading Words with the Letter H/h	92
Lesson 8.2	Reading Words with the Letter "h" Combinations: "sh," "wh," "ch," "th," "rh," "ph" and "gh"	93
Lesson 8.2	Reading Words with the Letter "h" Combinations: "sh," "wh," "ch," "th," "rh," "ph," "gh" and "sch"	94
Lesson 8.3	Reading Words with a Silent Letter "h"	95
Lesson 8.4	Reading Multisyllable Words	96
Lesson 8.4	Reading Multisyllable Words	97
Lesson 8.5	Proper and Common Nouns and Adjectives	98

Unit I

Lesson 9.1	Reading Words with the Letter I/i	99
Lesson 9.2	Reading Words with the Short Vowel "i" Sound	100
Lesson 9.2	Reading & Writing Words with the Short Vowel "i" Sound	101
Lesson 9.3	Reading Words with the Long Vowel "i" Sound	102
Lesson 9.3	Reading & Writing Words with the Long Vowel "i" Sound	103
Lessons 9.2 & 9.3	Reading Short Vowel and Long Vowel Words	104
Lesson 9.4	Reading Words with Letter "i" Vowel Pairs	105
Lesson 9.5	Reading Words with the Final Letter "i"	106
Lesson 9.6	Reading Letter "i" Words with the Schwa Vowel Sound	107

Lesson 9.7	Reading Words with the "ir" Letter Combination	108
Lesson 9.8	Reading Letter "i" Words with the Long Vowel "e" Sound	109
Lesson 9.9	Reading Words with a Silent Letter "i"	110
Unit Review	Reading Words with Vowel "i" Sounds: /ĭ/, /ī/, /ə/ & Silent	111
Lesson 9.10	Reading Multisyllable Words	112
Lesson 9.10	Reading Multisyllable Words	113
Lesson 9.11	Proper and Common Nouns and Adjectives	114

Unit J

Lesson 10.1	Reading Words with the Letter J/j	115
Lesson 10.2	Reading Multisyllable Words	116
Lesson 10.2	Reading Multisyllable Words	117
Lesson 10.3	Proper and Common Nouns and Adjectives	118

Unit K

Lesson 11.1	Reading Words with the Letter K/k	119
Lesson 11.2	Reading Words with the Letter "k" and "ck" Letter Combination	120
Lesson 11.3	Reading Words with the "kle" Letter Combination	121
Lesson 11.4	Reading Words with a Silent Letter "k"	122
Lesson 11.5	Reading Multisyllable Words	123
Lesson 11.5	Reading Multisyllable Words	124
Lesson 11.6	Proper and Common Nouns and Adjectives	125

Unit L

Lesson 12.1	Reading Words with the Letter L/l	126
Lesson 12.2	Reading Words with the Letter "l" Combinations: "fl," "pl" & "sl"	127
Lesson 12.3	Reading Words with a Silent Letter "l"	128
Lesson 12.4	Reading Multisyllable Words	129
Lesson 12.4	Reading Multisyllable Words	130
Lesson 12.5	Proper and Common Nouns and Adjectives	131

Unit M

Lesson 13.1	Reading Words with the Letter M/m	132
Lesson 13.2	Reading Words with a Silent Letter "m"	133
Lesson 13.3	Reading Multisyllable Words	134
Lesson 13.3	Reading Multisyllable Words	135
Lesson 13.4	Proper and Common Nouns and Adjectives	136

Unit N

Lesson 14.1	Reading Words with the Letter N/n	137
Lesson 14.2	Reading Words with the "ng" Letter Combination	138
Lesson 14.3	Reading Words with a Silent Letter "n"	139
Lesson 14.4	Reading Multisyllable Words	140
Lesson 14.4	Reading Multisyllable Words	141
Lesson 14.5	Proper and Common Nouns and Adjectives	142

Unit O

Lesson 15.1	Reading Words with the Letter O/o	143
Lesson 15.2	Reading Words with the Short Vowel "o" Sound	144
Lesson 15.2	Reading & Writing Words with the Short Vowel "o" Sound	145
Lesson 15.3	Reading Words with the Long Vowel "o" Sound	146
Lesson 15.3	Reading & Writing Words with the Long Vowel "o" Sound	147
Lessons 15.2 & 15.3	Reading Short Vowel and Long Vowel Words	148
Lesson 15.4	Reading Words with Letter "o" Vowel Pairs	149
Lesson 15.5	Reading Words with the Final Letter "o"	150
Lesson 15.6	Reading Letter "o" Words with the Schwa Vowel Sound	151
Lesson 15.7	Reading Words with Vowel "o" Sounds: /ŏ/, /ō/ & /$\overline{oo}$/	152
Lesson 15.8	Reading Words with the "or" Letter Combination	153
Lesson 15.8	Reading Words with the "or" Letter Combination	154
Lesson 15.9	Reading Words with a Silent Letter "o"	155
Unit Review	Reading Words with Vowel "o" Sounds: /ŏ/, /ō/, /ə/ & Silent	156
Lesson 15.10	Reading Multisyllable Words	157
Lesson 15.10	Reading Multisyllable Words	158

Lesson 15.11	Proper and Common Nouns and Adjectives	159

Unit P

Lesson 16.1	Reading Words with the Letter P/p	160
Lesson 16.2	Reading Words with the "ph" Letter Combination	161
Lesson 16.3	Reading Words with the "pr" Letter Combination	162
Lesson 16.4	Reading Words with the "pl" Letter Combination	163
Lesson 16.4	Reading Words with the "ple" Letter Combination	164
Lesson 16.5	Reading Words with a Silent Letter "p"	165
Lesson 16.6	Reading Multisyllable Words	166
Lesson 16.6	Reading Multisyllable Words	167
Lesson 16.7	Proper and Common Nouns and Adjectives	168

Unit Q

Lesson 17.1	Reading Words with the Letter Q/q	169
Lesson 17.2	Reading Words with the Letter "q" and "qu" Letter Combination	170
Lesson 17.2	Reading Words with the "qu" Letter Combination	171
Lesson 17.3	Reading Multisyllable Words	172
Lesson 17.3	Reading Multisyllable Words	173
Lesson 17.4	Proper and Common Nouns and Adjectives	174

Unit R

Lesson 18.1	Reading Words with the Letter R/r	175
Lesson 18.2	Reading Words with the Letter "r" Combinations: "br," "cr," "dr," "fr," "gr," "pr" and "tr"	176
Lesson 18.3	Reading Multisyllable Words	177
Lesson 18.3	Reading Multisyllable Words	178
Lesson 18.4	Proper and Common Nouns and Adjectives	179

Unit S

Lesson 19.1	Reading Words with the Letter S/s	180
Lesson 19.1	Reading Words with the Letter S/s	181

Lesson 19.2	Reading Words with the "sion," "sial" & "scious" Suffixes	182
Lesson 19.3	Reading Words with the "sch" Letter Combination	183
Lesson 19.4	Reading Words with the "scr," "shr," "spr" & "str" Letter Combinations	184
Lesson 19.5	Reading Words with the "sl" & "sle" Letter Combinations	185
Lesson 19.5	Reading Words with the "sle" Letter Combination	186
Lesson 19.6	Reading Words with the "sm" Letter Combination	187
Lesson 19.7	Reading Words with the "ss" Letter Combination	188
Lesson 19.8	Reading Words with a Silent Letter "s"	189
Lesson 19.9	Reading Multisyllable Words	190
Lesson 19.9	Reading Multisyllable Words	191
Lesson 19.10	Proper and Common Nouns and Adjectives	192

Unit T

Lesson 20.1	Reading Words with the Letter T/t	193
Lesson 20.2	Reading Words with the "thm" Letter Combination	194
Lesson 20.3	Reading Words with the "tion," "tial" & "tious" Suffixes	195
Lesson 20.4	Reading Words with the "tr" Letter Combination	196
Lesson 20.5	Reading Words with the "tle" Letter Combination	197
Lesson 20.6	Reading Words with the Letter "t" Sounds	198
Lesson 20.7	Reading Words with a Silent Letter "t"	199
Lesson 20.8	Reading Multisyllable Words	200
Lesson 20.8	Reading Multisyllable Words	201
Lesson 20.9	Proper and Common Nouns and Adjectives	202

Unit U

Lesson 21.1	Reading Words with the Letter U/u	203
Lesson 21.2	Reading Words with the Short Vowel "u" Sound	204
Lesson 21.2	Reading & Writing Words with the Short Vowel "u" Sound	205
Lesson 21.3	Reading Words with the Long Vowel "u" Sound	206
Lesson 21.3	Reading & Writing Words with the Long Vowel "u" Sound	207
Lessons 21.2 & 21.3	Reading Short Vowel and Long Vowel Words	208
Lesson 21.4	Reading Words with Letter "u" Vowel Pairs	209

Lesson 21.5	Reading Words with the Final Letter "u"	210
Lesson 21.6	Reading Letter "u" Words with the Schwa Vowel Sound	211
Lesson 21.7	Reading Words with the "ur" Letter Combination	212
Lesson 21.8	Reading Words with a Silent Letter "u"	213
Unit Review	Reading Words with Vowel "u" Sounds: /ŭ/, /o͞o/, /ə/ & Silent	214
Lesson 21.9	Reading Multisyllable Words	215
Lesson 21.9	Reading Multisyllable Words	216
Lesson 21.10	Proper and Common Nouns and Adjectives	217

Unit V

Lesson 22.1	Reading Words with the Letter V/v	218
Lesson 22.2	Reading Multisyllable Words	219
Lesson 22.2	Reading Multisyllable Words	220
Lesson 22.3	Proper and Common Nouns and Adjectives	221

Unit W

Lesson 23.1	Reading Words with the Letter W/w	222
Lesson 23.2	Reading Words with a Vowel before the Letter "w"	223
Lesson 23.3	Reading Words with a Silent "w" and "wr" Letter Combination	224
Lesson 23.3	Reading Words with a Silent Letter "w"	225
Lesson 23.4	Reading Multisyllable Words	226
Lesson 23.4	Reading Multisyllable Words	227
Lesson 23.5	Proper and Common Nouns and Adjectives	228

Unit X

Lesson 24.1	Reading Words with the Letter X/x	229
Lesson 24.1	Reading Words with the Letter X/x	230
Lesson 24.2	Reading Multisyllable Words	231
Lesson 24.2	Reading Multisyllable Words	232
Lesson 24.3	Proper and Common Nouns and Adjectives	233

Unit Y

Lesson 25.1	Reading Words with the Letter Y/y	234
Lesson 25.1	Reading Words with the Letter Y/y	235
Lesson 25.2	Reading Words with a Vowel before the Letter "y"	236
Lesson 25.3	Reading Words with the "cy" Letter Combination	237
Lesson 25.4	Reading Words with the Final Letter "y"	238
Lesson 25.5	Reading Words with the "yr" Letter Combination	239
Lesson 25.6	Reading Letter "y" Words with the Schwa Sound	240
Lesson 25.7	Reading Words with a Silent Letter "y"	241
Lesson 25.8	Reading Multisyllable Words	242
Lesson 25.8	Reading Multisyllable Words	243
Lesson 25.9	Proper and Common Nouns and Adjectives	244

Unit Z

Lesson 26.1	Reading Words with the Letter Z/z	245
Lesson 26.1	Reading Words with the Letter Z/z	246
Lesson 26.2	Reading Words with a Silent Letter "z"	247
Lesson 26.3	Reading Multisyllable Words	248
Lesson 26.3	Reading Multisyllable Words	249
Lesson 26.4	Proper and Common Nouns and Adjectives	250

Appendix

Appendix 1.0	Introduction of the Letter A/a	251
Appendix 2.0	Introduction of the Letter B/b	252
Appendix 2.0	Letter Recognition B/b	253
Appendix 3.0	Introduction of the Letter C/c	254
Appendix 3.0	Letter Recognition C/c	255
Appendix 4.0	Introduction of the Letter D/d	256
Appendix 4.0	Letter Recognition D/d	257
Appendix 5.0	Introduction of the Letter E/e	258
Appendix 6.0	Introduction of the Letter F/f	259
Appendix 6.0	Letter Recognition F/f	260

Appendix 7.0	Introduction of the Letter G/g	261
Appendix 7.0	Letter Recognition G/g	262
Appendix 8.0	Introduction of the Letter H/h	263
Appendix 8.0	Letter Recognition H/h	264
Appendix 9.0	Introduction of the Letter I/i	265
Appendix 10.0	Introduction of the Letter J/j	266
Appendix 10.0	Letter Recognition J/j	267
Appendix 11.0	Introduction of the Letter K/k	268
Appendix 11.0	Letter Recognition K/k	269
Appendix 12.0	Introduction of the Letter L/l	270
Appendix 12.0	Letter Recognition L/l	271
Appendix 13.0	Introduction of the Letter M/m	272
Appendix 13.0	Letter Recognition M/m	273
Appendix 14.0	Introduction of the Letter N/n	274
Appendix 14.0	Letter Recognition N/n	275
Appendix 15.0	Introduction of the Letter O/o	276
Appendix 16.0	Introduction of the Letter P/p	277
Appendix 16.0	Letter Recognition P/p	278
Appendix 17.0	Introduction of the Letter Q/q	279
Appendix 17.0	Letter Recognition Q/q	280
Appendix 18.0	Introduction of the Letter R/r	281
Appendix 18.0	Letter Recognition R/r	282
Appendix 19.0	Introduction of the Letter S/s	283
Appendix 19.0	Letter Recognition S/s	284
Appendix 20.0	Introduction of the Letter T/t	285
Appendix 20.0	Letter Recognition T/t	286
Appendix 21.0	Introduction of the Letter U/u	287
Appendix 22.0	Introduction of the Letter V/v	288
Appendix 22.0	Letter Recognition V/v	289
Appendix 23.0	Introduction of the Letter W/w	290
Appendix 23.0	Letter Recognition W/w	291

Appendix 24.0	Introduction of the Letter X/x	292
Appendix 24.0	Letter Recognition X/x	293
Appendix 25.0	Introduction of the Letter Y/y	294
Appendix 25.0	Letter Recognition Y/y	295
Appendix 26.0	Introduction of the Letter Z/z	296
Appendix 26.0	Letter Recognition Z/z	297

My Cup of Water

Name: _____ Date:___/___/_____ Score: _____

Lesson 1.1

Reading Words with the Letter A/a

✓ **Lesson Check Point**

 Directions: Read each target word. Find the letter "a" and put a check (✓) in the column that identifies its position: beginning, within or end.
지도: 각 대상 단어를 읽으십시오. 문자 "a"를 찾아 해당 위치를 나타내는 열에 확인 표시(✓)를 하십시오: 시작, 내부 또는 끝.

Target Words	Beginning (First Letter)	Within	End (Last Letter)
1. sofa			
2. basic			
3. April			
4. thankful			
5. formula			

 Directions: Read each target word. Read the words in the row and circle the word that has a different vowel "a" sound.
지도: 각 대상 단어를 읽으십시오. 행에 있는 단어를 읽고 모음 "a" 소리가 다른 단어에 동그라미를 치십시오.

Target Words				
6. clan	mass	play	can't	camp
7. plant	task	back	ants	plane
8. grass	hand	flame	nap	ask
9. stand	gate	rank	bass	has
10. bran	had	sand	raft	sauce

Name: _____ Date:___/___/_____ Score:_____

Lesson 1.2

Reading Words with the Short Vowel "a" Sound

✓ Lesson Check Point

 Directions: Read the words in the four boxes. Circle two words with the short vowel /ă/ sound. The anchor word for the short vowel /ă/ sound is apple.

지도: 네 개의 상자에 있는 단어를 읽으십시오. 짧은 모음 /ă/ 소리로 두 단어에 동그라미를 치십시오. 단모음 /ă/ 소리의 앵커 워드는apple입니다.

sake	track
wax	nail

lay	saw
pack	pad

lad	rattle
plane	car

tap	ram
ball	yarn

hat	calm
shape	van

place	tan
sale	and

 Directions: Read the words in the four boxes. Circle two words that rhyme. Rhyming words have the same ending sound, such as tap and map.

지도: 네 개의 상자에 있는 단어를 읽으십시오. 운이 맞는 두 단어에 동그라미를 치십시오. 운율이 있는 단어는 tap 및 map과 같이 끝 소리가 같습니다.

ape	fan
mall	can

snack	ball
tape	crack

palm	aunt
mass	grass

tax	day
wax	straw

law	fast
past	rain

glass	class
tall	pause

Name: _____ Date: ___/___/_____ Score: _____

Lesson 1.2

Reading & Writing Words with the Short Vowel "a" Sound

✓ **Lesson Check Point**

Directions: Read each sentence and underline three words with the short vowel /ă/ sound. Then, write the underlined words on the lines below. The anchor word for the short vowel /ă/ sound is <u>apple</u>.

지도: 각 문장을 읽고 세 단어에 짧은 모음 /ă/ 소리에 밑줄을 긋습니다. 그런 다음 밑줄 친 단어를 아래 줄에 쓰십시오. 단모음 /ă/ 소리의 기준어는 appple입니다.

Model

<u>Ann</u> raised her <u>hand</u> in <u>class</u>.

    Ann   hand   class
  _____   _____   _____

1. The large map is in the black sack.

   _____   _____   _____

2. My father's crystal glasses have cracks.

   _____   _____   _____

3. I can walk faster on the grass in the park.

   _____   _____   _____

4. The man has a large, tasty cake in his bag.

   _____   _____   _____

5. My awesome math teacher gave snacks to the class.

   _____   _____   _____

Name: _____ Date:___/___/_____ Score:_____

Lesson 1.3

Reading Words with the Long Vowel "a" Sound

✓ **Lesson Check Point**

 Directions: Read the words in the four boxes. Circle two words with the long vowel /ā/ sound. The anchor word for the long vowel /ā/ sound is <u>ape</u>.

지도: 네 개의 상자에 있는 단어를 읽으십시오. 장모음 /ā/ 소리로두단어에 동그라미를 치십시오. 장모음 /ā/ 소리의 기준어는 ape입니다.

fat	father
tape	ray

soda	hale
man	date

pages	nap
comma	bake

grass	rate
pale	plant

wail	sand
scale	map

state	cape
yam	taps

 Directions: Read the words in the four boxes. Circle two words that rhyme. Rhyming words have the same ending sound, such as <u>wait</u> and <u>date</u>.

지도: 네 개의 상자에 있는 단어를 읽으십시오. 운이 맞는 두 단어에 동그라미를 치십시오. 운율이 있는 단어는 wait 및 date와 같이 끝 소리가 같습니다.

idea	may
fast	sway

at	cake
take	alike

taste	waste
had	lack

face	sad
trace	can't

pain	asks
am	Dane

and	ago
game	tame

Name: _____ Date:___/___/_____ Score:_____

Lesson 1.3

Reading & Writing Words with the Long Vowel "a" Sound

✓ **Lesson Check Point**

Directions: Read each sentence and underline three words with the long vowel /ā/ sound. Then, write the underlined words on the lines below. The anchor word for the long vowel /ā/ sound is <u>ape</u>.

지도: 각 문장을 읽고 장모음 /ā/ 소리로 세 단어에 밑줄을 긋습니다. 그런 다음 밑줄 친 단어를 아래 줄에 쓰십시오. 장모음 /ā/ 소리의 기준어는 ape입니다.

Model

Ann has <u>grapes</u> and <u>cake</u> on her <u>plate</u>.

    grapes   cake   plate

1. She said, "It rained all day in Maine."

   _____   _____   _____

2. Diane ate two large bagels with grape jam.

   _____   _____   _____

3. Dave was brave to go into the dark cave alone.

   _____   _____   _____

4. It is not safe to wait on the train platform after dark.

   _____   _____   _____

5. Late last night, Alex baked large cakes in square pans.

   _____   _____   _____

Name: _____ Date: ___/___/_____ Score: _____

Review Lessons 1.2 & 1.3

Reading Short Vowel and Long Vowel Words

✓ **Lesson Check Point**

Directions: Read the target words in the word box. In the first column, write the words that have the short vowel /ǎ/ sound, as in the word <u>apple</u>. In the second column, write the words that have the long vowel /ā/ sound, as in the word <u>ape</u>.

지도: 단어 상자에 있는 대상 단어를 읽습니다. 첫 번째 열에는 apple이라는 단어에서와 같이 단모음 /ǎ/ 소리가 나는 단어를 씁니다. 두 번째 열에는 장모음이 포함된 단어를 쓰십시오 /ā/ 소리, 단어 ape에서와 같이.

Target Word Box				
trap	plane	gram	tape	asked
plant	same	land	snacks	paid
label	packs	cake	safe	late
crack	shape	pass	male	cap

Letter "a" has the /ǎ/ sound as in the word <u>apple</u>

Letter "a" has the /ā/ sound as in the word <u>ape</u>

Name: _____ Date: ___/___/_____ Score: _____

Lesson 1.4

Reading Words with the "age" Letter Combination

✓ **Lesson Check Point**

 Directions: Read each target word. Find the "age" letter combination and put a check (✓) in the column that correctly identifies its sounds.
지도: 각 대상 단어를 읽으십시오. "age" 문자 조합을 찾아 해당 소리를 올바르게 식별하는 열에 체크(✓)를 하십시오.

Target Words	"age" has the /ā/ + /j/ sounds as in the word stage	"age" has the /ĭ/ + /j/ sounds as in the word package	"age" has the /ä/ + /j/ or /ä/ + /zh/ sounds as in the word massage
1. pages			
2. fuselage			
3. average			
4. upstage			
5. entourage			

 Directions: Read each sentence and underline the word that has an "age" letter combination that has the /ĭ/ + /j/ sounds, as in the word package.
지도: 각 문장을 읽고 단어 package에서와 같이 /ĭ/ + /j/ 소리가 나는 "age" 문자 조합이 있는 단어에 밑줄을 긋습니다.

6. At my school, teenage students wear vintage shirts.

7. The teenage star and his entourage ate sausages and rice.

8. My agent encouraged everyone to have a relaxing massage.

9. The stage manager scheduled three performances in New York.

10. The search team found the airplane's fuselage in Anchorage, Alaska.

Name: _____ Date: ___/___/_____ Score: _____

Lesson 1.5

Reading Words with the "ai" Vowel Pair

✓ Lesson Check Point

 Directions: Read each target word. Circle the word in the column that has the same "ai" sound as the target word.
지도: 각 대상 단어를 읽으십시오. 목표 단어와 같은 "ai" 소리가 나는 열의 단어에 동그라미를 치십시오.

laid	a. face
	b. stand

plaid	a. apple
	b. main

rail	a. plaid
	b. date

brain	a. wage
	b. said

 Directions: Read each target word. Put a check (✓) under the correct column heading.
지도: 각 대상 단어를 읽으십시오. 올바른 열 제목 아래에 체크(✓)를 하십시오.

Target Words	Words have the long "a" sound as in the word <u>sail</u>	Words do not have the long "a" sound
1. plaid		
2. gain		
3. said		
4. train		

Learn To Read English With Directions In Korean   Copyrighted Material

Name: _____ Date:___/___/_____ Score:_____

Lesson 1.6

Reading Letter "a" Words with the Schwa Vowel Sound

✓ Lesson Check Point

 Directions: Read each target word. Circle the word in the column that has the same "a" sound as the target word.
지도: 각 대상 단어를 읽으십시오. 대상 단어와 동일한"a"소리가 나는 열의 단어에 동그라미를 치십시오.

| aware | a. collar |
| | b. table |

| vitamin | a. teenage |
| | b. about |

| around | a. circular |
| | b. apples |

| regular | a. educate |
| | b. across |

 Directions: Read each sentence and underline the letter "a" word that has the schwa vowel /ə/ sound. The anchor word for the letter "a" schwa vowel sound is sofa.
지도: 각 문장을 읽고 슈와 모음 /ə/ 소리가 있는 문자"a" 단어에 밑줄을 긋습니다. 문자"a" 슈와 모음 소리의 앵커 단어는 sofa입니다.

1. The large snakes are from Kenya.

2. Alex always adds sugar to his tea.

3. The artist will draw the map of Africa.

4. This Sunday, I will walk in the parade.

5. At the plaza, the cars are tan and black.

6. Mrs. Ansel's math class is very popular.

Name: _____ Date: ___/___/_____ Score: _____

Lesson 1.7

Reading Words with the "ar" Letter Combination

✓ Lesson Check Point

 Directions: Read each target word. Circle the word in the column that has the same "a" + "r" sounds as the target word.
지도: 각 대상 단어를 읽으십시오. 해당 열에 있는 단어에 동그라미를치십시오. 대상 단어와 동일한 "a" + "r" 소리가 있습니다.

yarn	a. regular
	b. chart

sugar	a. warn
	b. dollar

carrot	a. arrow
	b. cedar

scholar	a. grammar
	b. artist

 Directions: Read each target word. Put a check (✓) under the correct column heading.
지도: 각 대상 단어를 읽으십시오. 올바른 열 제목 아래에 체크(✓)를하십시오.

Target Words	"ar" has the /ă/ + /r/ sounds as in the word <u>baron</u>	"ar" has the /ə/ + /r/ sounds as in the word <u>dollar</u>	"ar" has the /ä/ + /r/ sounds as in the word <u>car</u>	"ar" has the /ô/ + /r/ sounds as in the word <u>war</u>
1. yarn				
2. sugar				
3. carrot				
4. scholar				

Name: _____ Date: ___/___/_____ Score: _____

Lesson 1.7

Reading Words with the "ar" Letter Combination

Dictionary Skills/ Vocabulary

✓ **Lesson Check Point**

Directions: Read each target word and its definition. Write the target word on the line in front of its meaning. Use a dictionary or the Internet to check your answers.

지도: 각 대상 단어와 그 정의를 읽으십시오. 의미 앞 줄에 대상단어 를 쓰십시오. 사전이나 인터넷을 사용하여 답을 확인하십시오.

Target Word Box				
Argentina	park	married	part	carriage

1. _____ a large South American country
2. _____ a vehicle that is pulled by a horse
3. _____ to have been joined in marriage
4. _____ an assigned role in a performance
5. _____ a place with trees, playgrounds and benches

Directions: Read each sentence and write the target word that correctly completes the sentence.

지도: 각 문장을읽고 다음과 같은 목표 단어를 쓰십시오. 장을올바르게 완성합니다.

6. Arnold is having a family barbecue at the _____.

7. Arsenio and I are getting _____ on March 31st.

8. The couple will have a _____ ride around the park.

9. My classmate, Arty, has a major _____ in the musical drama.

10. Do you know that Spanish is the official language of _____?

Name: _____ Date: ___/___/_____ Score: _____

Lesson 1.8

Reading Words with a Silent Letter "a"

✓ **Lesson Check Point**

Directions: Read the target words in the word box. Write the words that have a silent letter "a" in the first column. Write the words that do not have a silent letter "a" in the second column.

지도: 단어 상자에 있는 대상 단어를 읽습니다. 첫 번째 열에 묵음 문자 "a"가 있는 단어를 쓰십시오. 두 번째 열에 묵음 문자 "a"가 없는 단어를 쓰십시오.

Target Word Box				
heating	landing	chart	breadbox	many
assist	beautify	East	floating	oatmeal
camp	hand	coat	ready	teams
boar	flake	cars	half	sand

Letter "a" is silent   **Letter "a" has a letter "a" sound**

Name: _____   Date: ___/___/_____   Score: _____

Unit Review - A/a

Reading Words with Vowel "a" Sounds: /ă/, /ā/, /ə/ & Silent

✓ Lesson Check Point

Directions: Read each target word. Circle the word in the column that has the same "a" sound as the target word.

지도: 각 대상 단어를 읽으십시오. 대상 단어와 동일한 "a" 소리가 나는 열의 단어에 동그라미를 치십시오.

plane	a. zebras
	b. grapes

made	a. race
	b. past

stanza	a. umbrella
	b. flat

mamma	a. comma
	b. place

Directions: Read each target word. Put a check (✓) under the correct column heading.

지도: 각 대상 단어를 읽으십시오. 올바른 열 제목 아래에 체크(✓)를 하십시오.

Target Words	"a" has the /ă/ sound as in the word <u>apple</u>	"a" has the /ā/ sound as in the word <u>ate</u>	"a" has the /ə/ sound as in the word <u>sofa</u>	"a" is silent as in the word <u>boat</u>
1. plane				
2. made				
3. stanza				
4. mamma				

Name: _____ Date:___/___/_____ Score:_____

The Reading Challenge

Lesson 1.9

Reading Multisyllable Words

✓ **Lesson Check Point**

Directions: Read and divide each target word into syllables. Write each word and place a hyphen (-) between the syllables in the second column. Write the number of syllables in the third column. Use a dictionary or the Internet to check your answers.

지도: 각 대상 단어를 읽고 음절로 나눕니다. 각 단어를 쓰고 두 번째 열의 음절 사이에 하이픈(-)을 넣습니다. 세 번째 열에 음절 수를 쓰십시오. 사전이나 인터넷을 사용하여 답을 확인하십시오.

Target Words	Words Divided into Syllables	Number of Syllables
1. giant	_____	_____
2. constantly	_____	_____
3. observant	_____	_____
4. pregnancy	_____	_____
5. mousetrap	_____	_____
6. eyelashes	_____	_____
7. implanted	_____	_____
8. democrat	_____	_____
9. eggplant	_____	_____
10. servant	_____	_____

Name: _____ Date: ___/___/_____ Score: _____

The Reading Challenge

Lesson 1.9

Reading Multisyllable Words

✓ **Lesson Check Point**

 Directions: Read each target word. Circle the word in the row that is divided correctly into syllables. Use a dictionary or the Internet to check your answers.

지도: 각 대상 단어를 읽으십시오. 음절로 올바르게 나누어진 행에 있는 단어에 동그라미를 치십시오. 사전이나 인터넷을 사용하여 답을 확인하십시오.

Model

| important | a. im-por-tant (circled) | b. im-port-ant | c. im-porta-nt |

1. abundant	a. a-bun-dant	b. ab-un-dant	c. ab-und-ant
2. contestant	a. con-tes-tant	b. cont-es-tant	c. con-test-ant
3. advocate	a. ad-vo-cate	b. a-dvoc-ate	c. ad-voc-ate
4. dependent	a. dep-en-dent	b. de-pen-dent	c. de-pend-ent
5. elegant	a. e-leg-ant	b. el-e-gant	c. e-le-gant
6. answering	a. ans-wer-ing	b. a-nswe-ring	c. an-swer-ing
7. flamboyant	a. flam-boy-ant	b. flam-bo-yant	c. flam-boya-nt
8. ascendant	a. a-scen-dant	b. asc-en-dant	c. as-cen-dant

Name: _____ Date: ___/___/_____ Score: _____

Lesson 1.10

Reading and Writing

Proper and Common Nouns and Adjectives

Directions: Read the words in the word box. Put an (X) on the line next to each word that is written incorrectly. Remember that all proper nouns and proper adjectives are capitalized. Use a dictionary or the Internet to check your answers.

지도: 단어 상자에 있는 단어를 읽으십시오. 잘못 쓰여진 각 단어 옆의 줄에 (X)를 표시하십시오. 모든 고유 명사와 고유 형용사는 대문자임을 기억하십시오. 사전이나 인터넷을 사용하여 답을 확인하십시오.

Word Box		
__ africa	__ april	__ Alarming
__ apple Inc.	__ airport	__ alabama
__ angel	__ attraction	__ American
__ Afghanistan	__ Australian	__ Above

Directions: Read each unedited sentence and underline the word that is written incorrectly. Write each sentence correctly on the line.

지도: 편집되지 않은 각 문장을 읽고 잘못 쓰여진 단어에 밑줄을긋습 니다. 각 문장을 줄에 올바르게 쓰십시오.

Model

Andrew has a view of the <u>atlantic</u> Ocean from his apartment.
<u>Andrew has a view of the Atlantic Ocean from his apartment.</u>

1. Anna always Asks challenging questions about Asia.

_____

2. The Author wrote a book about ants and alligators.

_____

3. Our amazing, All-star athletes are competing in Athens.

_____

4. My Aunt said, "Many animals live in the Amazon Rainforest."

_____

Name: _____ Date: ___/___/_____ Score: _____

Lesson 2.1

Reading Words with the Letter B/b

✓ Lesson Check Point

Directions: Read each target word. Find the letter "b" and put a check (✓) in the column that identifies its position: beginning, within or end.
지도: 각 대상 단어를 읽으십시오. 문자"b"를 찾아 위치를 나타내는열: 시작, 내부 또는 끝에 체크(✓)를 하십시오.

Target Words	Beginning (First Letter)	Within	End (Last Letter)
1. tab			
2. limb			
3. bring			
4. about			
5. husband			

Directions: Read each sentence and underline the words that begin with the letter "b." Write all the underlined words in alphabetical order on the lines below.
지도: 각 문장을 읽고"b"로 시작하는 단어에 밑줄을 긋습니다. 밑줄친모든단어를 아래 줄에 알파벳 순서로 쓰십시오.

6. Adam has a big bat.

7. Ann has a black bag.

8. Andy's boats are blue.

9. The buds have bloomed.

10. The fat bees are by the flowers.

_____   _____   _____

_____   _____   _____

_____   _____
                _____

Name: _____ Date:___/___/_____ Score:_____

Lesson 2.2

Reading Words with the "br" Letter Combination

Dictionary Skills/ Vocabulary

 Lesson Check Point

 Directions: Read each target word and its definition. Write the letter of the definition on the line of each target word. Use a dictionary or the Internet to check your answers.
지도: 각 대상 단어와 그 정의를 읽으십시오. 각 대상 단어의 행에 정의의 문자를 씁니다. 사전이나 인터넷을 사용하여 답을 확인하십시오.

Target Words	Definitions
1. __ brakes	a. shiny, glowing reflection of light
2. __ bright	b. baked food product that is made from wheat
3. __ brook	c. separated into pieces as a result of a strong force
4. __ broke	d. a place where water flows along a small path
5. __ bread	e. device that slows down and stops a vehicle

 Directions: Read each sentence. Underline the word in the parentheses that correctly completes each sentence. Then, write the underlined word on the line.
지도: 각 문장을 읽으십시오. 각 문장을 올바르게 완성하는 괄호 안에 있는 단어에 밑줄을 긋습니다. 그런 다음 밑줄 친 단어를 줄에 쓰십시오.

6. Bret _____ the baseball bat. (bright, broke)

7. My bike's _____ are bad. (brakes, bright)

8. The sun at the bay is _____. (bread, bright)

9. Brian is sitting by the _____. (brook, brakes)

10. Brad always eats _____ for breakfast. (brook, bread)

Name: _____ Date: ___/___/_____ Score: _____

Lesson 2.3

Reading Words with the "bl" Letter Combination

Dictionary Skills/ Vocabulary

✓ Lesson Check Point

 Directions: Read each target word and its definition. Write the target word on the line in front of its meaning. Use a dictionary or the Internet to check your answers.
지도: 각 대상 단어와 그 정의를 읽으십시오. 의미 앞 줄에 대상단어 를 쓰십시오. 사전이나 인터넷을 사용하여 답을 확인하십시오.

Target Word Box				
blames	blouse	blind	blueberry	blanket

1. _____ to assign fault
2. _____ a sweet fruit
3. _____ a long loosely fitting shirt
4. _____ a person or animal's inability to see things
5. _____ a large cloth covering used to cover a bed

 Directions: Read each sentence. Underline the word in the parentheses that correctly completes each sentence. Then, write the underlined word on the line.
지도: 각 문장을 읽으십시오. 각 문장을 올바르게 완성하는 괄호 안에 있는 단어에 밑줄을 긋습니다. 그런 다음 밑줄 친 단어를 줄에 쓰십시오.

6. The _____ boys have Braille books. (blueberry, blind)

7. Bill's _____ has pictures of bats on it. (blind, blanket)

8. Beth washed her _____ with bleach. (blames, blouse)

9. Bob _____ me for eating the bananas. (blames, blanket)

10. The boys ate _____ bread at brunch. (blouse, blueberry)

Name: _____   Date: ___/___/_____   Score: _____

Lesson 2.3

Reading Words with the "ble" Letter Combination

✓ Lesson Check Point

 Directions: Read each target word. Find the "ble" letter combination and put a check (✓) in the column that identifies its position: beginning, within or end.
지도: 각 대상 단어를 읽으십시오. "ble" 문자 조합을 찾아 위치를 식별하는 열에 체크(✓)를 하십시오: 시작, 내부 또는 끝.

Target Words	Beginning (First 3 Letters)	Within	End (Last 3 Letters)
1. blew			
2. doublet			
3. capable			
4. terrible			
5. assembled			

 Directions: Read each target word. Put a check (✓) in the "yes" column if the "ble" letter combination has the /b/ + /ə/ + /l/ sounds. Put a check (✓) in the "no" column if the "ble" letter combination does not have the /b/ + /ə/ + /l/ sounds.
지도: 각 대상 단어를 읽으십시오. "ble" 문자 조합에/b/ + /ə/ + /l/ 소리가 있는 경우"yes" 열에 체크(✓)를 하십시오. "ble" 문자 조합에/b/ + /ə/ + /l/ 소리가 없으면"no"열에 체크(✓)를 하십시오.

Target Words	Yes	No
6. cable		
7. tablet		
8. emblem		
9. enjoyable		
10. convertible		

Name: _____ Date: ___/___/_____ Score: _____

Lesson 2.4

Reading Words with the "mb" Letter Combination

✓ **Lesson Check Point**

 Directions: Read each target word. Circle the word in the column that has the same "mb" sound(s) as the target word.

지도: 각 대상 단어를 읽으십시오. 대상 단어와 동일한 "mb" 소리가 있는 열의 단어에 동그라미를 치십시오.

lamb	a. remember
	b. entomb

crumb	a. crumble
	b. catacomb

number	a. thrombus
	b. numb

bombard	a. jumbo
	b. womb

 Directions: Read each target word. In the second column, write the number of letters in the word. In the third column, write the number of letters heard in the word.

지도: 각 대상 단어를 읽으십시오. 두 번째 열에는 단어의 글자 수를 씁니다. 세 번째 열에는 단어에서 들리는 글자 수를 쓰십시오.

Target Words	Number of letters in the word	Number of letters heard
1. lamb		
2. crumb		
3. number		
4. bombard		

Name: _____ Date: ___/___/_____ Score: _____

Lesson 2.4

Reading Words with the "bt" Letter Combination

✓ Lesson Check Point

 Directions: Read each target word. Circle the word in the column that has the same "bt" sound(s) as the target word.

지도: 각 대상 단어를 읽으십시오. 대상 단어와 동일한 "bt" 소리가 있는 열의 단어에 동그라미를 치십시오.

debt	a. obtuse
	b. subtle

debtors	a. doubting
	b. subtract

subtract	a. obtrude
	b. subtleness

subtropics	a. doubt
	b. obtain

 Directions: Read each target word. In the second column, write the number of letters in the word. In the third column, write the number of letters heard in the word.

지도: 각 대상 단어를 읽으십시오. 두 번째 열에는 단어의 글자 수를 씁니다. 세 번째 열에는 단어에서 들리는 글자 수를 쓰십시오.

Target Words	Number of letters in the word	Number of letters heard
1. debt		
2. debtors		
3. subtract		
4. subtropics		

Name: _____ Date: ___/___/_____ Score: _____

Lesson 2.5

Reading Words with a Silent "b"

✓ **Lesson Check Point**

 Directions: Read the target words in the word box. Write the words that have a silent letter "b" in the first column. Write the words that do not have a silent letter "b" in the second column.

지도: 단어 상자에 있는 대상 단어를 읽습니다. 첫 번째 열에 묵음 문자"b"가 있는 단어를 쓰십시오. 두 번째 열에 묵음 문자"b"가 없는 단어를 쓰십시오.

Target Word Box				
crumbs	indebted	behave	laboratory	combing
doubt	rebate	plumbing	burger	quibble
basket	beagle	lamb	subtlety	bonding
public	climbers	balance	thumb	beaver

Letter "b" is silent	Letter "b" has the /b/ sound

Name: _____ Date:___/___/_____ Score:_____

The Reading Challenge

Lesson 2.6

Reading Multisyllable Words

 Lesson Check Point

 Directions: Read and divide each target word into syllables. Write each word and place a hyphen (-) between the syllables in the second column. Write the number of syllables in the third column. Use a dictionary or the Internet to check your answers.

지도: 각 대상 단어를 읽고 음절로 나눕니다. 각 단어를 쓰고 두 번째 열의 음절 사이에 하이픈(-)을 넣습니다. 세 번째 열에 음절 수를 쓰십시오. 사전이나 인터넷을 사용하여 답을 확인하십시오.

Target Words	Words Divided into Syllables	Number of Syllables
1. absent	_____	_____
2. submit	_____	_____
3. table	_____	_____
4. tablet	_____	_____
5. absolutely	_____	_____
6. somebody	_____	_____
7. habitat	_____	_____
8. fabulous	_____	_____
9. observing	_____	_____
10. subtracting	_____	_____

Name: _____ Date:___/___/_____ Score: _____

The Reading Challenge

Lesson 2.6

Reading Multisyllable Words

✓ Lesson Check Point

 Directions: Read each target word. Circle the word in the row that is divided correctly into syllables. Use a dictionary or the Internet to check your answers.
지도: 각 대상 단어를 읽으십시오. 음절로 올바르게 나누어진 행에 있는 단어에 동그라미를 치십시오. 사전이나 인터넷을 사용하여 답을 확인하십시오.

Model

| because | (a. be-cause) | b. beca-use | c. b-ecause |

| 1. barbecue | a. bar-b-ecue | b. bar-becue | c. bar-be-cue |

| 2. brainstorm | a. brain-storm | b. brai-nst-orm | c. br-ain-storm |

| 3. belated | a. belat-ed | b. be-lat-ed | c. b-ela-ted |

| 4. barber | a. barb-er | b. bar-ber | c. ba-rber |

| 5. biweekly | a. bi-wee-kly | b. biw-eek-ly | c. bi-week-ly |

| 6. bathroom | a. bath-room | b. ba-throom | c. bathr-oom |

| 7. beagle | a. beag-le | b. bea-gle | c. be-agle |

| 8. background | a. back-ground | b. backgr-ound | c. ba-ckground |

Name: _____   Date:___/___/_____   Score: _____

Lesson 2.7

Reading and Writing

Proper and Common Nouns and Adjectives

Directions: Read the words in the word box. Put an (X) on the line next to each word that is written incorrectly. Remember that all proper nouns and proper adjectives are capitalized. Use a dictionary or the Internet to check your answers.

지도: 단어 상자에 있는 단어를 읽으십시오. 잘못 쓰여진 각 단어 옆의 줄에 (X)를 표시하십시오. 모든 고유 명사와 고유 형용사는 대문자임을 기억하십시오. 사전이나 인터넷을 사용하여 답을 확인하십시오.

Word Box		
__ Bronx	__ brazilian	__ British
__ bathtaB	__ biology	__ bulgaria
__ bangladesh	__ Bonanza	__ botswana
__ bittersweet	__ Brother Bob	__ Bonaparte

Directions: Read each unedited sentence and underline the word that is written incorrectly. Write each sentence correctly on the line.

지도: 편집되지 않은 각 문장을 읽고 잘못 쓰여진 단어에 밑줄을긋습 니다. 각 문장을 줄에 올바르게 쓰십시오.

Model
<u>brandon's</u> books are about big boats.
<u>Brandon's books are about big boats.</u>

1. Bess and Beth are at the Beach.

   _____

2. The Boy's bike is blue and brown.

   _____

3. bugs and birds are flying by the bay.

   _____

4. baby Ben has a big bear and a black boat.

   _____

Name: _____ Date:___/___/_____ Score:_____

Lesson 3.1

Reading Words with the Letter C/c

✓ Lesson Check Point

Directions: Read each target word. Find the letter "c" and put a check (✓) in the column that identifies its position: beginning, within or end.
지도: 각 대상 단어를 읽으십시오. 문자"c"를 찾아 위치를 나타내는 열: 시작, 내부 또는 끝에 체크(✓)를 하십시오.

Target Words	Beginning (First Letter)	Within	End (Last Letter)
1. zinc			
2. carrot			
3. fabric			
4. impacted			
5. protractor			

Directions: Read each sentence and underline the words that begin with the letter "c." Write all the underlined words in alphabetical order on the lines below.
지도: 각 문장을 읽고"c"로 시작하는 단어에 밑줄을 긋습니다. 밑줄 친 모든 단어를 아래 줄에 알파벳 순서로 쓰십시오.

6. The clock is on a big chain.

7. Andrew is counting the cats.

8. Bobby will climb up the cliff.

9. All the coins add up to ten cents.

10. Al said, "The chair is by my baby's crib."

_____   _____   _____

_____   _____   _____

_____

Name: _____ Date: ___/___/_____ Score: _____

Lesson 3.1

Reading Words with the Hard Letter "c"

✓ Lesson Check Point

Directions: Read each target word. Put a check (✓) under the correct column heading.

지도: 각 대상 단어를 읽으십시오. 올바른 열 제목 아래에 체크(✓)를 하십시오.

Target Words	Hard "c" has the /k/ sound as in the word cat	Soft "c" has the /s/ sound as in the word cell
1. cavity		
2. central		
3. century		
4. camping		
5. covering		

Directions: Read each sentence and underline the words that have the hard "c" sound, as in the word cat. Write all the underlined words in alphabetical order on the lines below.

지도: 각 문장을 읽고 단어 cat에서와 같이 단단한 "c" 소리가 나는 단어에 밑줄을 긋습니다. 아래 줄에 밑줄 친 단어를 알파벳 순서로 모두 쓰십시오.

6. Cindy likes to eat cake and candy.

7. Cyril is the coolest kid in his class.

8. The climbers did not see the icy cliff.

9. The experienced chemists can study animal cells.

10. My college campus has four large buildings in the city.

_____   _____   _____

_____   _____   _____

_____   _____   _____

_____

Learn To Read English With Directions In Korean   Copyrighted Material

Name: _____ Date:___/___/_____ Score:_____

Lesson 3.2

Reading Words with the Soft Letter "c"

Directions: Read each target word. Put a check (✓) under the correct column heading.

지도: 각 대상 단어를 읽으십시오. 올바른 열 제목 아래에 체크(✓)를하십시오.

Target Words	Hard "c" has the /k/ sound as in the word cat	Soft "c" has the /s/ sound as in the word cell
1. cub		
2. cab		
3. city		
4. grace		
5. recite		

Directions: Read each sentence and underline the words that have the soft "c" sound, as in the word cell. Write all the underlined words in alphabetical order on the lines below.

지도: 각 문장을 읽고 cell이라는 단어에서처럼 부드러운"c" 소리가 나는 단어에 밑줄을 긋습니다. 아래 줄에 밑줄 친 단어를 알파벳 순서로 모두 쓰십시오.

6. A cyclone is a strong wind that moves in a circle.

7. We will celebrate Cindy's birthday in the country.

8. While in the city, I ate cranberry and cinnamon candy.

9. The ceramic dishes and cereal bowls are in the cabinets.

10. We can repair the ceilings in the Central Street apartments.

_____ _____ _____

_____ _____ _____

_____ _____ _____

_____

Name: _____ Date:___/___/_____ Score:_____

Review Lessons 3.1 & 3.2

Reading Hard Letter "c" and Soft Letter "c" Words

Directions: Read the target words in the word box. In the first column, write the words with the letter "c" that have the /k/ sound, as in the word <u>cat</u>. In the second column, write the words with the letter "c" that have the /s/ sound, as in the word <u>cell</u>.

지도: 단어 상자에 있는 대상 단어를 읽으십시오. 첫 번째 열에는 cat라는 단어에서와 같이 /k/ 소리가 나는 문자"c"가 있는 단어를 씁니다. 두 번째 열에는 cell이라는 단어에서와 같이 /s/ 소리가 나는 문자"c"가 있는 단어를 씁니다.

Target Word Box				
cyst	car	cold	fence	icy
cider	places	candy	lacy	color
can	curl	come	cute	Tracy
face	cents	curb	cinch	camel

Hard letter "c"
has the
/k/ sound
as in the word
<u>cat</u>

Soft letter "c"
has the
/s/ sound
as in the word
<u>cell</u>

_____   _____
_____   _____
_____   _____
_____   _____
_____   _____
_____   _____
_____   _____
_____   _____

Name: _____ Date: ___/___/_____ Score: _____

Lesson 3.3

Reading Words with the "cr" Letter Combination

Dictionary Skills/ Vocabulary

✓ Lesson Check Point

 Directions: Read each target word and its definition. Write the letter of the definition on the line of each target word. Use a dictionary or the Internet to check your answers.
지도: 각 대상 단어와 그 정의를 읽으십시오. 각 대상 단어의 행에 정의의 문자를 씁니다. 사전이나 인터넷을 사용하여 답을 확인하십시오.

Target Words	Definitions
1. __ crabs	a. to have collided violently with another vehicle
2. __ crashed	b. shelled animals that live by and in water
3. __ creek	c. brittle texture of something that is easily broken
4. __ crispy	d. to have walked from one side to the other side
5. __ crossed	e. a stream of water that is smaller than a river

 Directions: Read each sentence. Underline the word in the parentheses that correctly completes each sentence. Then, write the underlined word on the line.
지도: 각 문장을 읽으십시오. 각 문장을 올바르게 완성하는 괄호 안에 있는 단어에 밑줄을 긋습니다. 그런 다음 밑줄 친 단어를 줄에 쓰십시오.

6. The children _____ the street. (crossed, creek)

7. My mommy's cookies are _____. (crispy, crashed)

8. Cindy and Chad had a picnic by the _____. (crispy, creek)

9. The big _____ live in a cold water creek. (crossed, crabs)

10. In the city, the cars _____ into one another. (crashed, crabs)

Name: _____ Date:___/___/_____ Score:_____

Lesson 3.4

Reading Words with the "cl" Letter Combination

Dictionary Skills/ Vocabulary

✓ **Lesson Check Point**

Directions: Read each target word and its definition. Write the target word on the line in front of its meaning. Use a dictionary or the Internet to check your answers.
지도: 각 대상 단어와 그 정의를 읽으십시오. 의미 앞 줄에 대상단어 를 쓰십시오. 사전이나 인터넷을 사용하여 답을 확인하십시오.

Target Word Box				
clapped	cleans	clock	close	clothes

1. _____ a near position
2. _____ a device used to indicate and display time
3. _____ to have hit the palms of one's hands together
4. _____ the process of removing dirt off of something
5. _____ garments used to cover and adorn a person's body

Directions: Read each sentence. Underline the word in the parentheses that correctly completes each sentence. Then, write the underlined word on the line.
지도: 각 문장을 읽으십시오. 각 문장을 올바르게 완성하는 괄호 안에있는 단어에 밑줄을 긋습니다. 그런 다음 밑줄 친 단어를 줄에 쓰십시오.

6. Cecil _____ the cabinets with bleach. (clock, cleans)

7. Cindy hangs her _____ in the closet. (clothes, close)

8. The audience _____ for the choir. (clapped, clothes)

9. Chad lives _____ to the country's capital. (cleans, close)

10. The _____ in the cabin tells the correct time. (clock, clapped)

Name: _____ Date:___/___/_____ Score: _____

Lesson 3.4

Reading Words with the "cle" Letter Combination

✓ Lesson Check Point

 Directions: Read each target word. Find the "cle" letter combination and put a check (✓) in the column that identifies its position: beginning, within or end.

지도: 각 대상 단어를 읽으십시오. "cle" 문자 조합을 찾아 위치를 식별하는열에 체크(✓)를 하십시오: 시작, 내부 또는 끝.

Target Words	Beginning (First 3 Letters)	Within	End (Last 3 Letters)
1. clerk			
2. cleave			
3. vehicle			
4. bicycle			
5. inclemently			

 Directions: Read each target word. Put a check (✓) in the "yes" column if the "cle" letter combination has the /k/ + /ə/ + /l/ sounds. Put a check (✓) in the "no" column if the "cle" letter combination does not have the /k/ + /ə/ + /l/ sounds.

지도: 각 대상 단어를 읽으십시오. "cle" 문자 조합에/k/ + /ə/ + /l/ 소리가있으 면"yes" 열에 체크(✓)를 하십시오. "cle" 문자 조합에/k/ + /ə/ + /l/ 소리가없으 면"no" 열에 체크(✓)를 하십시오.

Target Words	Yes	No
6. clerk		
7. cleave		
8. vehicle		
9. bicycle		
10. inclemently		

Name: _____   Date: ___/___/_____   Score: _____

Lesson 3.5

Reading Words with the "ct" Letter Combination

✓ Lesson Check Point

 Directions: Read each target word. Circle the word in the column that has the same "ct" sound(s) as the target word.
지도: 각 대상 단어를 읽으십시오. 대상 단어와 동일한 "ct" 소리가 있는 열의 단어에 동그라미를 치십시오.

affect	a. actual
	b. factor

product	a. abduction
	b. compact

practicing	a. acting
	b. induction

Connecticut	a. indict
	b. section

 Directions: Read each target word. Put a check (✓) under the correct column heading.
지도: 각 대상 단어를 읽으십시오. 올바른 열 제목 아래에 체크(✓)를 하십시오.

Target Words	"ct" has the /k/ + /t/ sounds as in the word <u>fact</u>	"ct" has the silent "c" + /t/ sound as in the word <u>indict</u>
1. affect		
2. product		
3. practicing		
4. Connecticut		

Name: _____ Date: ___/___/_____ Score: _____

Lesson 3.6

Reading Soft Letter "c" Words

✓ Lesson Check Point

 Directions: Read each target word. Circle the word in the column that has the same "cean," "cian," "cial," "cious" or "cient" sound as the target word.

지도: 각 대상 단어를 읽으십시오. 대상 단어와 동일한 "cean," "cian," "cial," "cious" 또는 "cient" 소리가 나는 열의 단어에 동그라미를 치십시오.

crucial	a. practical
	b. commercial

capricious	a. physician
	b. delicious

proficient	a. optician
	b. ancient

crustacean	a. clinician
	b. facial

 Directions: Read each target word. Put a check (✓) in the column that identifies the same "cean," "cian," "cial," "cious" or "cient" sound within the target word.

지도: 각 대상 단어를 읽으십시오. 대상 단어 내에서 동일한 "cean," "cian," "cial," "cious" 또는 "cient" 소리를 식별하는 열에 체크(✓)를 하십시오.

Target Words	"cean" has the /sh/+/ə/+/n/ sounds as in the word <u>ocean</u>	"cial" has the /sh/+/ə/+/l/ sounds as in the word <u>special</u>	"cious" has the /sh/+/ə/+/s/ sounds as in the word <u>delicious</u>	"cient" has the /sh/+/ə/+/n/+/t/ sounds as in the word <u>ancient</u>
1. crucial				
2. capricious				
3. proficient				
4. crustacean				

Name: _____ Date: ___/___/_____ Score: _____

Lesson 3.6

Reading Soft Letter "c" Words

Directions: Read the target words in the word box. In the first column, write the words with the letter "c" that have the /s/ sound, as in the word <u>cell</u>. In the second column, write the words with the letter "c" that have the /sh/ sound, as in the word <u>ocean</u>.

지도: 단어 상자에 있는 대상 단어를 읽으십시오. 첫 번째 열에는 cell이라는 단어에서와 같이 /s/ 소리가 나는 문자"c"가 있는 단어를 씁니다. 두 번째 열에는 다음과 같은 문자"c"가 포함된 단어를 쓰십시오. /sh/ 소리, ocean 이라는 단어에서처럼.

Target Word Box				
politician	fancy	deficient	musician	cider
ferocious	special	fence	nice	social
bicycle	excited	spicy	facial	cents
crustacean	circle	sufficient	city	magician

Soft letter "c" has the /s/ sound as in the word <u>cell</u>

Soft letter "c" has the /sh/ sound as in the word <u>ocean</u>

Name: _____ Date: ___/___/_____ Score: _____

Lesson 3.7

Reading Words with the "ch" Letter Combination

✓ **Lesson Check Point**

Directions: Read each target word. Circle the word in the column that has the same "ch" sound as the target word.
지도: 각 대상 단어를 읽으십시오. 대상 단어와 같은 "ch" 소리가 나는 열의 단어에 동그라미를 치십시오.

teach	a. speech
	b. chronic

character	a. choir
	b. ache

fuchsia	a. school
	b. yacht

chauffeur	a. chaos
	b. chef

Directions: Read each target word. Put a check (✓) under the correct column heading.
지도: 각 대상 단어를 읽으십시오. 올바른 열 제목 아래에 체크(✓)를 하십시오.

Target Words	"ch" has the /ch/ sound as in the word <u>chain</u>	"ch" has the /sh/ sound as in the word <u>chef</u>	"ch" has the /k/ sound as in the word <u>chaos</u>	"ch" is silent as in the word <u>yacht</u>
1. teach				
2. character				
3. fuchsia				
4. chauffeur				

Name: _____ Date: ___/___/_____ Score: _____

Lesson 3.8

Reading Words with the "cc" Letter Combination

✓ Lesson Check Point

Directions: Read each target word. Circle the word in the column that has the same "cc" sound(s) as the target word.

지도: 각 대상 단어를 읽으십시오. 대상 단어와 동일한 "cc" 소리가 나는 열의 단어에 동그라미를 치십시오.

succinct	a. occupy
	b. accept

success	a. access
	b. accomplish

acclaim	a. accord
	b. accident

account	a. broccoli
	b. accent

Directions: Read each target word. Put a check (✓) under the correct column heading.

지도: 각 대상 단어를 읽으십시오. 올바른 열 제목 아래에 체크(✓)를 하십시오.

Target Words	"cc" has the /k/ sound as in the word <u>soccer</u>	"cc" has the /k/ + /s/ sounds as in the word <u>accept</u>
1. succinct		
2. success		
3. acclaim		
4. account		

Name: _____   Date: ___/___/_____   Score: _____

Lesson 3.9

Reading Words with a Silent Letter "c"

✓ **Lesson Check Point**

Directions: Read the target words in the word box. Write the words that have a silent letter "c" in the first column. Write the words that do not have a silent letter "c" in the second column.

지도: 단어 상자에 있는 대상 단어를 읽으십시오. 첫 번째 열에 묵음 문자 "c"가 있는 단어를 쓰십시오. 두 번째 열에 묵음 문자 "c"가 없는 단어를 쓰십시오.

Target Word Box				
corner	scuba	scent	cycle	score
essence	domestic	clocks	collar	acquit
abscess	descend	fascinate	ascent	scene
adolescent	escalator	disciple	recruit	fuchsia

Letter "c" is silent   **Letter "c" has the /k/, /s/ or /sh/ sound**

Name: _____ Date: ___/___/_____ Score: _____

The Reading Challenge

Lesson 3.10

Reading Multisyllable Words

✓ **Lesson Check Point**

Directions: Read and divide each target word into syllables. Write each word and place a hyphen (-) between the syllables in the second column. Write the number of syllables in the third column. Use a dictionary or the Internet to check your answers.

지도: 각 대상 단어를 읽고 음절로 나눕니다. 각 단어를 쓰고 두 번째 열의 음절 사이에 하이픈(-)을 넣습니다. 세 번째 열에 음절 수를 쓰십시오. 사전이나 인터넷을 사용하여 답을 확인하십시오.

Target Words	Words Divided into Syllables	Number of Syllables
1. cardinal	_____	_____
2. chamber	_____	_____
3. cockroach	_____	_____
4. cauliflower	_____	_____
5. cylinder	_____	_____
6. conjunction	_____	_____
7. casual	_____	_____
8. complexion	_____	_____
9. category	_____	_____
10. California	_____	_____

Name: _____ Date: ___/___/_____ Score: _____

The Reading Challenge

Lesson 3.10

Reading Multisyllable Words

✓ Lesson Check Point

Directions: Read each target word. Circle the word in the row that is divided correctly into syllables. Use a dictionary or the Internet to check your answers.

지도: 각 대상 단어를 읽으십시오. 음절로 올바르게 나누어진 행에 있는 단어에 동그라미를 치십시오. 사전이나 인터넷을 사용하여 답을 확인하십시오.

Model

| calculus | a. calcu-lus | b. (cal-cu-lus) | c. cal-culus |

| 1. clinical | a. clin-i-cal | b. clini-cal | c. clin-ic-al |

| 2. cockatoo | a. co-ck-atoo | b. cock-a-too | c. cocka-too |

| 3. coconut | a. coco-nut | b. co-conut | c. co-co-nut |

| 4. clerical | a. cler-i-cal | b. cleri-cal | c. cle-ri-cal |

| 5. citizen | a. cit-izen | b. cit-i-zen | c. ci-tiz-en |

| 6. condition | a. con-di-tion | b. cond-i-tion | c. co-ndi-tion |

| 7. congruent | a. co-ngru-ent | b. con-gru-ent | c. con-g-ruent |

| 8. constitute | a. cons-tit-ute | b. const-i-tute | c. con-sti-tute |

Learn To Read English With Directions In Korean

Name: _____ Date: ___/___/_____ Score: _____

Lesson 3.11

Reading and Writing

Proper and Common Nouns and Adjectives

Directions: Read the words in the word box. Put an (X) on the line next to each word that is written incorrectly. Remember that all proper nouns and proper adjectives are capitalized. Use a dictionary or the Internet to check your answers.

지도: 단어 상자에 있는 단어를 읽으십시오. 잘못 쓰여진 각 단어 옆의 줄에 (X)를 표시하십시오. 모든 고유 명사와 고유 형용사는 대문자임을 기억하십시오. 사전이나 인터넷을 사용하여 답을 확인하십시오.

Word Box		
___ City	___ closet	___ Curtain
___ capital	___ CriCket	___ Cutting
___ Columbus	___ canyon	___ Costa Rica
___ Cousin Charles	___ cherokee	___ carson city

Directions: Read each unedited sentence and underline the word that is written incorrectly. Write each sentence correctly on the line.

지도: 편집되지 않은 각 문장을 읽고 잘못 쓰여진 단어에 밑줄을 긋습 니다. 각 문장을 줄에 올바르게 쓰십시오.

Model
The <u>Camp</u> in Cleveland is closed.
The camp in Cleveland is closed.

1. chad is carrying his bag of rice.
   _____

2. The climate in central America is not cold.
   _____

3. The Coffee and cocoa in our cups are cold.
   _____

4. Charles and Cecil are Characters in my cool book.
   _____

Name: _____ Date: ___/___/_____ Score: _____

Lesson 4.1

Reading Words with the Letter D/d

✓ Lesson Check Point

Directions: Read each target word. Find the letter "d" and put a check (✓) in the column that identifies its position: beginning, within or end.
지도: 각 대상 단어를 읽으십시오. 문자"d"를 찾아 위치를 나타내는 열에 체크(✓)를 하십시오: 시작, 내부 또는 끝.

Target Words	Beginning (First Letter)	Within	End (Last Letter)
1. hold			
2. dollar			
3. holiday			
4. darling			
5. kingdom			

Directions: Read each sentence and underline the words that begin with the letter "d." Write all the underlined words in alphabetical order on the lines below.
지도: 각 문장을 읽고 문자"d"로 시작하는 단어에 밑줄을 긋습니다. 아래 줄에 밑줄 친 단어를 알파벳 순서로 모두 쓰십시오.

6. My daughter is an excellent doctor.

7. Fred ate deep-fried chicken for dinner.

8. The detective drives his blue car to the city.

9. My mom drove directly to the college campus.

10. I asked about the dangers of the hot desert sun.

_____   _____   _____
_____   _____   _____
_____   _____   _____
            _____

Name: _____ Date: ___/___/_____ Score: _____

Lesson 4.2

Reading Letter "d" Words with the /d/ Sound & /j/ Sound

✓ Lesson Check Point

Directions: Read each target word. Circle the word in the column that has the same "d" sound as the target word.
지도: 각 대상 단어를 읽으십시오. 대상 단어와 "d" 소리가 같은 열의 단어에 동그라미를 치십시오.

cordial	a. schedule
	b. dental

indirect	a. education
	b. model

advance	a. doctor
	b. nodule

glandular	a. bedrock
	b. educated

Directions: Read each target word. Put a check (✓) under the correct column heading.
지도: 각 대상 단어를 읽으십시오. 올바른 열 제목 아래에 체크(✓)를 하십시오.

Target Words	"d" has the /d/ sound as in the word <u>doctor</u>	"d" has the /j/ sound as in the word <u>educate</u>
1. cordial		
2. indirect		
3. advance		
4. glandular		

Name: _____ Date:___/___/_____ Score:_____

Lesson 4.2

Reading Words with the "dr" Letter Combination

Dictionary Skills/ Vocabulary

✓ **Lesson Check Point**

 Directions: Read each target word and its definition. Write the letter of the definition on the line of each target word. Use a dictionary or the Internet to check your answers.
지도: 각 대상 단어와 그 정의를 읽으십시오. 각 대상 단어의 행에 정의의 문자를 씁니다. 사전이나 인터넷을 사용하여 답을 확인하십시오.

Target Words	Definitions
1. __ dress up	a. a musical instrument
2. __ drive	b. to operate a car, train or bus
3. __ drum	c. pictures made with an artist's tool
4. __ dramatic	d. to wear fancy clothes for a special event
5. __ drawings	e. the act of showing feelings during a performance

 Directions: Read each sentence. Underline the word in the parentheses that correctly completes each sentence. Then, write the underlined word on the line.
지도: 각 문장을 읽으십시오. 각 문장을 올바르게 완성하는 괄호 안에 있는 단어에 밑줄을 긋습니다. 그런 다음 밑줄 친 단어를 줄에 쓰십시오.

6. We will _____ out of the driveway. (dress up, drive)

7. Danny's _____ were skillfully done. (drive, drawings)

8. David played the _____ at the concert. (drum, dramatic)

9. At the show, Diana did a _____ dance. (dramatic, drive)

10. Everyone in my class will _____ for the dance. (dress up, drawings)

Name: _____ Date:___/___/_____ Score: _____

Lesson 4.3

Reading Words with the "ed" Suffix/ Past Tense Verbs

✓ **Lesson Check Point**

Directions: Read each target word. Circle the word in the column that has the same "ed" sound(s) as the target word.

지도: 각 대상 단어를 읽으십시오. 대상 단어와 동일한"ed" 소리(들)가있는열의 단어에 동그라미를 치십시오.

fixed	a. framed
	b. ripped

saved	a. cooked
	b. tamed

started	a. plotted
	b. produced

stopped	a. rested
	b. licked

Directions: Read each target word. Put a check (✓) under the correct column heading.

지도: 각 대상 단어를 읽으십시오. 올바른 열 제목 아래에 체크(✓)를하십시오.

Target Words	"ed" has the /ĭ/ + /d/ sounds as in the word <u>rested</u>	"ed" has the /d/ sound as in the word <u>hugged</u>	"ed" has the /t/ sound as in the word <u>tipped</u>
1. fixed			
2. saved			
3. started			
4. stopped			

Name: _____ Date: ___/___/_____ Score: _____

Lesson 4.4

Reading Words with a Silent Letter "d"

✓ **Lesson Check Point**

 Directions: Read the target words in the word box. Write the words that have a silent letter "d" in the first column. Write the words that do not have a silent letter "d" in the second column.

지도: 단어 상자에 있는 대상 단어를 읽으십시오. 첫 번째 열에 묵음문자 "d"가 있는 단어를 쓰십시오. 두 번째 열에 묵음 문자"d"가 없는 단어를 쓰십시오.

Target Word Box				
sedge	candy	saddle	fridge	fade
dollar	deck	radiant	radish	drink
bridge	denim	adjective	doctor	nudge
cartridge	pendant	knowledge	Windsor	Wednesday

Letter "d" is silent	Letter "d" has the /d/ sound

Name: _____ Date: ___/___/_____ Score: _____

The Reading Challenge

Lesson 4.5

Reading Multisyllable Words

✓ Lesson Check Point

Directions: Read and divide each target word into syllables. Write each word and place a hyphen (-) between the syllables in the second column. Write the number of syllables in the third column. Use a dictionary or the Internet to check your answers.

지도: 각 대상 단어를 읽고 음절로 나눕니다. 각 단어를 쓰고 두 번째 열의 음절 사이에 하이픈(-)을 넣습니다. 세 번째 열에 음절 수를 쓰십시오. 사전이나 인터넷을 사용하여 답을 확인하십시오.

Target Words	Words Divided into Syllables	Number of Syllables
1. dentistry	_____	_____
2. dialect	_____	_____
3. development	_____	_____
4. disembark	_____	_____
5. denominate	_____	_____
6. department	_____	_____
7. description	_____	_____
8. demanding	_____	_____
9. designer	_____	_____
10. dependent	_____	_____

Name: _____ Date:___/___/_____ Score: _____

The Reading Challenge

Lesson 4.5

Reading Multisyllable Words

✓ Lesson Check Point

 Directions: Read each target word. Circle the word in the row that is divided correctly into syllables. Use a dictionary or the Internet to check your answers.
지도: 각 대상 단어를 읽으십시오. 음절로 올바르게 나누어진 행에 있는 단어에 동그라미를 치십시오. 사전이나 인터넷을 사용하여 답을 확인하십시오.

Model

dictionary	a. di-ction-ary	b. dic-tion-ar-y (circled)	c. dic-tiona-ry
1. deception	a. dec-ep-tion	b. de-cep-tion	c. de-ce-ption
2. database	a. da-ta-base	b. dat-a-base	c. da-tab-ase
3. delinquent	a. del-in-quent	b. de-lin-quent	c. delin-qu-ent
4. disengage	a. dis-en-gage	b. di-sen-gage	c. dis-eng-age
5. drapery	a. dra-pe-ry	b. drap-er-y	c. drape-r-y
6. decided	a. de-cide-d	b. de-ci-ded	c. de-cid-ed
7. duplicate	a. du-pli-cate	b. dup-li-cate	c. du-plic-ate
8. diagnosis	a. dia-gno-sis	b. di-ag-no-sis	c. diagn-o-sis

Name: _____ Date: ___/___/_____ Score: _____

Lesson 4.6

Reading and Writing

Proper and Common Nouns and Adjectives

✓ Lesson Check Point

Directions: Read the words in the word box. Put an (X) on the line next to each word that is written incorrectly. Remember that all proper nouns and proper adjectives are capitalized. Use a dictionary or the Internet to check your answers.

지도: 단어 상자에 있는 단어를 읽으십시오. 잘못 쓰여진 각 단어 옆의줄에 (X)를 표시하십시오. 모든 고유 명사와 고유 형용사는 대문자임을 기억하십시오. 사전이나 인터넷을 사용하여 답을 확인하십시오.

Word Box		
___ dr.	___ Dove	___ Desk
___ dutch	___ Delhi	___ driver
___ Detroit	___ Dominica	___ distant
___ Dessert	___ december	___ Damascus

Directions: Read each unedited sentence and underline the word that is written incorrectly. Write each sentence correctly on the line.

지도: 편집되지 않은 각 문장을 읽고 잘못 쓰여진 단어에 밑줄을긋습 니다. 각 문장을 줄에 올바르게 쓰십시오.

Model
Dan said, "My daughter's name is <u>donna</u>."
<u>Dan said, "My daughter's name is Donna."</u>

1. After dinner, I ate dad's donuts.
   _____

2. dina designed a cute denim dress.
   _____

3. Daniel dug a Ditch by the bushes.
   _____

4. detroit Diner has delicious dishes.
   _____

Name: _____ Date:___/___/_____ Score: _____

Lesson 5.1

Reading Words with the Letter E/e

✓ Lesson Check Point

 Directions: Read each target word. Find the letter "e" and put a check (✓) in the column that identifies its position: beginning, within or end.
지도: 각 대상 단어를 읽으십시오. 문자"e"를 찾아 체크 표시(✓)위치를식 별하는 열에서 시작, 내부 또는 끝.。

Target Words	Beginning (First Letter)	Within	End (Last Letter)
1. east			
2. alive			
3. exact			
4. heater			
5. annex			

 Directions: Read each target word. Read the words in the row and circle the word that has a different vowel "e" sound.
지도: 각 대상 단어를 읽으십시오. 줄에 있는 단어를 읽고 모음"e" 소리가 다른 단어에 동그라미를 치세요.

Target Words				
6. help	tend	he	sell	rent
7. check	bell	rest	cent	she
8. shell	west	clef	me	step
9. bless	be	get	red	sent
10. French	self	the	dent	desk

Name: _____ Date:___/___/_____ Score:_____

Lesson 5.2

Reading Words with the Short Vowel "e" Sound

✓ **Lesson Check Point**

Directions: Read the words in the four boxes. Circle two words with the short vowel /ĕ/ sound. The anchor word for the short vowel /ĕ/ sound is <u>egg</u>.

지도: 네 개의 상자에 있는 단어를 읽으십시오. 짧은 모음 /ĕ/ 소리로 두 단어에 동그라미를 치십시오. 단모음 /ĕ/ 소리의 앵커 워드는 egg입니다.

were	send		great	dean		please	bred
dwell	scheme		peg	belt		we	spend

blend	sea		bet	these		spell	Ted
rend	she		take	den		leaf	be

Directions: Read the words in the four boxes. Circle two words that rhyme. Rhyming words have the same ending sound, such as <u>set</u> and <u>wet</u>.

지도: 네 개의 상자에 있는 단어를 읽으십시오. 운이 맞는 두 단어에동그라미를 치십시오. 운율이 있는 단어는 set 및 wet와 같이 끝 소리가같습니다.

Ben	leap		lead	they		nest	heat
her	ten		wreck	peck		west	break

meal	sell		tend	send		smell	melt
tell	where		these	bent		bend	felt

Name: _____ Date:___/___/_____ Score:_____

Lesson 5.2

Reading & Writing Words with the Short Vowel "e" Sound

✓ **Lesson Check Point**

Directions: Read each sentence and underline three words with the short vowel /ĕ/ sound. Then, write the underlined words on the lines below. The anchor word for the short vowel /ĕ/ sound is <u>egg</u>.

지도: 각 문장을 읽고 세 단어에 짧은 모음 /ĕ/ 소리에 밑줄을 긋습니다. 그런 다음 밑줄 친 단어를 아래 줄에 쓰십시오. 단모음 /ĕ/ 소리의 기준 어는 egg입니다.

Model

She placed her <u>legs</u> on the <u>wet</u> <u>deck</u>.

    legs   wet   deck

1. At the campsite, he fell into the deep red well.

   _____   _____   _____

2. Do you know whether Beth ironed her blue dress?

   _____   _____   _____

3. At Mr. Eastman's house, the pets made a mess in the den.

   _____   _____   _____

4. On Tuesday, the men slept in the green and orange tents.

   _____   _____   _____

5. In December, I saw Lewis with ten extremely large emblems.

   _____   _____   _____

Name: _____ Date: ___/___/_____ Score: _____

Lesson 5.3

Reading Words with the Long Vowel "e" Sound

✓ **Lesson Check Point**

 Directions: Read the words in the four boxes. Circle two words with the long vowel /ē/ sound. The anchor word for the long vowel /ē/ sound is <u>me</u>.

지도: 네 개의 상자에 있는 단어를 읽으십시오. 장모음 /ē/ 소리로두단어에 동그라미를 치십시오. 장모음 /ē/ 소리의 기준어는 me입니다.

pelt	text
tree	meat

great	weak
wet	three

best	crease
peace	fear

grease	belt
pearl	cleave

knee	peck
bear	teal

eels	team
spell	lent

 Directions: Read the words in the four boxes. Circle two words that rhyme. Rhyming words have the same ending sound, such as <u>beep</u> and <u>reap</u>.

지도: 네 개의 상자에 있는 단어를 읽으십시오. 운이 맞는 두 단어에동그라미를 치십시오. 운율이 있는 단어는 beep 및 reap과 같이 끝 소리가같습니다.

peak	crest
beard	seek

speck	apples
real	peel

blest	cream
heart	dream

meal	spent
deal	tear

please	ease
smell	head

lets	cheat
treat	stress

Name: _____ Date: ___/___/_____ Score: _____

Lesson 5.3

Reading & Writing Words with the Long Vowel "e" Sound

✓ **Lesson Check Point**

Directions: Read each sentence and underline three words with the long vowel /ē/ sound. Then, write the underlined words on the lines below. The anchor word for the long vowel /ē/ sound is <u>me</u>.

지도: 각 문장을 읽고 장모음 /ē/ 소리로 세 단어에 밑줄을 긋습니다. 그런 다음 밑줄 친 단어를 아래 줄에 쓰십시오. 장모음 /ē/ 소리의 기준어는 me 입니다.

Model

<u>We</u> are <u>reading</u> an article entitled, "<u>Eagles</u> Bird of Prey."

  We   reading   Eagles
 _____ _____ _____

1. The dean is speaking about our ten athletic teams.

 _____ _____ _____

2. At three o'clock, she began to eat bread and eggs.

 _____ _____ _____

3. Sheila and Peter are reading interesting articles.

 _____ _____ _____

4. Steve said, "One pound of meat has more protein than ten eggs."

 _____ _____ _____

5. My teacher began her lesson with three facts about the planet Venus.

 _____ _____ _____

Name: _____   Date:___/___/_____   Score:_____

Review Lessons 5.2 & 5.3

Reading Short Vowel and Long Vowel Words

✓ **Lesson Check Point**

Directions: Read the target words in the word box. In the first column, write the words that have the short vowel /ĕ/ sound, as in the word <u>e</u>gg. In the second column, write the words that have the long vowel /ē/ sound, as in the word m<u>e</u>.

지도: 단어 상자에 있는 대상 단어를 읽으십시오. 첫 번째 칸에는 egg라는 단어처럼 단모음 /ĕ/ 소리가 나는 단어를 씁니다. 두 번째 칸에는 me라는 단어처럼 장모음 /ē/ 소리가 나는 단어를 쓰세요.

Target Word Box				
defeat	stem	supreme	stream	press
coffee	never	flesh	between	stress
help	speech	next	dress	ceiling
ever	complete	deplete	check	asleep

Letter "e" has the /ĕ/ sound as in the word <u>e</u>gg

Letter "e" has the /ē/ sound as in the word m<u>e</u>

Name: _____ Date:___/___/_____ Score:_____

Lesson 5.4

Reading Words with Letter "e" Vowel Pairs

✓ Lesson Check Point

 Directions: Read each target word. Circle the word in the column that has the same vowel "ea," "ee," "ei," "eo" or "eu" sound as the target word.
지도: 각 대상 단어를 읽으십시오. 같은 모음 "ea," "ee," "ei," "eo" 또는 "eu"가 대상 단어와 동일한 열의 단어에 동그라미를 치십시오.

ream	a. health
	b. teal

heat	a. peel
	b. bread

protein	a. asleep
	b. hear

streusel	a. mean
	b. Europe

 Directions: Read each target word. Put a check (✓) under the correct column heading.
지도: 각 대상 단어를 읽으십시오. 올바른 열 제목 아래에 체크(✓)를 하십시오.

Target Words	Words have the long "e" sound as in the word <u>tea</u>	Words do not have the long "e" sound
1. ream		
2. heat		
3. protein		
4. streusel		

Name: _____ Date: ___/___/_____ Score: _____

Lesson 5.5

Reading Words with the Final Letter "e"

✓ **Lesson Check Point**

 Directions: Read each target word. Find the letter "e" and put a check (✓) in the column that identifies its position within the syllable.
지도: 각 대상 단어를 읽으십시오. 문자"e"를 찾아 체크 표시(✓)음절내에서 위치를 식별하는 열에서.

Target Words	"e" is at the end of a one syllable word	"e" is at the end of the first syllable	"e" is at the end of a multi-syllable word
1. he			
2. me			
3. hero			
4. r<u>e</u>fresh			
5. becom<u>e</u>			

 Directions: Read each target word. Put a check (✓) under the correct column heading.
지도: 각 대상 단어를 읽으십시오. 올바른 열 제목 아래에 체크(✓)를 하십시오.

Target Words	"e" has the /ĕ/ sound as in the word <u>egg</u>	"e" has the /ē/ sound as in the word <u>me</u>	"e" has the /ə/ sound as in the word <u>item</u>	"e" is silent as in the word <u>great</u>
6. either				
7. pollen				
8. resting				
9. Europe				
10. urgently				

Name: _____ Date: ___/___/_____ Score: _____

Lesson 5.6

Reading Letter "e" Words with the Schwa Vowel Sound

✓ **Lesson Check Point**

 Directions: Read each target word. Circle the word in the column that has the same "e" sound as the target word.
지도: 각 대상 단어를 읽으십시오. 목표 단어와 같은 "e" 소리가 나는 열의 단어에 동그라미를 치십시오.

| letter | a. systems |
| | b. eggplant |

| celebrate | a. reap |
| | b. answer |

| elephant | a. father |
| | b. eating |

| problem | a. labels |
| | b. beeping |

 Directions: Read each sentence and underline the letter "e" word that has the schwa vowel /ə/ sound. The anchor word for the letter "e" schwa vowel sound is item.
지도: 각 문장을 읽고 슈와 모음 /ə/ 소리가 있는 문자 "e" 단어에 밑줄을 긋습니다. "e" 슈와 모음 소리의 앵커 단어는 item입니다.

1. You will benefit from reading this book.

2. Today, Emma began to shiver from fear.

3. Curried chicken with rice tastes very good.

4. My friend, Pete, made a profound statement.

5. Eddie painted an elephant for his art project.

6. There is oxygen in the large blue and white tank.

Name: _____ Date: ___/___/_____ Score: _____

Lesson 5.7

Reading Words with the "er" Letter Combination

Dictionary Skills/ Vocabulary

✓ Lesson Check Point

Directions: Read each target word and its definition. Write the letter of the definition on the line of each target word. Use a dictionary or the Internet to check your answers.
지도: 각 대상 단어와 그 정의를 읽으십시오. 각 대상 단어의 행에 정의의 문자를 씁니다. 사전이나 인터넷을 사용하여 답을 확인하십시오.

Target Words	Definitions
1. ___ ferry	a. sweet fruit
2. ___ brother	b. meal eaten in the evening
3. ___ periscope	c. a boat that sails across a body of water
4. ___ supper	d. a viewing instrument that has a system of lenses
5. ___ blackberries	e. a male person who has the same parent(s) as another

Directions: Read each sentence and write the target word that correctly completes the sentence.
지도: 각 문장을 읽고 문장을 올바르게 완성하는 목표 단어를 쓰십시오.

6. The _____ is floating under the city bridge.

7. Are you going to put _____ on your cereal?

8. Jerry always looks through his big _____.

9. My sister and _____ like to eat sweet cherries.

10. Tonight, we are going to have herring for _____.

Name: _____ Date: ___/___/_____ Score: _____

Lesson 5.8

Reading Words with the "eu" and "ew" Letter Combinations

✓ **Lesson Check Point**

 Directions: Read each sentence and underline the word that has a silent letter "e."
지도: 각 문장을 읽고 묵음 문자 "e"가 있는 단어에 밑줄을 긋습니다.

Model
My father said, "The apricot streusel is very tasty."

1. The eulogy at Eddie's funeral was very touching.

2. Lieutenant Glen has been a soldier for ten years.

3. Eleven of my friends went to Europe for an exciting vacation.

4. Prior to the wedding, Edwina will sew my white bridal gown.

 Directions: Read each sentence and underline the word with an "eu" or "ew" letter combination that has the long vowel /yōō/ or /ōō/ sound, as in the words feud and flew.
지도: 각 문장을 읽고 단어 feud 그리고 flew에서와 같이 장모음 /yōō/ 또는 /ōō/ 소리가 있는 "eu" 또는 "ew" 문자 조합으로 단어에 밑줄을 긋습니다.

5. Emily likes to wear neutral colors.

6. Edward chews his baked granola bar very slowly.

7. The artist drew a picture of an eagle and her eaglets.

8. Eugene's favorite television show is "The Price is Right."

9. The patients in the hospital are being treated for rheumatic fever.

10. Dr. Edmond said that Annie's rheumatism is a very painful condition.

Name: _____ Date: ___/___/_____ Score: _____

Lesson 5.9

Reading Words with the "ey" Letter Combination

✓ Lesson Check Point

Directions: Read each target word. Put a check (✓) under the correct column heading.

지도: 각 대상 단어를 읽으십시오. 올바른 열 제목 아래에 체크(✓)를 하십시오.

Target Words	"ey" has the long /ē/ sound as in the word honey	"ey" has the long /ā/ sound as in the word hey
1. they're		
2. journey		
3. odyssey		
4. obeyed		

Directions: Read each sentence and underline the word with the "ey" letter combination. Put a check (✓) under the correct column heading.

지도: 각 문장을 읽고 "ey" 문자 조합으로 단어에 밑줄을 긋습니다. 올바른 열 제목 아래에 체크(✓)를 하십시오.

	"ey" has the long /ē/ sound as in the word honey	"ey" has the long /ā/ sound as in the word hey
5. I completed an extremely long survey.		
6. He should obey the class rules.		
7. They like to eat eggs for breakfast.		
8. The new medley sounds very good.		
9. I like parsley flakes on my sandwich.		
10. It is difficult to convey the message.		

Name: _____ Date: ___/___/_____ Score: _____

Lesson 5.10

Reading Words with a Silent Letter "e"

✓ Lesson Check Point

Directions: Read the target words in the word box. Write the words that have a silent letter "e" in the first column. Write the words that do not have a silent letter "e" in the second column.

지도: 단어 상자에 있는 대상 단어를 읽으십시오. 첫 번째 열에 묵음 문자 "e"가 있는 단어를 쓰십시오. 두 번째 열에 묵음 문자 "e"가 없는 단어를 쓰십시오.

Target Word Box				
beat	intake	water	cube	denting
ate	tea	blue	mule	life
bone	wife	the	lively	reading
sea	me	space	meat	elephant

Letter "e" is silent   **Letter "e" has a letter "e" sound**

Name: _____ Date:___/___/_____ Score:_____

Unit Review - E/e

Reading Words with Vowel "e" Sounds: /ĕ/, /ē/, /ə/ & Silent

✓ **Lesson Check Point**

 Directions: Read each target word. Circle the word in the column that has the same "e" sound as the target word.

지도: 각 대상 단어를 읽으십시오. 목표 단어와 같은 "e" 소리가 나는 열의 단어에 동그라미를 치십시오.

belts	a. cakes
	b. legs

peanuts	a. cheese
	b. edge

eating	a. asleep
	b. melt

oxygen	a. bled
	b. label

 Directions: Read each target word. Put a check (✓) under the correct column heading.

지도: 각 대상 단어를 읽으십시오. 올바른 열 제목 아래에 체크(✓)를 하십시오.

Target Words	"e" has the /ĕ/ sound as in the word <u>egg</u>	"e" has the /ē/ sound as in the word <u>me</u>	"e" has the /ə/ sound as in the word <u>item</u>	"e" is silent as in the word <u>great</u>
1. belts				
2. peanuts				
3. eating				
4. oxygen				

Name: _____ Date: ___/___/_____ Score: _____

The Reading Challenge

Lesson 5.11

Reading Multisyllable Words

✓ **Lesson Check Point**

Directions: Read and divide each target word into syllables. Write each word and place a hyphen (-) between the syllables in the second column. Write the number of syllables in the third column. Use a dictionary or the Internet to check your answers.

지도: 각 대상 단어를 읽고 음절로 나눕니다. 각 단어를 쓰고 두 번째 열의 음절 사이에 하이픈(-)을 넣습니다. 세 번째 열에 음절 수를 쓰십시오. 사전이나 인터넷을 사용하여 답을 확인하십시오.

Target Words	Words Divided into Syllables	Number of Syllables
1. nutshell	_____	_____
2. increasing	_____	_____
3. emblem	_____	_____
4. stairwell	_____	_____
5. exceeding	_____	_____
6. airmen	_____	_____
7. drunken	_____	_____
8. eggshell	_____	_____
9. repeated	_____	_____
10. fasten	_____	_____

Unit E
Lesson 5.11

Name: _____ Date: ___/___/_____ Score: _____

The Reading Challenge

Lesson 5.11

Reading Multisyllable Words

 Lesson Check Point

 Directions: Read each target word. Circle the word in the row that is divided correctly into syllables. Use a dictionary or the Internet to check your answers.

지도: 각 대상 단어를 읽으십시오. 음절로 올바르게 나누어진 행에 있는 단어에 동그라미를 치십시오. 사전이나 인터넷을 사용하여 답을 확인하십시오.

Model

| megabyte | a. me-ga-byte | b. meg-a-byte (circled) | c. me-gaby-te |

Target	a	b	c
1. ecosystem	a. eco-sys-tem	b. e-co-sys-tem	c. eco-syst-em
2. segregate	a. se-gre-gate	b. se-greg-ate	c. seg-re-gate
3. countrymen	a. coun-trym-en	b. count-ry-men	c. coun-try-men
4. woodpecker	a. wood-peck-er	b. wood-pec-ker	c. woo-dpeck-er
5. gardening	a. gard-en-ing	b. gar-de-ning	c. gar-den-ing
6. legislate	a. leg-is-late	b. le-gis-late	c. leg-isl-ate
7. comprehend	a. comp-re-hend	b. com-preh-end	c. com-pre-hend
8. dividend	a. div-i-dend	b. di-vid-end	c. div-id-end

Name: _____ Date: ___/___/_____ Score: _____

Lesson 5.12

Reading and Writing

Proper and Common Nouns and Adjectives

✓ **Lesson Check Point**

Directions: Read the words in the word box. Put an (X) on the line next to each word that is written incorrectly. Remember that all proper nouns and proper adjectives are capitalized. Use a dictionary or the Internet to check your answers.
지도: 단어 상자에 있는 단어를 읽으십시오. 잘못 쓰여진 각 단어 옆의 줄에 (X)를 표시하십시오. 모든 고유 명사와 고유 형용사는 대문자임을 기억하십시오. 사전이나 인터넷을 사용하여 답을 확인하십시오.

Word Box		
___ EssEx	___ edition	___ elbow
___ English	___ elaborate	___ ecuador
___ Eskimo	___ Egyptology	___ Education
___ eastern european	___ erie Channel	___ Middle east

Directions: Read each unedited sentence and underline the word that is written incorrectly. Write each sentence correctly on the line.
지도: 편집되지 않은 각 문장을 읽고 잘못 쓰여진 단어에 밑줄을 긋습 니다. 각 문장을 줄에 올바르게 쓰십시오.

Model
All my friends are Excited about the class trip to Europe.
All my friends are excited about the class trip to Europe.

1. My friend, Elias, speaks english extremely well.
   _____

2. Mr. edison developed a battery for the electric car.
   _____

3. This evening, Dr. Edwards Examined Elliot's eyes.
   _____

4. Eileen's e-ticket to edinburgh will expire on April eleventh.
   _____

Name: _____ Date:___/___/_____ Score:_____

Lesson 6.1

Reading Words with the Letter F/f

✓ Lesson Check Point

Directions: Read each target word. Find the letter "f" and put a check (✓) in the column that identifies its position: beginning, within or end.
지도: 각 대상 단어를 읽으십시오. 문자 "f"를 찾아 체크 표시(✓)위치를 식별하는 열에서 시작, 내부 또는 끝.

Target Words	Beginning (First Letter)	Within	End (Last Letter)
1. leaf			
2. fresh			
3. flipped			
4. comfort			
5. defrost			

Directions: Read each sentence and underline the words that begin with the letter "f." Write all the underlined words in alphabetical order on the lines below.
지도: 각 문장을 읽고"f"로 시작하는 단어에 밑줄을 긋습니다. 밑줄친모든 단어를 아래 줄에 알파벳 순서로 쓰십시오.

6. Did you know the fox had fleas?

7. Annie said, "The field is far away."

8. Last January, Bobby ate a lot of fast food.

9. The children like to have fun at the fountain.

10. In the afternoon, the flock of birds flew away.

_____   _____   _____
_____   _____   _____
_____   _____   _____
              _____

Name: _____ Date:___/___/_____ Score:_____

Lesson 6.2

Reading Words with the "fr" Letter Combination

Dictionary Skills/ Vocabulary

✓ Lesson Check Point

Directions: Read each target word and its definition. Write the letter of the definition on the line of each target word. Use a dictionary or the Internet to check your answers.
지도: 각 대상 단어와 그 정의를 읽으십시오. 각 대상 단어의 행에 정의의 문자를 씁니다. 사전이나 인터넷을 사용하여 답을 확인하십시오.

Target Words	Definitions
1. __ frames	a. facial expression indicating displeasure
2. __ French	b. language spoken in France
3. __ front	c. the first or forward position
4. __ frowns	d. something made solid by extreme cold
5. __ frozen	e. borders around an object, such as a picture

Directions: Read each sentence. Underline the word in the parentheses that correctly completes each sentence. Then, write the underlined word on the line.
지도: 각 문장을 읽으십시오. 각 문장을 올바르게 완성하는 괄호 안에 있는 단어에 밑줄을 긋습니다. 그런 다음 밑줄 친 단어를 줄에 쓰십시오.

6. The food in the freezer is _____. (frame, frozen)

7. Flo puts her drawings in beautiful _____. (frames, frozen)

8. Freda speaks _____ and Finnish fluently. (frowns, French)

9. The whiteboard is in _____ of the classroom. (front, French)

10. Happy clowns do not have _____ on their faces. (frowns, frames)

Name: _____   Date: ___/___/_____   Score: _____

Lesson 6.3

Reading Words with the "fl" Letter Combination

Dictionary Skills/ Vocabulary

✓ Lesson Check Point

Directions: Read each target word and its definition. Write the target word on the line in front of its meaning. Use a dictionary or the Internet to check your answers.
지도: 각 대상 단어와 그 정의를 읽으십시오. 의미 앞 줄에 대상 단어를 쓰십시오. 사전이나 인터넷을 사용하여 답을 확인하십시오.

Target Word Box				
flag	flavor	flu	flute	flying

1. _____ the taste of food
2. _____ a woodwind instrument
3. _____ to travel through the air with wings
4. _____ a sickness caused by an acute viral infection
5. _____ a designed fabric used as a country's symbol

Directions: Read each sentence. Underline the word in the parentheses that correctly completes each sentence. Then, write the underlined word on the line.
지도: 각 문장을 읽으십시오. 각 문장을 올바르게 완성하는 괄호 안에 있는 단어에 밑줄을 긋습니다. 그런 다음 밑줄 친 단어를 줄에 쓰십시오.

6. Fred is in bed with the bad _____. (flag, flu)

7. Francis enjoys _____ in the airplane. (flying, flavor)

8. The Japanese _____ is white and red. (flag, flute)

9. Flossy is learning to play the _____ in class. (flute, flu)

10. Flex's fried chicken is full of _____. (flavor, flying)

Name: _____ Date: ___/___/_____ Score: _____

Lesson 6.3

Reading Words with the "fle" Letter Combination

✓ **Lesson Check Point**

 Directions: Read each target word. Find the "fle" letter combination and put a check (✓) in the column that identifies its position: beginning, within or end.

지도: 각 대상 단어를 읽으십시오. "fle" 문자 조합을 찾아해당 위치를식별 하는열에 체크(✓)를 하십시오: 시작, 내부 또는 끝.

Target Words	Beginning (First 3 Letters)	Within	End (Last 3 Letters)
1. fled			
2. baffle			
3. waffle			
4. deflect			
5. inflexed			

 Directions: Read each target word. Put a check (✓) in the "yes" column if the "fle" letter combination has the /f/ + /ə/ + /l/ sounds. Put a check (✓) in the "no" column if the "fle" letter combination does not have the /f/ + /ə/ + /l/ sounds.

지도: 각 대상 단어를 읽으십시오. "fle" 문자 조합에/f/ + /ə/ + /l/ 소리가있으면 "yes" 열에 체크(✓)를 하십시오. "fle" 문자 조합에/f/ + /ə/ + /l/ 소리가"no" 아 니오" 열에 체크(✓)를 하십시오.

Target Words	Yes	No
6. fled		
7. baffle		
8. waffle		
9. deflect		
10. inflexed		

Name: _____ Date: ___/___/_____ Score: _____

Lesson 6.4

Reading Words with the "ft," "lf" and "ff" Letter Combinations

Dictionary Skills/ Vocabulary

✓ Lesson Check Point

Directions: Read each target word and its definition. Write the letter of the definition on the line of each target word. Use a dictionary or the Internet to check your answers.
지도: 각 대상 단어와 그 정의를 읽으십시오. 각 대상 단어의 행에 정의의 문자를 씁니다. 사전이나 인터넷을 사용하여 답을 확인하십시오.

Target Words	Definitions
1. __ staff	a. not hard or firm
2. __ golf	b. an athletic game
3. __ cliff	c. people who work for a company
4. __ soft	d. vehicles driving along the road
5. __ traffic	e. a high and steep area of overhanging soil and rock

Directions: Read each sentence and write the target word that correctly completes the sentence.
지도: 각 문장을 읽고 다음과 같은 목표 단어를 쓰십시오. 장을 올바르게 완성합니다.

6. My family enjoys sleeping on _____ beds.

7. The _____ on the road is backed up to Main Street.

8. My dad's company is hiring new _____ members.

9. Fred and Francis are playing _____ on the course.

10. During the camping trip, the boys climbed up a high _____.

Name: _____   Date:___/___/_____   Score:_____

Lesson 6.5

Reading Words with a Silent Letter "f"

✓ **Lesson Check Point**

Directions: Read the target words in the word box. Write the words that have a silent letter "f" in the first column. Write the words that do not have a silent letter "f" in the second column.

지도: 단어 상자에 있는 대상 단어를 읽으십시오. 첫 번째 열에 묵음문자 "f"가 있는 단어를 쓰십시오. 두 번째 열에 묵음 문자"f"가 없는 단어를 쓰십시오.

Target Word Box				
effort	infant	off	friend	afraid
buffer	before	stiff	figure	rainfall
official	graffiti	waffle	confront	stuffy
suffer	effect	fitting	filter	refer

Letter "f" is silent

Letter "f" has the /f/ sound

Name: _____ Date:___/___/_____ Score:_____

Lesson 6.6

Reading Singular and Plural forms of Words Ending in "-f" & "-fe"

✓ Lesson Check Point

Directions: Read each target word. Put a check (✓) in the second column if the plural form of the target word ends with "-ves." Put a check (✓) in the third column if the plural form of the target word ends with "-s" or "-es."
지도: 각 대상 단어를 읽으십시오. 대상 단어의 복수형이"-ves"로 끝나는 경우 두 번째 열에 체크(✓)를 하십시오. 대상 단어의 복수형이"-s" 또는 "-es."로 끝나는 경우 세 번째 열에 체크(✓)를 하십시오.

Target Words	The plural form of the target word ends with "-ves"	The plural form of the target word ends with "-s" or "-es"
1. roof		
2. calf		
3. knife		
4. chief		
5. belief		

Directions: Read each sentence. Complete each sentence by writing the plural form of the word on the line.
지도: 각 문장을 읽으십시오. 단어의 복수형을 줄에 써서 각 문장을완성 하세요.

6. In autumn, the _____ change color. (leaf)

7. The two dull _____ cannot cut the bread. (knife)

8. On Friday, five bold _____ robbed the bank. (thief)

9. Lifeguards are stationed by the pool to save _____. (life)

10. During the storm, the shingles on the _____ blew away. (roof)

Name: _____ Date: ___/___/_____ Score: _____

The Reading Challenge

Lesson 6.7

Reading Multisyllable Words

✓ **Lesson Check Point**

Directions: Read and divide each target word into syllables. Write each word and place a hyphen (-) between the syllables in the second column. Write the number of syllables in the third column. Use a dictionary or the Internet to check your answers.

지도: 각 대상 단어를 읽고 음절로 나눕니다. 각 단어를 쓰고 두 번째 열의 음절 사이에 하이픈(-)을 넣습니다. 세 번째 열에 음절 수를 쓰십시오. 사전이나 인터넷을 사용하여 답을 확인하십시오.

Target Words	Words Divided into Syllables	Number of Syllables
1. finalist	_____	_____
2. facade	_____	_____
3. flowery	_____	_____
4. folding	_____	_____
5. formula	_____	_____
6. failure	_____	_____
7. fluctuate	_____	_____
8. foolish	_____	_____
9. freedom	_____	_____
10. frequency	_____	_____

Learn To Read English With Directions In Korean

Name: _____ Date: ___/___/_____ Score: _____

The Reading Challenge

Lesson 6.7

Reading Multisyllable Words

✓ **Lesson Check Point**

Directions: Read each target word. Circle the word in the row that is divided correctly into syllables. Use a dictionary or the Internet to check your answers.

지도: 각 대상 단어를 읽으십시오. 음절로 올바르게 나누어진 행에 있는 단어에 동그라미를 치십시오. 사전이나 인터넷을 사용하여 답을 확인하십시오.

Model

| factory | a. fac-tor-y | b. fac-to-ry | c. fa-cto-ry |

1. forgetful	a. for-get-ful	b. fo-rget-ful	c. forg-et-ful
2. faculty	a. fac-u-lty	b. fa-cult-y	c. fac-ul-ty
3. fabulous	a. fab-u-lous	b. fa-bul-ous	c. fab-ulo-us
4. financial	a. fi-nan-cial	b. fin-an-cial	c. fin-anc-ial
5. foliage	a. fo-li-age	b. fol-i-age	c. fo-lia-ge
6. foreigner	a. fore-ign-er	b. fore-ig-ner	c. for-eign-er
7. focusing	a. fo-cus-ing	b. foc-us-ing	c. foc-u-sing
8. falsify	a. fal-sif-y	b. fals-i-fy	c. fal-si-fy

Name: _____ Date: ___/___/_____ Score: _____

Lesson 6.8

Reading and Writing

Proper and Common Nouns and Adjectives

✓ Lesson Check Point

Directions: Read the words in the word box. Put an (X) on the line next to each word that is written incorrectly. Remember that all proper nouns and proper adjectives are capitalized. Use a dictionary or the Internet to check your answers.

지도: 단어 상자에 있는 단어를 읽으십시오. 잘못 쓰여진 각 단어 옆의 줄에 (X)를 표시하십시오. 모든 고유 명사와 고유 형용사는 대문자임을 기억하십시오. 사전이나 인터넷을 사용하여 답을 확인하십시오.

Word Box		
__ Farmer	__ frog	__ france
__ Friend	__ female	__ fingers
__ french	__ frankfort	__ finnish
__ Fort Lee	__ Franklin	__ Fred's Diner

Directions: Read each unedited sentence and underline the word that is written incorrectly. Write each sentence correctly on the line.

지도: 편집되지 않은 각 문장을 읽고 잘못 쓰여진 단어에 밑줄을긋습 니다. 각 문장을 줄에 올바르게 쓰십시오.

Model
Fiji is my <u>Florist's</u> favorite holiday destination.
<u>Fiji is my florist's favorite holiday destination.</u>

1. Flo said, "China is in the far East."
_____

2. Frank is visiting Aunt flossy in Florida.
_____

3. franklin and Francis were born in Frankfort.
_____

4. On friday, Florence wore a fancy dress to the dance.
_____

Name: _____   Date: ___/___/_____   Score: _____

Lesson 7.1

Reading Words with the Letter G/g

✓ Lesson Check Point

Directions: Read each target word. Find the letter "g" and put a check (✓) in the column that identifies its position: beginning, within or end.
지도: 각 대상 단어를 읽으십시오. 문자"g"를 찾아 체크 표시(✓)위치를 식별하는 열에서 시작, 내부 또는 끝.

Target Words	Beginning (First Letter)	Within	End (Last Letter)
1. judge			
2. loving			
3. sibling			
4. grammar			
5. hamburger			

Directions: Read each sentence and underline the words that begin with the letter "g." Write all the underlined words in alphabetical order on the lines below.
지도: 각 문장을 읽고 문자"g"로 시작하는 단어에 밑줄을 긋습니다. 밑줄 친 모든 단어를 아래 줄에 알파벳 순서로 쓰십시오.

6. The goldfish is in a glass bowl.

7. On Saturday, I am going to the art gallery.

8. On Sundays, Grace enjoys singing gospel music.

9. Annie is growing beautiful flowers in her garden.

10. The graphic designer drew a great logo for my business card.

_____   _____   _____
_____   _____   _____
_____   _____   _____
              _____

Name: _____ Date: ___/___/_____ Score: _____

Lesson 7.1

Reading Words with the Hard Letter "g"

✓ **Lesson Check Point**

Directions: Read each target word. Put a check (✓) under the correct column heading.

지도: 각 대상 단어를 읽으십시오. 올바른 열 제목 아래에 체크(✓)를 하십시오.

Target Words	Hard "g" has the /g/ sound as in the word **gum**	Soft "g" has the /j/ sound as in the word **gem**
1. girls		
2. giant		
3. glossy		
4. gender		
5. garden		

Directions: Read each sentence and underline the words that have the hard "g" sound. The anchor word for the hard "g" sound is <u>gum</u>. Write all the underlined words in alphabetical order on the lines below.

지도: 각 문장을 읽고 단단한 "g" 소리가 나는 단어에 밑줄을 긋습니다. 단단한 "g" 소리의 기준어는 gum입니다. 밑줄 친 모든 단어를 아래 줄에 알파벳 순서로 쓰십시오.

6. Ginny's gift was a colorful globe.

7. George is guilty of grabbing the balloons.

8. The giant likes to eat grapes and garlic cloves.

9. In Guyana, the skilled gymnasts are very gracious.

10. Two groups of students are going to visit Germany.

_____   _____   _____

_____   _____   _____

_____   _____   _____

_____

Name: _____ Date: ___/___/_____ Score: _____

Lesson 7.2

Reading Words with the Soft Letter "g"

✓ Lesson Check Point

Directions: Read each target word. Put a check (✓) under the correct column heading.

지도: 각 대상 단어를 읽으십시오. 올바른 열 제목 아래에 체크(✓)를 하십시오.

Target Words	Soft "g" has the /j/ or /zh/ sound as in the words gem & massage	Hard "g" has the /g/ sound as in the word gum	Both soft "g" and hard "g" sounds as in the word gauge
1. give			
2. emerge			
3. apology			
4. garages			
5. geographical			

Directions: Read each sentence and underline the words that have the soft "g" sound. The anchor word for the soft "g" sound is gem. Write all the underlined words in alphabetical order on the lines below.

지도: 각 문장을 읽고 부드러운"g" 소리가 나는 단어에 밑줄을 긋습니다. 부드러운"g" "g" 소리의 기준어는 gem입니다. 밑줄 친 모든 단어를 아래 줄에 알파벳 순서로 쓰십시오.

6. The gentle giant did not break the gate.

7. Gilbert gave me two oranges and a big gyro.

8. Mr. Green said, "The two geese are in a huge cage."

9. My guest took a guided tour of Genie's gymnasium.

10. There is a picture of a gigantic gorilla on the next page.

_____   _____   _____
_____   _____   _____
_____   _____   _____
                  _____

Name: _____ Date:___/___/_____ Score:_____

Review Lessons 7.1 & 7.2

Reading Hard Letter "g" and Soft Letter "g" Words

Directions: Read each target word. Put a check (✓) under the correct column heading.

지도: 각 대상 단어를 읽으십시오. 올바른 열 제목 아래에 체크(✓)를 하십시오.

Target Words	Soft "g" has the /j/ or /zh/ sound as in the words gem & massage	Hard "g" has the /g/ sound as in the word gum	Both soft "g" and hard "g" sounds as in the word gauge
1. griddle			
2. change			
3. analogy			
4. girlfriend			
5. geography			

Directions: Read each sentence and underline the words that have the hard "g" sound. The anchor word for the hard "g" sound is gum. Write all the underlined words in alphabetical order on the lines below.

지도: 각 문장을 읽고 단단한 "g" 소리가 나는 단어에 밑줄을 긋습니다. 단단한 "g" 소리의 기준어는 gum입니다. 밑줄 친 모든 단어를 아래 줄에 알파벳 순서로 쓰십시오.

6. George gave each child a toy kangaroo.

7. Gina designed a great maze in the garden.

8. Geron received golf clubs as a birthday gift.

9. Gene is allergic to an ingredient in orange gum.

10. Grandma said, "The magic gel is in a gold bottle."

_____   _____   _____
_____   _____   _____
_____   _____   _____
             _____

Learn To Read English With Directions In Korean

Name: _____ Date: ___/___/_____ Score: _____

Review Lessons 7.1 & 7.2

Reading Hard Letter "g" and Soft Letter "g" Words

Directions: Read the target words in the word box. In the first column, write the words with the letter "g" that have the /g/ sound, as in the word <u>gum</u>. In the second column, write the words with the letter "g" that have the /j/ sound, as in the word <u>gem</u>.

지도: 단어 상자에 있는 대상 단어를 읽으십시오. 첫 번째 열에는단어 gum 에서와 같이 /g/ 소리가 나는 문자"g"가 있는 단어를 씁니다. 두 번째열에 "g"가 포함된 단어를 쓰십시오. /j/ 소리, gem이라는 단어에서와 같이.

Target Word Box				
page	gesture	good	gene	green
garden	gills	ginger	gift	gentle
cage	ago	orange	gypsy	grade
gulp	bag	large	figure	German

Hard letter "g" has the /g/ sound as in the word <u>gum</u>

Soft letter "g" has the /j/ sound as in the word <u>gem</u>

Name: _____ Date:___/___/_____ Score:_____

Lesson 7.3

Reading Words with the "gr" Letter Combination

Dictionary Skills/ Vocabulary

✓ **Lesson Check Point**

Directions: Read each target word and its definition. Write the letter of the definition on the line of each target word. Use a dictionary or the Internet to check your answers.
지도: 각 대상 단어와 그 정의를 읽으십시오. 각 대상 단어의 행에 정의의 문자를 씁니다. 사전이나 인터넷을 사용하여 답을 확인하십시오.

Target Words	Definitions
1. __ grilled	a. the color of leaves and plant stems
2. __ gravity	b. characteristic of distinction and importance
3. __ great	c. force that keeps things grounded
4. __ green	d. kindness and politeness in a person's character
5. __ gracious	e. to have cooked food on parallel bars over a fire

Directions: Read each sentence. Underline the word in the parentheses that correctly completes each sentence. Then, write the underlined word on the line.
지도: 각 문장을 읽으십시오. 각 문장을 올바르게 완성하는 괄호 안에 있는 단어에 밑줄을 긋습니다. 그런 다음 밑줄 친 단어를 줄에 쓰십시오.

6. The _____ grass is growing. (grilled, green)

7. At the barbecue, my dad _____ the chicken. (great, grilled)

8. Gloria is always _____ and charming. (gracious, green)

9. The _____ citizens received service awards. (gravity, great)

10. _____ stops things from floating upward. (Gracious, Gravity)

Name: _____   Date:___/___/_____   Score:_____

Lesson 7.4

Reading Words with the "gl" Letter Combination

Dictionary Skills/ Vocabulary

✓ Lesson Check Point

Directions: Read each target word and its definition. Write the target word on the line in front of its meaning. Use a dictionary or the Internet to check your answers.
지도: 각 대상 단어와 그 정의를 읽으십시오. 의미 앞 줄에 대상 단어를 쓰십시오. 사전이나 인터넷을 사용하여 답을 확인하십시오.

Target Word Box				
glamorous	glass	glasses	gloves	glows

1. _____ having glamour
2. _____ protective coverings for hands
3. _____ to reflect light through an object
4. _____ a container used for drinking hot or cold beverages
5. _____ a pair of lenses fitted into a frame that a person wears to see

Directions: Read each sentence. Underline the word in the parentheses that correctly completes each sentence. Then, write the underlined word on the line.
지도: 각 문장을 읽으십시오. 각 문장을 올바르게 완성하는 괄호 안에 있는 단어에 밑줄을 긋습니다. 그런 다음 밑줄 친 단어를 줄에 쓰십시오.

6. My doctor always wears latex _____. (glows, gloves)

7. The computer screen _____ in the dark. (gloves, glows)

8. Greg wears _____ to see things at a distance. (glasses, glass)

9. Gloria likes to drink her coffee with a crystal _____. (glows, glass)

10. The girls bought _____ dresses for the concert. (glamorous, glasses)

Name: _____ Date: ___/___/_____ Score: _____

Lesson 7.4

Reading Words with the "gle" Letter Combination

✓ Lesson Check Point

 Directions: Read each target word. Find the "gle" letter combination and put a check (✓) in the column that identifies its position: beginning, within or end.

지도: 각 대상 단어를 읽으십시오. "gle" 문자 조합을 찾아 위치를 식별하는 열에 체크(✓)를 하십시오: 시작, 내부 또는 끝.

Target Words	Beginning (First 3 Letters)	Within	End (Last 3 Letters)
1. ringlet			
2. dangle			
3. bungle			
4. gleamed			
5. Glenwood			

 Directions: Read each target word. Put a check (✓) in the "yes" column if the "gle" letter combination has the /g/ + /ə/ + /l/ sounds. Put a check (✓) in the "no" column if the "gle" letter combination does not have the /g/ + /ə/ + /l/ sounds.

지도: 각 대상 단어를 읽으십시오. "gle" 문자 조합에 /g/ + /ə/ + /l/ 소리가 있으면 "yes" 열에 체크(✓)를 하십시오. "gle" 문자 조합에 /g/ + /ə/ + /l/ 소리가 없으면 "no" 열에 체크(✓)를 하십시오.

Target Words	Yes	No
6. ringlet		
7. dangle		
8. bungle		
9. gleamed		
10. Glenwood		

Name: _____ Date: ___/___/_____ Score: _____

Lesson 7.5

Reading Words with the "gh" Letter Combination

✓ Lesson Check Point

 Directions: Read each target word. Circle the word in the column that has the same "gh" sound as the target word.

지도: 각 대상 단어를 읽으십시오. 대상 단어와 같은 "gh" 소리가 나는 열의 단어에 동그라미를 치십시오.

ghost	a. ghastly
	b. rough

weight	a. enough
	b. thigh

insight	a. laughing
	b. weigh

coughing	a. mighty
	b. tougher

 Directions: Read each target word. Put a check (✓) under the correct column heading.

지도: 각 대상 단어를 읽으십시오. 올바른 열 제목 아래에 체크(✓)를하십시오.

Target Words	"gh" has the /g/ sound as in the word <u>ghetto</u>	"gh" has the /f/ sound as in the word <u>laugh</u>	"gh" is silent as in the word <u>light</u>
1. ghost			
2. weight			
3. insight			
4. coughing			

Name: _____ Date:___/___/_____ Score:_____

Lesson 7.6

Reading Words with the "gn" Letter Combination

✓ Lesson Check Point

 Directions: Read each target word. Circle the word in the column that has the same "gn" sound(s) as the target word.
지도: 각 대상 단어를 읽으십시오. 대상 단어와 같은 "gn" 소리가 나는 열의 단어에 동그라미를 치십시오.

| ignore | a. aligned |
| | b. recognition |

| ignition | a. diagnostic |
| | b. alignment |

| vignette | a. magnified |
| | b. benign |

| champagne | a. ignorant |
| | b. designer |

 Directions: Read each target word. Put a check (✓) under the correct column heading.
지도: 각 대상 단어를 읽으십시오. 올바른 열 제목 아래에 체크(✓)를 하십시오.

Target Words	"gn" has the /g/ + /n/ sounds as in the word <u>ignite</u>	"gn" has the silent "g" + /n/ sound as in the word <u>sign</u>
1. ignore		
2. ignition		
3. vignette		
4. champagne		

Name: _____ Date: ___/___/_____ Score: _____

Lesson 7.7

Reading Words with a Silent Letter "g"

✓ **Lesson Check Point**

Directions: Read the target words in the word box. Write the words that have a silent letter "g" in the first column. Write the words that do not have a silent letter "g" in the second column.

지도: 단어 상자에 있는 대상 단어를 읽으십시오. 첫 번째 열에 묵음문자 "g"가 있는 단어를 쓰십시오. 두 번째 열에 묵음 문자 "g"가 없는 단어를 쓰십시오.

Target Word Box				
signal	ago	Ghana	goat	campaign
clog	thigh	bright	gloves	foreign
design	program	magic	sign	tight
bologna	good	goggle	smug	snuggle

Letter "g" is silent **Letter "g" has the /g/ or /j/ sound**

Name: _____ Date: ___/___/_____ Score: _____

The Reading Challenge

Lesson 7.8

Reading Multisyllable Words

✓ **Lesson Check Point**

 Directions: Read and divide each target word into syllables. Write each word and place a hyphen (-) between the syllables in the second column. Write the number of syllables in the third column. Use a dictionary or the Internet to check your answers.

지도: 각 대상 단어를 읽고 음절로 나눕니다. 각 단어를 쓰고 두 번째 열의 음절 사이에 하이픈(-)을 넣습니다. 세 번째 열에 음절 수를 쓰십시오. 사전이나 인터넷을 사용하여 답을 확인하십시오.

Target Words	Words Divided into Syllables	Number of Syllables
1. goalkeeper	_____	_____
2. government	_____	_____
3. gasoline	_____	_____
4. guarantee	_____	_____
5. gelatin	_____	_____
6. glorified	_____	_____
7. gathering	_____	_____
8. Grenada	_____	_____
9. generalize	_____	_____
10. glamorous	_____	_____

Name: _____ Date:___/___/_____ Score:_____

The Reading Challenge

Lesson 7.8

Reading Multisyllable Words

✓ **Lesson Check Point**

 Directions: Read each target word. Circle the word in the row that is divided correctly into syllables. Use a dictionary or the Internet to check your answers.

지도: 각 대상 단어를 읽으십시오. 음절로 올바르게 나누어진 행에 있는 단어에 동그라미를 치십시오. 사전이나 인터넷을 사용하여 답을 확인하십시오.

Model

| galaxy | a. ga-lax-y | b. gal-ax-y | c. gal-a-xy |

1. generate	a. ge-ner-ate	b. gen-er-ate	c. gen-era-te
2. gigabyte	a. gig-a-byte	b. gi-ga-byte	c. gig-aby-te
3. gardenia	a. ga-rde-nia	b. gar-de-nia	c. gar-den-ia
4. gondola	a. go-ndo-la	b. go-ndol-a	c. gon-do-la
5. generous	a. gen-er-ous	b. ge-ner-ous	c. gen-ero-us
6. gradual	a. grad-u-al	b. gra-du-al	c. grad-ua-l
7. gasoline	a. gas-o-line	b. ga-soline	c. gas-oli-ne
8. gestation	a. gest-a-tion	b. ge-stat-ion	c. ges-ta-tion

Name: _____ Date: ___/___/_____ Score: _____

Lesson 7.9

Reading and Writing

Proper and Common Nouns and Adjectives

✓ **Lesson Check Point**

Directions: Read the words in the word box. Put an (X) on the line next to each word that is written incorrectly. Remember that all proper nouns and proper adjectives are capitalized. Use a dictionary or the Internet to check your answers.

지도: 단어 상자에 있는 단어를 읽으십시오. 잘못 쓰여진 각 단어 옆의 줄에 (X)를 표시하십시오. 모든 고유 명사와 고유 형용사는 대문자임을 기억하십시오. 사전이나 인터넷을 사용하여 답을 확인하십시오.

Word Box		
___ Guyana	___ Greek	___ guam
___ georgia	___ Glacier	___ great
___ Gesture	___ guardian	___ Guitar
___ Grandfather	___ Gentleman	___ Germany

Directions: Read each unedited sentence and underline the word that is written incorrectly. Write each sentence correctly on the line.

지도: 편집되지 않은 각 문장을 읽고 잘못 쓰여진 단어에 밑줄을 긋습 니다. 각 문장을 줄에 올바르게 쓰십시오.

Model
Ginger and <u>gene</u> are going to Georgetown, Guyana.
Ginger and Gene are going to Georgetown, Guyana.

1. The Gorgeous gymnast is from Gibraltar.
   _____

2. On Friday, gina was gossiping about Gene.
   _____

3. Ginger bought a glamorous Gold ring from Guatemala.
   _____

4. I saw a gracious gazelle at the famous Golden gate Zoo.
   _____

Name: _____   Date: ___/___/_____   Score: _____

Lesson 8.1

Reading Words with the Letter H/h

✓ Lesson Check Point

Directions: Read each target word. Find the letter "h" and put a check (✓) in the column that identifies its position: beginning, within or end.
지도: 각 대상 단어를 읽으십시오. 문자"h"를 찾아 체크 표시(✓)위치를 식별하는 열에서 시작, 내부 또는 끝.

Target Words	Beginning (First Letter)	Within	End (Last Letter)
1. Utah			
2. teach			
3. horse			
4. helper			
5. Fahrenheit			

Directions: Read each sentence and underline the words that begin with the letter "h." Write all the underlined words in alphabetical order on the lines below.
지도: 각 문장을 읽고 "h"로 시작하는 단어에 밑줄을 긋습니다. 밑줄 친 모든 단어를 아래 줄에 알파벳 순서로 쓰십시오.

6. Pat's high chair is very heavy.

7. Henry broke Samantha's heart.

8. Ashley is holding a very big hammer.

9. Brenda puts green herbs in the hummus.

10. The hacker accessed Harry's email account.

_____   _____   _____
_____   _____   _____
_____   _____   _____
            _____

Name: _____ Date: ___/___/_____ Score: _____

Lesson 8.2

Reading Words with the Letter "h" Combinations:
"sh," "wh," "ch," "th," "rh," "ph" and "gh"

✓ Lesson Check Point

 Directions: Read the target words in the word box. Identify the words with the following letter combinations: "sh," "wh," "ch," "th," "rh," "ph" and "gh." Write the word on the line that shows the position of the letter combination: beginning, within or end.

지도: 단어 상자에 있는 대상 단어를 읽으십시오. "sh," "wh," "ch," "th," "rh," "ph" 및 "gh" 문자 조합으로 단어를 식별합니다. 문자 조합의 위치를 나타내는 줄에 단어를 쓰십시오: 시작, 내부 또는 끝.

Target Word Box				
white	myrrh	phonics	echo	laughed
birthday	shake	letterhead	triumph	rich
rhetoric	chorus	theme	north	tough
flywheel	finish	telephone	ghetto	wishes

	Beginning	Within	End
sh	1. _____	2. _____	3. _____
wh	4. _____	5. _____	
ch	6. _____	7. _____	8. _____
th	9. _____	10. _____	11. _____
rh	12. _____	13. _____	14. _____
ph	15. _____	16. _____	17. _____
gh	18. _____	19. _____	20. _____

Learn To Read English With Directions In Korean

Name: _____ Date: ___/___/_____ Score: _____

Lesson 8.2

Reading Words with the Letter "h" Combinations:
"sh," "wh," "ch," "th," "rh," "ph," "gh" and "sch"

✓ **Lesson Check Point**

Directions: Read the target words in the word box. Identify the words with the following letter combinations: "sh," "wh," "ch," "th," "rh," "ph," "gh" and "sch." Write the target word that correctly completes each sentence on the line.

지도: 단어 상자에 있는 대상 단어를 읽습니다: "sh," "wh," "ch," "th," "rh," "ph," "gh" 및"sch"의 문자 조합으로 단어를 식별합니다. 각 문장을 올바르게 완성하는 대상 단어를 줄에 쓰십시오.

Target Word Box		
white	school	laughed
teacher	ship	elephant
through		rhombus
shortbread		phone

1. My family and I saw a big _____ at the circus.

2. My science _____ wrote three facts on the board.

3. Sharon wore her new _____ shoes to school.

4. My parents bought me three notebooks for _____.

5. The diamond-shaped figure is called a _____.

6. The cruise _____ sailed from New York to Florida.

7. Everyone _____ at Grandma's funny jokes.

8. The children walked _____ the rain without umbrellas.

9. Alexandria is unable to sync her _____ to the computer.

10. The bakers baked _____ cookies with three ingredients.

Name: _____ Date: ___/___/_____ Score: _____

Lesson 8.3

Reading Words with a Silent Letter "h"

✓ Lesson Check Point

Directions: Read the target words in the word box. Write the words that have a silent letter "h" in the first column. Write the words that do not have a silent letter "h" in the second column.

지도: 단어 상자에 있는 대상 단어를 읽습니다. 첫 번째 열에 묵음문자 "h"가 있는 단어를 쓰십시오. 두 번째 열에 묵음 문자"h"가 없는 단어를 쓰십시오.

Target Word Box				
manhood	behind	honest	prohibit	ought
overhaul	whisk	honorarium	inherit	helpful
bought	right	spaghetti	houses	manhole
shorthand	heirs	rehearse	exhume	rhyme

Letter "h" is silent   **Letter "h" has the /h/ sound**

Name: _____ Date: ___/___/_____ Score: _____

The Reading Challenge

Lesson 8.4

Reading Multisyllable Words

✓ Lesson Check Point

Directions: Read and divide each target word into syllables. Write each word and place a hyphen (-) between the syllables in the second column. Write the number of syllables in the third column. Use a dictionary or the Internet to check your answers.

지도: 각 대상 단어를 읽고 음절로 나눕니다. 각 단어를 쓰고 두 번째 열의 음절 사이에 하이픈(-)을 넣습니다. 세 번째 열에 음절 수를 쓰십시오. 사전이나 인터넷을 사용하여 답을 확인하십시오.

Target Words	Words Divided into Syllables	Number of Syllables
1. hibernate	_____	_____
2. hallway	_____	_____
3. helicopter	_____	_____
4. holdover	_____	_____
5. headstrong	_____	_____
6. hazardous	_____	_____
7. historic	_____	_____
8. humorous	_____	_____
9. heartbroken	_____	_____
10. homework	_____	_____

Unit H
Lesson 8.4

Name: _____ Date: ___/___/_____ Score: _____

The Reading Challenge

Lesson 8.4

Reading Multisyllable Words

✓ **Lesson Check Point**

Directions: Read each target word. Circle the word in the row that is divided correctly into syllables. Use a dictionary or the Internet to check your answers.

지도: 각 대상 단어를 읽으십시오. 음절로 올바르게 나누어진 행에 있는 단어에 동그라미를 치십시오. 사전이나 인터넷을 사용하여 답을 확인하십시오.

Model

| heroic | a. he-roi-c | b. her-o-ic | c. he-ro-ic ⟵(circled) |

1. histogram	a. his-to-gram	b. hi-sto-gram	c. his-tog-ram
2. hab-i-tat	a. ha-bi-tat	b. ha-bit-at	c. hab-i-tat
3. hospital	a. hos-pi-tal	b. hos-pit-al	c. ho-spi-tal
4. hamburger	a. ham-burg-er	b. hamb-urg-er	c. hamb-ur-ger
5. habitual	a. hab-it-ual	b. hab-i-tual	c. ha-bit-u-al
6. handicap	a. hand-i-cap	b. han-di-cap	c. hand-ic-ap
7. holiday	a. hol-i-day	b. ho-lid-ay	c. ho-li-day
8. humorous	a. hum-or-ous	b. hum-o-rous	c. hu-mor-ous

Name: _____   Date: ___/___/_____   Score: _____

Lesson 8.5

Reading and Writing

Proper and Common Nouns and Adjectives

✓ Lesson Check Point

Directions: Read the words in the word box. Put an (X) on the line next to each word that is written incorrectly. Remember that all proper nouns and proper adjectives are capitalized. Use a dictionary or the Internet to check your answers.

지도: 단어 상자에 있는 단어를 읽으십시오. 잘못 쓰여진 각 단어 옆의 줄에 (X)를 표시하십시오. 모든 고유 명사와 고유 형용사는 대문자임을 기억하십시오. 사전이나 인터넷을 사용하여 답을 확인하십시오.

Word Box		
__ Haiti	__ hawk	__ Hotel
__ Horizon	__ House	__ herself
__ Heather	__ holland	__ horses
__ hinduism	__ Hannah	__ honduras

Directions: Read each unedited sentence and underline the word that is written incorrectly. Write each sentence correctly on the line.

지도: 편집되지 않은 각 문장을 읽고 잘못 쓰여진 단어에 밑줄을 긋습 니다. 각 문장을 줄에 올바르게 쓰십시오.

Model
Mr. Hitt has a big house on <u>hope</u> Avenue.
<u>Mr. Hitt has a big house on Hope Avenue.</u>

1. Hadia and Henry are standing in the Hallway.
   _____

2. The best Hamburgers are sold at Harpo's Diner.
   _____

3. Hollywood is producing a movie entitled, "The house of Hearts."
   _____

4. The Hacker broke into Hartford Hospital's computer database.
   _____

Name: _____ Date: ___/___/_____ Score: _____

Lesson 9.1

Reading Words with the Letter I/i

✓ Lesson Check Point

 Directions: Read each target word. Find the letter "i" and put a check (✓) in the column that identifies its position: beginning, within or end.
지도: 각 대상 단어를 읽으십시오. 문자 "i"를 찾아 체크 표시(✓)위치를 식별하는 열에서 시작, 내부 또는 끝.

Target Words	Beginning (First Letter)	Within	End (Last Letter)
1. blink			
2. octopi			
3. certify			
4. iceberg			
5. alumni			

 Directions: Read each target word. Read the words in the row and circle the word that has a different vowel "i" sound.
지도: 각 대상 단어를 읽으십시오. 행에 있는 단어를 읽고 모음 "i" 소리가 다른 단어에 동그라미를 치십시오.

Target Words				
6. pink	fib	did	him	like
7. ring	bride	kid	bit	fig
8. gift	jig	blip	drive	hint
9. fish	flit	lime	brim	hid
10. pick	cite	kit	fill	silk

Name: _____ Date:___/___/_____ Score:_____

Lesson 9.2

Reading Words with the Short Vowel "i" Sound

✓ **Lesson Check Point**

 Directions: Read the words in the four boxes. Circle two words with the short vowel /ĭ/ sound. The anchor word for the short vowel /ĭ/ sound is <u>insect</u>.

지도: 네 개의 상자에 있는 단어를 읽으십시오. 짧은 모음/ĭ/ 소리로 두 단어에 동그라미를 치십시오. 단모음/ĭ/ 소리의 기준어는 insect입니다.

ripe	did		wish	link		click	vice
lid	five		fine	dime		wipe	bring

wide	size		dish	wing		sing	dive
stick	flint		miles	wild		dine	limp

 Directions: Read the words in the four boxes. Circle two words that rhyme. Rhyming words have the same ending sound, such as <u>hip</u> and <u>dip</u>.

지도: 네 개의 상자에 있는 단어를 읽으십시오. 운이 맞는 두 단어에동그라미를 치십시오. 운율이 있는 단어는 hip와dip과 같이 끝 소리가같습니다.

trim	fire		hive	grip		tire	pipe
tide	brim		tile	trip		skip	ship

flip	snip		swim	dice		file	gift
wire	pile		skim	ride		lift	hire

Name: _____ Date: ___/___/_____ Score: _____

Lesson 9.2

Reading & Writing Words with the Short Vowel "i" Sound

✓ **Lesson Check Point**

Directions: Read each sentence and underline three words with the short vowel /ĭ/ sound. Then, write the underlined words on the lines below. The anchor word for the short vowel /ĭ/ sound is <u>insect</u>.

지도: 각 문장을 읽고 세 단어에 짧은 모음 /ĭ/ 소리에 밑줄을 긋습니다. 그런 다음 밑줄 친 단어를 아래 줄에 쓰십시오. 단모음 /ĭ/ 소리의 기준 어는 insect입니다.

Model

<u>Jim</u> placed a <u>big</u> cup of ice on the <u>windowsill</u>.

    Jim   big   windowsill

1. Gil's white shirt did not fit.

   _____   _____   _____

2. Isaac drinks white skim milk.

   _____   _____   _____

3. Jim likes to sit on top of the hill.

   _____   _____   _____

4. Will you miss the five kids from Iceland?

   _____   _____   _____

5. My friends, Irene and Tim, ate six tortilla chips.

   _____   _____   _____

Name: _____ Date: ___/___/_____ Score: _____

Lesson 9.3

Reading Words with the Long Vowel "i" Sound

✓ **Lesson Check Point**

 Directions: Read the words in the four boxes. Circle two words with the long vowel /ī/ sound. The anchor word for the long vowel /ī/ sound is <u>ice</u>.

지도: 네 개의 상자에 있는 단어를 읽으십시오. 장모음/ī/ 소리로두단어에 동그라미를 치십시오. 장모음/ī/ 소리의 기준어는 ice입니다.

tile	wing	cling	dine	trick	milk
side	grill	chain	cite	hide	lime

rite	lice	price	click	hive	item
main	brick	disk	pile	sink	Spain

 Directions: Read the words in the four boxes. Circle two words that rhyme. Rhyming words have the same ending sound, such as <u>rice</u> and <u>nice</u>.

지도: 네 개의 상자에 있는 단어를 읽으십시오. 운이 맞는 두 단어에동그라미를 치십시오. 운율이 있는 단어는 rice와 nice와 같은 끝 소리가같습니다.

file	stick	wide	lint	mist	rink
clip	mile	side	mill	mice	dice

trip	tile	nice	wish	limb	skip
pile	king	ski	vice	pipe	ripe

Name: _____ Date: ___/___/_____ Score: _____

Lesson 9.3

Reading & Writing Words with the Long Vowel "i" Sound

✓ **Lesson Check Point**

Directions: Read each sentence and underline three words with the long vowel /ī/ sound. Then, write the underlined words on the lines below. The anchor word for the long vowel /ī/ sound is <u>ice</u>.

지도: 각 문장을 읽고 장모음/ī/ 소리로 세 단어에 밑줄을 긋습니다. 그런 다음 밑줄 친 단어를 아래 줄에 쓰십시오. 장모음/ī/ 소리의 기준어는 ice 입니다.

Model

David and <u>I</u> flew our big, <u>white</u> <u>kite</u> along the riverbank.

    I   white   kite
_____   _____   _____

1. The child likes to hide in the old mill.

   _____   _____   _____

2. At night, Jim drives his car for miles.

   _____   _____   _____

3. He will win a prize for the ninth time.

   _____   _____   _____

4. At five o'clock, the bride simply smiled at William.

   _____   _____   _____

5. His wife admires the six firefighters for their bravery.

   _____   _____   _____

Name: _____ Date: ___/___/_____ Score: _____

Review Lessons 9.2 & 9.3

Reading Short Vowel and Long Vowel Words

✓ **Lesson Check Point**

Directions: Read the target words in the word box. In the first column, write the words that have the short vowel /ĭ/ sound, as in the word <u>insect</u>. In the second column, write the words that have the long vowel /ī/ sound, as in the word <u>ice</u>.

지도: 단어 상자에 있는 대상 단어를 읽습니다. 첫 번째 열에는 insect라는 단어와 같이 단모음/ĭ/ 소리가 나는 단어를 씁니다. 두 번째 열에는 ice 라는 단어에서처럼 장모음/ī/ 소리가 나는 단어를 씁니다.

Target Word Box				
lion	blimp	hike	mild	lie
dill	tiger	bring	tried	fine
fish	miss	king	fried	ring
dice	fiber	cinch	spring	click

Letter "i" has the /ĭ/ sound as in the word <u>insect</u>

Letter "i" has the /ī/ sound as in the word <u>ice</u>

Name: _____ Date: ___/___/_____ Score: _____

Lesson 9.4

Reading Words with Letter "i" Vowel Pairs

✓ Lesson Check Point

 Directions: Read each target word. Circle the word in the column that has the same vowel "ia," "ie," "io" or "iu" sound(s) as the target word.
지도: 각 대상 단어를 읽으십시오. 대상 단어와 같은 모음 "ia," "ie," "io" 또는 "iu" 소리가 있는 열의 단어에 동그라미를 치십시오.

fried	a. diet
	b. tried

podium	a. dialing
	b. bacteria

opinion	a. reunion
	b. client

appliance	a. aquarium
	b. reliable

 Directions: Read each target word. Put a check (✓) under the correct column heading.
지도: 각 대상 단어를 읽으십시오. 올바른 열 제목 아래에 체크(✓)를 하십시오.

Target Words	Words have the long "i" sound as in the word <u>dial</u>	Words do not have the long "i" sound
1. fried		
2. podium		
3. opinion		
4. appliance		

Name: _____ Date: ___/___/_____ Score: _____

Lesson 9.5

Reading Words with the Final Letter "i"

✓ **Lesson Check Point**

Directions: Read each target word. Find the letter "i" and put a check (✓) in the column that identifies its position within the syllable.
지도: 각 대상 단어를 읽으십시오. 문자"i"를 찾아 체크 표시(✓)음절내에서 위치를 식별하는 열에서.

Target Words	"i" is at the end of a one syllable word	"i" is at the end of the first syllable	"i" is at the end of a multi-syllable word
1. I			
2. hi			
3. alibī			
4. dinette			
5. bifocal			

Directions: Read each target word. Put a check (✓) under the correct column heading.
지도: 각대상 단어를 읽으십시오. 올바른 열 제목 아래에체크(✓)를하십시오.

Target Words	"i" has the /ĭ/ sound as in the word insect	"i" has the /ī/ sound as in the word bike	"i" has the /ə/ sound as in the word pencil	"i" is silent as in the word maid
6. raised				
7. fashion				
8. lipstick				
9. tiger				
10. uniform				

Name: _____ Date: ___/___/_____ Score: _____

Lesson 9.6

Reading Letter "i" Words with the Schwa Vowel Sound

✓ **Lesson Check Point**

 Directions: Read each target word. Circle the word in the column that has the same "i" sound as the target word.
지도: 각 대상 단어를 읽으십시오. 목표 단어와 동일한"i" 소리가 나는 열의 단어에 동그라미를 치십시오.

incred**i**ble	a. insect
	b. notify

simpl**i**fy	a. binocular
	b. pink

sim**i**lar	a. ripping
	b. amplify

nostr**i**ls	a. fishing
	b. carnival

 Directions: Read each sentence and underline the letter "i" word that has the schwa vowel /ə/ sound. The anchor word for the letter "i" schwa vowel sound is <u>pencil</u>.
지도: 각 문장을 읽고 슈와 모음 /ə/ 소리가 있는 문자"i" 단어에 밑줄을 긋습니다. 문자"i" 슈와 모음 소리의 앵커 단어는 pencil입니다.

1. The animals in the zoo are excited.

2. Those five children are simply beautiful.

3. The principal approved the school's signs.

4. Irene and her family like to ski in Iceland.

5. The filing cabinets have important documents.

6. Every student is required to wear the school uniform.

Name: _____ Date: ___/___/_____ Score: _____

Lesson 9.7

Reading Words with the "ir" Letter Combination

Dictionary Skills/ Vocabulary

✓ Lesson Check Point

Directions: Read each target word and its definition. Write the letter of the definition on the line of each target word. Use a dictionary or the Internet to check your answers.

지도: 각 대상 단어와 그 정의를 읽으십시오. 각 대상 단어의 행에 정의의 문자를 씁니다. 사전이나 인터넷을 사용하여 답을 확인하십시오.

Target Words	Definitions
1. ___ thirst	a. the position before the second
2. ___ squirt	b. having a desire to drink something
3. ___ dirt	c. the upper, brown layer of the earth; garden soil
4. ___ first	d. the use of circular motions to mix or blend something
5. ___ stirred	e. to squeeze liquid out of something

Directions: Read each sentence and write the target word that completes the sentence.

지도: 각 문장을 읽고 다음과 같은 목표 단어를 쓰십시오. 장을 올바르게 완성합니다.

6. We planted the seeds deep into the _____.

7. Bertha admires her _____ grade teacher.

8. Iris _____ low-fat milk into her Spanish coffee.

9. I drank a cold glass of water to quench my _____.

10. She will _____ chocolate syrup on her ice cream.

Name: _____ Date:___/___/_____ Score:_____

Lesson 9.8

Reading Letter "i" Words with the Long Vowel "e" Sound

✓ Lesson Check Point

Directions: Read each target word. Circle the word in the column that has the same "i" sound as the target word.

지도: 각 대상 단어를 읽으십시오. 목표 단어와 동일한"i" 소리가 나는 열의 단어에 동그라미를 치십시오.

kiwi	a. pilgrim
	b. deli

Hindi	a. ski
	b. silently

chili	a. giant
	b. maxi

pizza	a. taxi
	b. license

Directions: Read each sentence and underline the letter "i" word that has the long vowel /ē/ sound. Then, write the word on the line. The anchor word, taxi, has a letter "i" that has the long vowel /ē/ sound.

지도: 각 문장을 읽고 장모음 /ē/ 소리가 나는"i" 단어에 밑줄을 긋습니다. 그런 다음 줄에 단어를 쓰십시오. 앵커 단어인 taxi에는 장모음 /ē/ 소리를 나타내는 문자"i"가 있습니다.

1. I plan to ride in a yellow taxicab. _____

2. Nick and Jim will join the Marine Corps. _____

3. In the winter, the Rivers family likes to ski. _____

4. The African safari ride costs sixty-six dollars. _____

5. Isaac and Allison ate pepperoni rolls for dinner. _____

6. The chef sprinkled paprika on her stuffed eggs. _____

Learn To Read English With Directions In Korean

Name: _____ Date: ___/___/_____ Score: _____

Lesson 9.9

Reading Words with a Silent Letter "i"

✓ **Lesson Check Point**

Directions: Read the target words in the word box. Write the words that have a silent letter "i" in the first column. Write the words that do not have a silent letter "i" in the second column.

지도: 단어 상자에 있는 대상 단어를 읽습니다. 첫 번째 열에 묵음문자 "i"가 있는 단어를 쓰십시오. 두 번째 열에 묵음 문자"i"가 없는 단어를 쓰십시오.

Target Word Box				
vain	likes	pipe	civil	waist
insects	suits	lines	rails	cruise
inside	instant	tails	dinner	obtained
finding	detailed	gripping	Jamaican	attained

Letter "i" is silent   Letter "i" has a letter "i" sound

Name: _____ Date: ___/___/_____ Score: _____

Unit Review - I/i

Reading Words with Vowel "i" Sounds: /ĭ/, /ī/, /ə/ & Silent

✓ **Lesson Check Point**

Directions: Read each target word. Circle the word in the column that has the same "i" sound as the target word.
지도: 각 대상 단어를 읽으십시오. 목표 단어와 동일한 "i" 소리가 나는 열의 단어에 동그라미를 치십시오.

nice	a. item
	b. slim

again	a. ring
	b. bait

sister	a. paid
	b. trip

inform	a. dishes
	b. taxi

Directions: Read each target word. Put a check (✓) under the correct column heading.
지도: 각 대상 단어를 읽으십시오. 올바른 열 제목 아래에 체크(✓)를 하십시오.

Target Words	"i" has the /ĭ/ sound as in the word <u>insect</u>	"i" has the /ī/ sound as in the word <u>bike</u>	"i" has the /ə/ sound as in the word <u>pencil</u>	"i" is silent as in the word <u>maid</u>
1. nice				
2. again				
3. sister				
4. inform				

Name: _____ Date: ___/___/_____ Score: _____

The Reading Challenge

Lesson 9.10

Reading Multisyllable Words

✓ **Lesson Check Point**

Directions: Read and divide each target word into syllables. Write each word and place a hyphen (-) between the syllables in the second column. Write the number of syllables in the third column. Use a dictionary or the Internet to check your answers.

지도: 각 대상 단어를 읽고 음절로 나눕니다. 각 단어를 쓰고 두 번째 열의 음절 사이에 하이픈(-)을 넣습니다. 세 번째 열에 음절 수를 쓰십시오. 사전이나 인터넷을 사용하여 답을 확인하십시오.

Target Words	Words Divided into Syllables	Number of Syllables
1. tiger		
2. silently		
3. outsider		
4. relief		
5. national		
6. wishing		
7. compiling		
8. regional		
9. visionary		
10. graciously		

Name: _____ Date: ___/___/_____ Score: _____

The Reading Challenge

Lesson 9.10

Reading Multisyllable Words

✓ Lesson Check Point

Directions: Read each target word. Circle the word in the row that is divided correctly into syllables. Use a dictionary or the Internet to check your answers.

지도: 각 대상 단어를 읽으십시오. 음절로 올바르게 나누어진 행에 있는 단어에 동그라미를 치십시오. 사전이나 인터넷을 사용하여 답을 확인하십시오.

Model

| interesting | a. in-ter-est-ing (circled) | b. int-er-est-ing | c. inte-rest-ing |

1. scientific	a. sci-en-tif-ic	b. scien-ti-fic	c. sci-en-ti-fic
2. uniform	a. un-i-form	b. u-ni-form	c. u-nif-orm
3. ingredient	a. in-gre-di-ent	b. in-gre-dient	c. ing-red-i-ent
4. nutrient	a. nu-tri-ent	b. nut-ri-ent	c. nut-rie-nt
5. impatient	a. im-pat-ient	b. im-pa-tient	c. i-mpa-tient
6. tastier	a. tas-ti-er	b. ta-sti-er	c. tast-i-er
7. position	a. po-si-tion	b. pos-it-ion	c. pos-i-tion
8. mediate	a. me-di-ate	b. med-i-ate	c. med-iat-e

Name: _____ Date: ___/___/_____ Score: _____

Lesson 9.11

Reading and Writing

Proper and Common Nouns and Adjectives

✓ Lesson Check Point

Directions: Read the words in the word box. Put an (X) on the line next to each word that is written incorrectly. Remember that all proper nouns and proper adjectives are capitalized. Use a dictionary or the Internet to check your answers.

지도: 단어 상자에 있는 단어를 읽으십시오. 잘못 쓰여진 각 단어 옆의 줄에 (X)를 표시하십시오. 모든 고유 명사와 고유 형용사는 대문자임을 기억하십시오. 사전이나 인터넷을 사용하여 답을 확인하십시오.

Word Box		
___ inca	___ India	___ identify
___ Italy	___ index	___ Industry
___ ireland	___ irrigate	___ Ice cream
___ impressive	___ iberian	___ Illusionist

Directions: Read each unedited sentence and underline the word that is written incorrectly. Write each sentence correctly on the line.

지도: 편집되지 않은 각 문장을 읽고 잘못 쓰여진 단어에 밑줄을긋습 니다. 각 문장을 줄에 올바르게 쓰십시오.

Model
New Delhi and Indore are beautiful cities in <u>india</u>.
<u>New Delhi and Indore are beautiful cities in India.</u>

1. My friend, Indira, attends Intel institute.
   _____

2. The Itla family has an interesting indian heritage.
   _____

3. One day, Irwin will Investigate cases in Italy and Indonesia.
   _____

4. Irene wrote a report about the ivory Coast for International Day.
   _____

Name: _____ Date: ___/___/_____ Score: _____

Lesson 10.1

Reading Words with the Letter J/j

✓ **Lesson Check Point**

Directions: Read each target word. Find the letter "j" and put a check (✓) in the column that identifies its position: beginning, within or end.
지도: 각 대상 단어를 읽으십시오. 문자"j"를 찾아 체크 표시(✓)위치를 식별하는 열에서 시작, 내부 또는 끝.

Target Words	Beginning (First Letter)	Within	End (Last Letter)
1. jump			
2. jewel			
3. adjust			
4. rejoice			
5. rejuvenate			

Directions: Read each sentence and underline the words that begin with the letter "j." Write all the underlined words in alphabetical order on the lines below.
지도: 각 문장을 읽고"j"로 시작하는 단어에 밑줄을 긋습니다. 밑줄친모든 단어를 아래 줄에 알파벳 순서로 쓰십시오.

6. Bob joined the jazz band.

7. Jimmy enjoys eating jellybeans.

8. Mr. Adams has a new job as a janitor.

9. Everyone is joyous at the country jamboree.

10. Gianna's denim jacket has a jaguar on the back.

_____   _____   _____
_____   _____   _____
_____   _____   _____
            _____

Name: _____ Date:___/___/_____ Score:_____

The Reading Challenge

Lesson 10.2

Reading Multisyllable Words

✓ **Lesson Check Point**

Directions: Read and divide each target word into syllables. Write each word and place a hyphen (-) between the syllables in the second column. Write the number of syllables in the third column. Use a dictionary or the Internet to check your answers.

지도: 각 대상 단어를 읽고 음절로 나눕니다. 각 단어를 쓰고 두 번째 열의 음절 사이에 하이픈(-)을 넣습니다. 세 번째 열에 음절 수를 쓰십시오. 사전이나 인터넷을 사용하여 답을 확인하십시오.

Target Words	Words Divided into Syllables	Number of Syllables
1. jingle		
2. joker		
3. juror		
4. jaguar		
5. jersey		
6. journey		
7. justice		
8. jockey		
9. jumper		
10. jargon		

Name: _____ Date: ___/___/_____ Score: _____

The Reading Challenge

Lesson 10.2

Reading Multisyllable Words

✓ **Lesson Check Point**

Directions: Read each target word. Circle the word in the row that is divided correctly into syllables. Use a dictionary or the Internet to check your answers.

지도: 각 대상 단어를 읽으십시오. 음절로 올바르게 나누어진 행에 있는 단어에 동그라미를 치십시오. 사전이나 인터넷을 사용하여 답을 확인하십시오.

Model

| janitor | a. ja-ni-tor | b. jan-it-or | c. jan-i-tor (circled) |

1. jeweler	a. jew-el-er	b. jewe-le-r	c. je-wel-er
2. jubilee	a. ju-bil-ee	b. jub-i-lee	c. ju-bi-lee
3. joining	a. join-ing	b. jo-in-ing	c. jo-ining
4. jeopardy	a. jeop-ard-y	b. jeo-pard-y	c. jeop-ar-dy
5. journalist	a. jour-na-list	b. journ-a-list	c. jour-nal-ist
6. jovial	a. jov-i-al	b. jo-vi-al	c. jovi-al
7. judicial	a. ju-di-cial	b. jud-i-cial	c. ju-dic-ial
8. jamboree	a. jamb-o-ree	b. jam-bo-ree	c. jam-bor-ee

Name: _____ Date:___/___/_____ Score:_____

Lesson 10.3

Reading and Writing

Proper and Common Nouns and Adjectives

✓ **Lesson Check Point**

Directions: Read the words in the word box. Put an (X) on the line next to each word that is written incorrectly. Remember that all proper nouns and proper adjectives are capitalized. Use a dictionary or the Internet to check your answers.

지도: 단어 상자에 있는 단어를 읽으십시오. 잘못 쓰여진 각 단어 옆의 줄에 (X)를 표시하십시오. 모든 고유 명사와 고유 형용사는 대문자임을 기억하십시오. 사전이나 인터넷을 사용하여 답을 확인하십시오.

Word Box		
___ Joke	___ july	___ James
___ june	___ jargon	___ jewel
___ Japan	___ Jungle	___ Jigsaw
___ Jordan	___ jefferson	___ January

Directions: Read each unedited sentence and underline the word that is written incorrectly. Write each sentence correctly on the line.

지도: 편집되지 않은 각 문장을 읽고 잘못 쓰여진 단어에 밑줄을긋습 니다. 각 문장을 줄에 올바르게 쓰십시오.

Model
Joey and his family live in New <u>jersey</u>.
<u>Joey and his family live in New Jersey.</u>

1. The Janitor has a good job.
   _____

2. Joseph and james are going to Japan.
   _____

3. In Jamaica, people eat Jerk chicken for dinner.
   _____

4. We are taking a Journey along the Jordan River.
   _____

Name: _____   Date: ___/___/_____   Score: _____

Lesson 11.1

Reading Words with the Letter K/k

✓ Lesson Check Point

Directions: Read each target word. Find the letter "k" and put a check (✓) in the column that identifies its position: beginning, within or end.
지도: 각 대상 단어를 읽으십시오. 문자"k"를 찾아 체크 표시(✓)위치를 식별하는 열에서 시작, 내부 또는 끝.

Target Words	Beginning (First Letter)	Within	End (Last Letter)
1. shark			
2. kitchen			
3. ketchup			
4. folktale			
5. comeback			

Directions: Read each sentence and underline the words that begin with the letter "k." Write all the underlined words in alphabetical order on the lines below.
지도: 각 문장을 읽고 문자"k"로 시작하는 단어에 밑줄을 긋습니다. 밑줄 친 모든 단어를 아래 줄에 알파벳 순서로 쓰십시오.

6. Kidney beans taste great with ketchup.

7. The three kids are eating in the kitchen.

8. The five kittens are staying in the kennel.

9. Kelvin's kite is flying high above the trees.

10. The powerful kingdom was guarded by knights.

_____   _____   _____
_____   _____   _____
_____   _____   _____
                _____

Name: _____ Date: ___/___/_____ Score: _____

Lesson 11.2

Reading Words with the Letter "k" and "ck" Letter Combination

 Lesson Check Point

Directions: Read each target word. Put a check (✓) in the second column if the target word has one vowel. Put a check (✓) in the third column if the target word has two vowels.

지도: 각 대상 단어를 읽으십시오. 대상 단어에 모음이 하나 있는 경우 두 번째 열에 체크(✓)를 합니다. 대상 단어에 두 개의 모음이 있는경우제삼 열에 체크(✓)를 합니다.

Target Words	Words with 1 Vowel	Words with 2 Vowels
1. rack		
2. take		
3. sock		
4. seek		
5. lock		

Directions: Read each target word in the first column and write the number of vowels within the word in the second column. Read each target word in the third column and write the number of vowels within the word in the fourth column.

지도: 첫 번째 열의 각 대상 단어를 읽고 두 번째 열의 단어 내 모음 수를 쓰십시오. 세 번째 열의 각 대상 단어를 읽고 네 번째 열의 단어에 포함된 모음의 수를 쓰십시오.

Target Words	Number of Vowels	Target Words	Number of Vowels
6. back		bake	
7. pick		pike	
8. stoke		stock	
9. stack		stake	
10. make		Mack	

Name: _____ Date:___/___/_____ Score:_____

Lesson 11.3

Reading Words with the "kle" Letter Combination

✓ Lesson Check Point

 Directions: Read each target word. Find the "kle" letter combination and put a check (✓) in the column that identifies its position: beginning, within or end.

지도: 각 대상 단어를 읽으십시오. "kle" 문자 조합을 찾아 해당 위치를 식별하는 열에 체크(✓)를 하십시오: 시작, 내부 또는 끝.

Target Words	Beginning (First 3 Letters)	Within	End (Last 3 Letters)
1. shackle			
2. anklets			
3. wrinkled			
4. unbuckle			
5. kleptomaniac			

 Directions: Read each target word. Put a check (✓) in the "yes" column if the "kle" letter combination has the /k/ + /ə/ + /l/ sounds. Put a check (✓) in the "no" column if the "kle" letter combination does not have the /k/ + /ə/ + /l/ sounds.

지도: 각 대상 단어를 읽으십시오. "kle" 문자 조합에/k/ + /ə/ + /l/ 소리가있으 면"yes" 열에 체크(✓)를 하십시오. "kle" 문자 조합에/k/ + /ə/ + /l/ 소리가없으 면"no" 열에 체크(✓)를 하십시오.

Target Words	Yes	No
6. shackle		
7. anklets		
8. wrinkled		
9. unbuckle		
10. kleptomaniac		

Name: _____ Date: ___/___/_____ Score: _____

Lesson 11.4

Reading Words with a Silent Letter "k"

✓ **Lesson Check Point**

Directions: Read the target words in the word box. Write the words that have a silent letter "k" in the first column. Write the words that do not have a silent letter "k" in the second column.

지도: 단어 상자에 있는 대상 단어를 읽으십시오. 첫 번째 열에 묵음문자 "k"가 있는 단어를 쓰십시오. 두 번째 열에 묵음 문자"k"가 없는 단어를 쓰십시오.

Target Word Box				
knife	knits	knots	knew	keys
kneel	knish	leaking	knight	know
keeping	kangaroo	kerosene	market	knack
knowledge	breaking	keyboard	forsake	knuckles

Letter "k" is silent

Letter "k" has the /k/ sound

Name: _____ Date: ___/___/_____ Score: _____

The Reading Challenge

Lesson 11.5

Reading Multisyllable Words

✓ **Lesson Check Point**

Directions: Read and divide each target word into syllables. Write each word and place a hyphen (-) between the syllables in the second column. Write the number of syllables in the third column. Use a dictionary or the Internet to check your answers.

지도: 각 대상 단어를 읽고 음절로 나눕니다. 각 단어를 쓰고 두 번째 열의 음절 사이에 하이픈(-)을 넣습니다. 세 번째 열에 음절 수를 쓰십시오. 사전이나 인터넷을 사용하여 답을 확인하십시오.

Target Words	Words Divided into Syllables	Number of Syllables
1. kazoo	_____	_____
2. kidney	_____	_____
3. knocker	_____	_____
4. kosher	_____	_____
5. keycard	_____	_____
6. Kansas	_____	_____
7. kindred	_____	_____
8. kinetic	_____	_____
9. kayak	_____	_____
10. keeping	_____	_____

Unit K
Lesson 11.5

Name: _____ Date: ___/___/_____ Score: _____

The Reading Challenge

Lesson 11.5

Reading Multisyllable Words

✓ **Lesson Check Point**

Directions: Read each target word. Circle the word in the row that is divided correctly into syllables. Use a dictionary or the Internet to check your answers.

지도: 각 대상 단어를 읽으십시오. 음절로 올바르게 나누어진 행에 있는 단어에 동그라미를 치십시오. 사전이나 인터넷을 사용하여 답을 확인하십시오.

Model

kangaroo	a. kang-a-roo	b. kan-ga-roo (circled)	c. kan-gar-oo

1. kerosene	a. ker-o-sene	b. ker-os-ene	c. ke-ro-sene

2. kneecap	a. knee-cap	b. kn-ee-cap	c. kn-eec-ap

3. Korean	a. K-ore-an	b. Kor-e-an	c. Ko-re-an

4. kneeling	a. kneel-ing	b. knee-ling	c. kne-eling

5. keeper	a. kee-per	b. keep-er	c. ke-eper

6. kinship	a. kinsh-ip	b. ki-nship	c. kin-ship

7. knowing	a. know-ing	b. kno-wing	c. knowi-ng

8. koala	a. ko-al-a	b. k-oa-la	c. ko-a-la

Learn To Read English With Directions In Korean

Name: _____ Date: ___/___/_____ Score: _____

Lesson 11.6

Reading and Writing

Proper and Common Nouns and Adjectives

✓ **Lesson Check Point**

Directions: Read the words in the word box. Put an (X) on the line next to each word that is written incorrectly. Remember that all proper nouns and proper adjectives are capitalized. Use a dictionary or the Internet to check your answers.
지도: 단어 상자에 있는 단어를 읽으십시오. 잘못 쓰여진 각 단어 옆의 줄에 (X)를 표시하십시오. 모든 고유 명사와 고유 형용사는 대문자임을 기억하십시오. 사전이나 인터넷을 사용하여 답을 확인하십시오.

Word Box					
___	korea	___	kuwait	___	Korean
___	kennel	___	Kicking	___	kitchen
___	Kansas	___	Keycard	___	key West
___	ketchup	___	Kwanzaa	___	Kangaroo

Directions: Read each unedited sentence and underline the word that is written incorrectly. Write each sentence correctly on the line.
지도: 편집되지 않은 각 문장을 읽고 잘못 쓰여진 단어에 밑줄을 긋습 니다. 각 문장을 줄에 올바르게 쓰십시오.

Model
Helen <u>keller</u> was a kind person.
<u>Helen Keller was a kind person.</u>

1. In kuwait, kids like to kick their soccer balls.

_____

2. The State of kansas is located in America's heartland.

_____

3. The Kennedy kids enjoy eating klondike ice cream bars.

_____

4. key West and Key Largo are islands off the coast of Florida.

_____

Name: _____ Date: ___/___/_____ Score: _____

Lesson 12.1

Reading Words with the Letter L/l

✓ **Lesson Check Point**

Directions: Read each target word. Find the letter "l" and put a check (✓) in the column that identifies its position: beginning, within or end.
지도: 각 대상 단어를 읽으십시오. 문자"l"을 찾아 체크 표시(✓)위치를 식별하는 열에서 시작, 내부 또는 끝.

Target Words	Beginning (First Letter)	Within	End (Last Letter)
1. like			
2. curl			
3. bowl			
4. lunch			
5. helper			

Directions: Read each sentence and underline the words that begin with the letter "l." Write all the underlined words in alphabetical order on the lines below.
지도: 각 문장을 읽고 문자"l"로 시작하는 단어에 밑줄을 긋습니다. 밑줄 친 모든 단어를 아래 줄에 알파벳 순서로 쓰십시오.

6. I brought my laptop to the library.

7. David applied a handful of lotion to his legs.

8. Everyone knows Abigail loves to write letters.

9. On Friday, the lawyer wrote a legal document.

10. My family and I had liver and lettuce for dinner.

_____   _____   _____
_____   _____   _____
_____   _____
_____

Name: _____ Date:___/___/_____ Score:_____

Lesson 12.2

Reading Words with the Letter "l" Combinations: "fl," "pl" & "sl"

Dictionary Skills/ Vocabulary

✓ **Lesson Check Point**

 Directions: Read each target word and its definition. Write the target word on the line in front of its meaning. Use a dictionary or the Internet to check your answers.

지도: 각 대상 단어와 그 정의를 읽으십시오. 의미 앞 줄에 대상단어 를 쓰십시오. 사전이나 인터넷을 사용하여 답을 확인하십시오.

Target Word Box				
flew	plants	plastic	sleep	slide

1. _____ living things that are grown in soil
2. _____ a flexible man-made material that can be shaped
3. _____ to move in a downward motion on a slippery surface
4. _____ traveled through the air with wings
5. _____ closing eyes and going into a periodic state of rest

 Directions: Read each sentence. Underline the word in the parentheses that correctly completes each sentence. Then, write the underlined word on the line.

지도: 각 문장을 읽으십시오. 각 문장을 올바르게 완성하는 괄호 안에 있는 단어에 밑줄을 긋습니다. 그런 다음 밑줄 친 단어를 줄에 쓰십시오.

6. At camp, the campers will _____ on bunk beds. (sleep, flew)

7. Pam loves to _____ down the hill with her sled. (plants, slide)

8. Early in the morning, the birds _____ over the pond. (flew, plastic)

9. The _____ in Grandma's garden are colorful. (slide, plants)

10. Paul's comb is made with a strong _____ material. (sleep, plastic)

Name: _____ Date: ___/___/_____ Score: _____

Lesson 12.3

Reading Words with a Silent Letter "l"

✓ **Lesson Check Point**

Directions: Read the target words in the word box. Write the words that have a silent letter "l" in the first column. Write the words that do not have a silent letter "l" in the second column.

지도: 단어 상자에 있는 대상 단어를 읽으십시오. 첫 번째 열에 묵음문자 "l"이 있는 단어를 쓰십시오. 두 번째 열에 묵음 문자"l"이 없는 단어를 쓰십 시오.

Target Word Box				
love	calf	tail	half	yolk
should	hello	balm	chalk	letter
salmon	ladder	dental	closed	would
Lincoln	telephone	laughs	perfectly	lower

Letter "l" is silent	Letter "l" has the /l/ sound

Unit L Lesson 12.3

Name: _____   Date: ___/___/_____   Score: _____

The Reading Challenge

Lesson 12.4

Reading Multisyllable Words

✓ **Lesson Check Point**

Directions: Read and divide each target word into syllables. Write each word and place a hyphen (-) between the syllables in the second column. Write the number of syllables in the third column. Use a dictionary or the Internet to check your answers.

지도: 각 대상 단어를 읽고 음절로 나눕니다. 각 단어를 쓰고 두 번째 열의 음절 사이에 하이픈(-)을 넣습니다. 세 번째 열에 음절 수를 쓰십시오. 사전이나 인터넷을 사용하여 답을 확인하십시오.

Target Words	Words Divided into Syllables	Number of Syllables
1. linguistic		
2. laughing		
3. lighting		
4. ligament		
5. likely		
6. lexicon		
7. lavender		
8. leftover		
9. lasting		
10. languish		

Name: _____   Date: ___/___/_____   Score: _____

The Reading Challenge

Lesson 12.4

Reading Multisyllable Words

✓ **Lesson Check Point**

Directions: Read each target word. Circle the word in the row that is divided correctly into syllables. Use a dictionary or the Internet to check your answers.

지도: 각 대상 단어를 읽으십시오. 음절로 올바르게 나누어진 행에 있는 단어에 동그라미를 치십시오. 사전이나 인터넷을 사용하여 답을 확인하십시오.

Model

liberty	a. li-ber-ty	b. (lib-er-ty)	c. lib-ert-y

1. Latino	a. Lat-i-no	b. Lat-in-o	c. La-ti-no

2. leverage	a. le-ver-age	b. lev-e-rage	c. lev-er-age

3. liberate	a. li-ber-ate	b. lib-e-rate	c. lib-er-ate

4. limousine	a. lim-ou-sine	b. li-mou-sine	c. lim-o-usine

5. lyrical	a. lyr-i-cal	b. ly-ri-cal	c. lyr-ic-al

6. lexicon	a. le-xi-con	b. lex-ic-on	c. lex-i-con

7. library	a. lib-rar-y	b. li-brar-y	c. li-bra-ry

8. ligament	a. lig-a-ment	b. li-ga-ment	c. li-gam-ent

Learn To Read English With Directions In Korean   Copyrighted Material

Name: _____ Date: ___/___/_____ Score: _____

Lesson 12.5

Reading and Writing

Proper and Common Nouns and Adjectives

Directions: Read the words in the word box. Put an (X) on the line next to each word that is written incorrectly. Remember that all proper nouns and proper adjectives are capitalized. Use a dictionary or the Internet to check your answers.

지도: 단어 상자에 있는 단어를 읽으십시오. 잘못 쓰여진 각 단어 옆의 줄에 (X)를 표시하십시오. 모든 고유 명사와 고유 형용사는 대문자임을 기억하십시오. 사전이나 인터넷을 사용하여 답을 확인하십시오.

Word Box		
___ Lagos	___ Libya	___ lima
___ Lunch	___ Lemonade	___ London
___ Laptop	___ living room	___ landlord
___ License	___ Long Island	___ liverpool

Directions: Read each unedited sentence and underline the word that is written incorrectly. Write each sentence correctly on the line.

지도: 편집되지 않은 각 문장을 읽고 잘못 쓰여진 단어에 밑줄을 긋습 니다. 각 문장을 줄에 올바르게 쓰십시오.

Model
I am studying <u>latin</u> at Lutheran Life Academy.
<u>I am studying Latin at Lutheran Life Academy.</u>

1. My family ate Lunch at Long Beach, New York.

_____

2. Larry said, "The Largest city in Nigeria is Lagos."

_____

3. We visited London and liverpool on the same day.

_____

4. The labrador Peninsula is a large peninsula in Eastern Canada.

_____

Name: _____ Date: ___/___/_____ Score: _____

Lesson 13.1

Reading Words with the Letter M/m

✓ Lesson Check Point

Directions: Read each target word. Find the letter "m" and put a check (✓) in the column that identifies its position: beginning, within or end.
지도: 각 대상 단어를 읽으십시오. 문자"m"을 찾아 체크 표시(✓)위치 를 식별하는 열에서 시작, 내부 또는 끝.

Target Words	Beginning (First Letter)	Within	End (Last Letter)
1. hermit			
2. mother			
3. summer			
4. romance			
5. upstream			

Directions: Read each sentence and underline the words that begin with the letter "m." Write all the underlined words in alphabetical order on the lines below.
지도: 각 문장을 읽고 문자"m"으로 시작하는 단어에 밑줄을 긋습니다. 밑줄 친 모든 단어를 아래 줄에 알파벳 순서로 쓰십시오.

6. His sister, Mercy, wrote a great manuscript.

7. Dr. Mingo's class is reading a book about Mexico.

8. The mail carrier placed the letters in the mailbox.

9. Grandma bought mandarin oranges at the market.

10. Our friend, Max, sailed along the great Mississippi River.

_____ _____ _____
_____ _____ _____
_____ _____ _____
             _____

Name: _____ Date: ___/___/_____ Score: _____

Lesson 13.2

Reading Words with a Silent Letter "m"

✓ Lesson Check Point

Directions: Read each target word. Find the letter "m" and put a check (✓) in the column that identifies its position: beginning, within or end.
지도: 각 대상 단어를 읽으십시오. 문자 "m"을 찾아 체크 표시(✓)위치 를 식별하는 열에서 시작, 내부 또는 끝.

Target Words	Beginning (First Letter)	Within	End (Last Letter)
1. monkey			
2. immune			
3. symmetry			
4. globalism			
5. mnemonic			

Directions: Read each target word. Put a check (✓) in the "yes" column if the target word has a silent letter "m." Put a check (✓) in the "no" column if the target word does not have a silent letter "m."
지도: 각 대상 단어를 읽으십시오. 대상 단어에 묵음 "m"이 있는 경우 "yes" 열에 체크(✓) 표시 대상 단어에 묵음 "m"이 없는 경우 "no" 열에체크 (✓) 표시.

Target Words	Yes	No
6. monkey		
7. immune		
8. symmetry		
9. globalism		
10. mnemonic		

Learn To Read English With Directions In Korean   Copyrighted Material

Name: _____ Date: ___/___/_____ Score: _____

The Reading Challenge

Lesson 13.3

Reading Multisyllable Words

✓ **Lesson Check Point**

Directions: Read and divide each target word into syllables. Write each word and place a hyphen (-) between the syllables in the second column. Write the number of syllables in the third column. Use a dictionary or the Internet to check your answers.

지도: 각 대상 단어를 읽고 음절로 나눕니다. 각 단어를 쓰고 두 번째 열의 음절 사이에 하이픈(-)을 넣습니다. 세 번째 열에 음절 수를 쓰십시오. 사전이나 인터넷을 사용하여 답을 확인하십시오.

Target Words	Words Divided into Syllables	Number of Syllables
1. meditate	_____	_____
2. master	_____	_____
3. medium	_____	_____
4. Mexico	_____	_____
5. musical	_____	_____
6. mother	_____	_____
7. mustard	_____	_____
8. mystery	_____	_____
9. membrane	_____	_____
10. multiply	_____	_____

Name: _____ Date: ___/___/_____ Score: _____

The Reading Challenge

Lesson 13.3

Reading Multisyllable Words

✓ **Lesson Check Point**

Directions: Read each target word. Circle the word in the row that is divided correctly into syllables. Use a dictionary or the Internet to check your answers.

지도: 각 대상 단어를 읽으십시오. 음절로 올바르게 나누어진 행에 있는 단어에 동그라미를 치십시오. 사전이나 인터넷을 사용하여 답을 확인하십시오.

Model

| magazine | a. mag-a-zine (circled) | b. ma-ga-zine | c. mag-az-ine |

1. Milwaukee	a. Mil-wa-ukee	b. Mil-wau-kee	c. Mil-wauk-ee
2. monarchy	a. mon-ar-chy	b. mo-nar-chy	c. mon-archy
3. mediate	a. me-di-ate	b. med-i-ate	c. me-dia-te
4. magnetic	a. mag-net-ic	b. mag-ne-tic	c. magn-et-ic
5. Mercury	a. Merc-u-ry	b. Me-rcu-ry	c. Mer-cu-ry
6. mosquito	a. mos-qui-to	b. mo-squi-to	c. mos-quit-o
7. microwave	a. micr-o-wave	b. mic-ro-wave	c. mi-cro-wave
8. memento	a. mem-en-to	b. mem-e-nto	c. me-men-to

Name: _____ Date: ___/___/_____ Score: _____

Lesson 13.4

Reading and Writing

Proper and Common Nouns and Adjectives

Directions: Read the words in the word box. Put an (X) on the line next to each word that is written incorrectly. Remember that all proper nouns and proper adjectives are capitalized. Use a dictionary or the Internet to check your answers.
지도: 단어 상자에 있는 단어를 읽으십시오. 잘못 쓰여진 각 단어 옆의 줄에 (X)를 표시하십시오. 모든 고유 명사와 고유 형용사는 대문자임을 기억하십시오. 사전이나 인터넷을 사용하여 답을 확인하십시오.

Word Box		
___ miser	___ Mecca	___ Malta
___ muffins	___ manners	___ Master
___ malaysia	___ Millionaire	___ Monarch
___ massachusetts	___ manchester	___ Mexico

Directions: Read each unedited sentence and underline the word that is written incorrectly. Write each sentence correctly on the line.
지도: 편집되지 않은 각 문장을 읽고 잘못 쓰여진 단어에 밑줄을긋습 니다. 각 문장을 줄에 올바르게 쓰십시오.

Model
My son, Mark, is going to attend MIT in <u>massachusetts</u>.
<u>My son, Mark, is going to attend MIT in Massachusetts.</u>

1. Miss Miller will Marry Mr. McShine next month.
   _____

2. My teacher, mr. Mann, lives in Martha's Vineyard.
   _____

3. Every morning, my friend, molly, eats multi-grain cereal.
   _____

4. In the morning, Matthew loves to listen to mozart's music.
   _____

Name: _____ Date: ___/___/_____ Score: _____

Lesson 14.1

Reading Words with the Letter N/n

✓ Lesson Check Point

Directions: Read each target word. Find the letter "n" and put a check (✓) in the column that identifies its position: beginning, within or end.
지도: 각 대상 단어를 읽으십시오. 문자"n"을 찾아 체크 표시(✓)위치를 식별하는 열에서 시작, 내부 또는 끝.

Target Words	Beginning (First Letter)	Within	End (Last Letter)
1. freshen			
2. noodle			
3. number			
4. transfer			
5. linguistic			

Directions: Read each sentence and underline the words that begin with the letter "n." Write all the underlined words in alphabetical order on the lines below.
지도: 각 문장을 읽고"n"으로 시작하는 단어에 밑줄을 긋습니다. 밑줄 친 모든 단어를 아래 줄에 알파벳 순서로 쓰십시오.

6. Jack wrote a note in his blue notebook.

7. Andrew narrated the play entitled, "Our Nation."

8. My grandmother is nibbling on nachos and cheese.

9. Newton wrote the numerator above the denominator.

10. Native Americans navigated their canoes along the Mississippi River.

_____   _____   _____
_____   _____   _____
_____   _____   _____
_____

Name: _____ Date:___/___/_____ Score: _____

Lesson 14.2

Reading Words with the "ng" Letter Combination

✓ Lesson Check Point

 Directions: Read each target word. Circle the word in the column that has the same "ng" sound(s) as the target word.
지도: 각 대상 단어를 읽으십시오. 대상 단어와 같은"ng" 소리가 나는 열의 단어에 동그라미를 치십시오.

engulf	a. manger
	b. engage

mango	a. linguist
	b. change

hanger	a. ranger
	b. younger

challenger	a. arranging
	b. angle

 Directions: Read each target word. Put a check (✓) under the correct column heading.
지도: 각 대상 단어를 읽으십시오. 올바른 열 제목 아래에 체크(✓)를하십시오.

Target Words	"ng" has the /n/ + /g/ sounds as in the word ingrain	"ng" has the /n/ + /j/ sounds as in the word ginger	"ng" has the /ng/ sound as in the word bang	"ng" has the /ng/ + /g/ sounds as in the word congress
1. engulf				
2. mango				
3. hanger				
4. challenger				

Name: _____ Date: ___/___/_____ Score: _____

Lesson 14.3

Reading Words with a Silent Letter "n"

✓ **Lesson Check Point**

Directions: Read the target words in the word box. Write the words that have a silent letter "n" in the first column. Write the words that do not have a silent letter "n" in the second column.

지도: 단어 상자에 있는 대상 단어를 읽으십시오. 첫 번째 열에 묵음문자 "n"이 있는 단어를 쓰십시오. 두 번째 열에 묵음 문자"n"이 없는 단어를 쓰십시오.

Target Word Box				
inner	needle	hymn	annex	solemn
frozen	bundle	handle	network	expanse
cannon	columns	landmark	chimneys	autumn
condemn	dominate	cinnamon	comments	column

Letter "n" is silent | **Letter "n" has the /n/ sound**

Name: _____ Date: ___/___/_____ Score: _____

The Reading Challenge

Lesson 14.4

Reading Multisyllable Words

✓ **Lesson Check Point**

Directions: Read and divide each target word into syllables. Write each word and place a hyphen (-) between the syllables in the second column. Write the number of syllables in the third column. Use a dictionary or the Internet to check your answers.

지도: 각 대상 단어를 읽고 음절로 나눕니다. 각 단어를 쓰고 두 번째 열의 음절 사이에 하이픈(-)을 넣습니다. 세 번째 열에 음절 수를 쓰십시오. 사전이나 인터넷을 사용하여 답을 확인하십시오.

Target Words	Words Divided into Syllables	Number of Syllables
1. nucleus	_____	_____
2. nobleman	_____	_____
3. nightly	_____	_____
4. nebula	_____	_____
5. navel	_____	_____
6. needless	_____	_____
7. ninety	_____	_____
8. noodle	_____	_____
9. negative	_____	_____
10. nervously	_____	_____

Name: _____ Date: ___/___/_____ Score: _____

The Reading Challenge

Lesson 14.4

Reading Multisyllable Words

✓ Lesson Check Point

 Directions: Read each target word. Circle the word in the row that is divided correctly into syllables. Use a dictionary or the Internet to check your answers.

지도: 각 대상 단어를 읽으십시오. 음절로 올바르게 나누어진 행에 있는 단어에 동그라미를 치십시오. 사전이나 인터넷을 사용하여 답을 확인하십시오.

Model

| napkin | a. na-pkin | b. napk-in | c. nap-kin ⭕ |

| 1. nephew | a. neph-ew | b. ne-phew | c. nep-hew |

| 2. nature | a. nat-ure | b. na-ture | c. natu-re |

| 3. nursery | a. nurse-r-y | b. nurs-er-y | c. nur-ser-y |

| 4. nominee | a. nom-i-nee | b. no-mi-nee | c. no-min-ee |

| 5. nitrogen | a. nit-ro-gen | b. ni-tro-gen | c. nit-rog-en |

| 6. Nevada | a. Nev-ad-a | b. Ne-va-da | c. Ne-vad-a |

| 7. negative | a. ne-ga-tive | b. neg-a-tive | c. ne-gat-ive |

| 8. nectarine | a. nec-ta-rine | b. nect-a-rine | c. nec-tar-ine |

Name: _____ Date: ___/___/_____ Score: _____

Lesson 14.5

Reading and Writing

Proper and Common Nouns and Adjectives

✓ **Lesson Check Point**

Directions: Read the words in the word box. Put an (X) on the line next to each word that is written incorrectly. Remember that all proper nouns and proper adjectives are capitalized. Use a dictionary or the Internet to check your answers.

지도: 단어 상자에 있는 단어를 읽으십시오. 잘못 쓰여진 각 단어 옆의 줄에 (X)를 표시하십시오. 모든 고유 명사와 고유 형용사는 대문자임을 기억하십시오. 사전이나 인터넷을 사용하여 답을 확인하십시오.

Word Box		
___ needy	___ nectar	___ negative
___ Nepal	___ Nibble	___ Newscast
___ new York	___ newark	___ New Mexico
___ niagara Falls	___ Neglect	___ New Amsterdam

Directions: Read each unedited sentence and underline the word that is written incorrectly. Write each sentence correctly on the line.

지도: 편집되지 않은 각 문장을 읽고 잘못 쓰여진 단어에 밑줄을 긋습 니다. 각 문장을 줄에 올바르게 쓰십시오.

Model
Nick and Nancy live in the <u>netherlands</u>.
<u>Nick and Nancy live in the Netherlands.</u>

1. I bought my gold Necklace in Nigeria.
   _____

2. New York State is next to new Jersey.
   _____

3. The Newspaper article is about Nicaragua.
   _____

4. My Nephew, Nat, navigated his boat along the Nile River.
   _____

Name: _____ Date: ___/___/_____ Score: _____

Lesson 15.1

Reading Words with the Letter O/o

✓ Lesson Check Point

 Directions: Read each target word. Find the letter "o" and put a check (✓) in the column that identifies its position: beginning, within or end.
지도: 각 대상 단어를 읽으십시오. 문자"o"를 찾아 체크 표시(✓)위치 를 식별하는 열에서 시작, 내부 또는 끝.

Target Words	Beginning (First Letter)	Within	End (Last Letter)
1. office			
2. house			
3. turbo			
4. object			
5. going			

 Directions: Read each target word. Read the words in the row and circle the word that has a different vowel "o" sound.
지도: 각 대상 단어를 읽으십시오. 행에 있는 단어를 읽고 모음"o" 소리가 다른 단어에 동그라미를 치십시오.

Target Words				
6. most	boat	poke	cope	mob
7. doing	going	who	to	move
8. colder	bone	no	dot	poet
9. chosen	boxes	ago	float	hose
10. popping	knock	roll	lost	sock

Name: _____ Date:___/___/_____ Score: _____

Lesson 15.2

Reading Words with the Short Vowel "o" Sound

✓ Lesson Check Point

 Directions: Read the words in the four boxes. Circle two words with the short vowel /ŏ/ or /ô/ sound. The anchor word for the short vowel /ŏ/ and /ô/ sounds is <u>frog</u>.

지도: 네 개의 상자에 있는 단어를 읽으십시오. 짧은 모음/ŏ/ 또는 /ô/ 소리로 두 단어에 동그라미를 치십시오. 단모음/ŏ/ 및 /ô/ 소리의 앵커 단어는 frog입니다.

cone	boast		poem	jock		knock	cold
snob	mock		boat	hog		bolt	blotch

open	soft		toll	frost		lot	almost
floss	old		soap	stock		fold	hog

 Directions: Read the words in the four boxes. Circle two words that rhyme. Rhyming words have the same ending sound, such as <u>hot</u> and <u>not</u>.

지도: 네 개의 상자에 있는 단어를 읽으십시오. 운이 맞는 두 단어에동그라미를 치십시오. 운율이 있는 단어는 hot 및 not과 같이 끝 소리가같습니다.

dot	pot		yolk	clock		most	open
cold	cargo		yo-yo	block		pop	top

log	so		box	fox		doc	joke
fog	over		scold	token		mold	wok

Name: _____ Date: ___/___/_____ Score: _____

Lesson 15.2

Reading & Writing Words with the Short Vowel "o" Sound

✓ **Lesson Check Point**

Directions: Read each sentence and underline three words with the short vowel /ŏ/ or /ô/ sound. Then, write the underlined words on the lines below. The anchor word for the short vowel /ŏ/ and /ô/ sounds is <u>frog</u>.

지도: 각 문장을 읽고 짧은 모음/ŏ/ 또는 /ô/ 소리로 세 단어에 밑줄을 긋습니다. 그런 다음 밑줄 친 단어를 아래 줄에 쓰십시오. 단모음/ŏ/ 및 /ô/ 소리의 앵커 단어는 frog입니다.

Model

Everyone saw the <u>frog</u> <u>hop</u> close to the <u>rock</u>.

    frog   hop   rock

1. Bob will jog around one block.

   _____   _____   _____

2. Owen dropped the hot pot by the oven.

   _____   _____   _____

3. My boss crossed the street and bought codfish.

   _____   _____   _____

4. Odessa tossed the oversized frog back into the pond.

   _____   _____   _____

5. Tom and Ricardo have three animals: an ox, a cat and a hog.

   _____   _____   _____

Name: _____ Date:___/___/_____ Score:_____

Lesson 15.3

Reading Words with the Long Vowel "o" Sound

✓ Lesson Check Point

 Directions: Read the words in the four boxes. Circle two words with the long vowel /ō/ sound. The anchor word for the long vowel /ō/ sound is open.

지도: 네 개의 상자에 있는 단어를 읽으십시오. 장모음 /ō/ 소리로 두 단어에 동그라미를 치십시오. 장모음 /ō/ 소리의 기준어는 open입니다.

note	stop		flop	loaf		blond	roam
plot	foam		soft	vote		shock	lobe

gloss	gloat		lock	stock		floss	nose
robe	doll		doe	goat		over	slot

 Directions: Read the words in the four boxes. Circle two words that rhyme. Rhyming words have the same ending sound, such as hope and soap.

지도: 네 개의 상자에 있는 단어를 읽으십시오. 운이 맞는 두 단어에 동그라미를 치십시오. 운율이 있는 단어는 hope 및 soap과 같이 끝 소리가 같습니다.

chop	troll		bond	dome		long	coal
toast	bowl		float	throat		mock	goal

soak	poke		rope	most		hose	rose
hose	moss		load	rode		cope	dock

Name: _____ Date: ___/___/_____ Score: _____

Lesson 15.3

Reading & Writing Words with the Long Vowel "o" Sound

✓ **Lesson Check Point**

Directions: Read each sentence and underline three words with the long vowel /ō/ sound. Then, write the underlined words on the lines below. The anchor word for the long vowel /ō/ sound is <u>open</u>.

지도: 각 문장을 읽고 장모음 /ō/소리로 세 단어에 밑줄을 긋습니다. 그런 다음 밑줄 친 단어를 아래 줄에 쓰십시오. 장모음 /ō/ 소리의 앵커 단어는 open입니다.

Model

We will <u>go</u> to the <u>rodeo</u> and <u>limbo</u> competitions for fun.

　　　go　　　　　　　　rodeo　　　　　　　　limbo

1. The motel's lunch combo has two donuts for dessert.

　　_____　　　_____　　　_____

2. The outstanding critic said, "Carlo's company logo is so-so."

　　_____　　　_____　　　_____

3. The new apartment condo is going to become available in October.

　　_____　　　_____　　　_____

4. The disc jockey will play disco music as we go under the limbo bar.

　　_____　　　_____　　　_____

5. I read a poem about nomads who traveled along the Atlantic Ocean.

　　_____　　　_____　　　_____

Name: _____   Date: ___/___/_____   Score: _____

Review Lessons 15.2 & 15.3

Reading Short Vowel and Long Vowel Words

✓ **Lesson Check Point**

Directions: Read the target words in the word box. In the first column, write the words that have the short vowel /ŏ/ or /ô/ sound, as in the word <u>frog</u>. In the second column, write the words that have the long vowel /ō/ sound, as in the word <u>open</u>.

지도: 단어 상자에 있는 대상 단어를 읽으십시오. 첫 번째 열에는 frog라는 단어에서와 같이 단모음 /ŏ/ 또는 /ô/ 소리가 나는 단어를 씁니다. 두번째 열에는 open이라는 단어에서와 같이 장모음 /ō/ 소리가 나는 단어를 씁니다.

Target Word Box				
close	mom	solar	poster	oval
almost	colder	ocean	boxers	patrol
conflict	hotter	jogging	proceed	doctor
dropping	swollen	stopped	mopping	potting

Letter "o" has the /ŏ/ or /ô/ sound as in the word <u>frog</u>

Letter "o" has the /ō/ sound as in the word <u>open</u>

Name: _____ Date:___/___/_____ Score: _____

Lesson 15.4

Reading Words with Letter "o" Vowel Pairs

✓ Lesson Check Point

 Directions: Read each target word. Circle the word in the column that has the same vowel "oa," "oe," "oo" or "ou" sound(s) as the target word.
지도: 각 대상 단어를 읽으십시오. 대상 단어와 동일한 모음 "oa," "oe," "oo" 또는 "ou" 소리가 있는 열의 단어에 동그라미를 치십시오.

scout	a. goalie
	b. flounder

moan	a. aloe
	b. pounds

toast	a. lagoon
	b. banjoes

oboe	a. roast
	b. typhoon

 Directions: Read each target word. Put a check (✓) under the correct column heading.
지도: 각 대상 단어를 읽으십시오. 올바른 열 제목 아래에 체크(✓)를 하십시오.

Target Words	Words have the long "o" sound as in the word <u>coat</u>	Words do not have the long "o" sound
1. scout		
2. moan		
3. toast		
4. oboe		

Name: _____ Date: ___/___/_____ Score: _____

Lesson 15.5

Reading Words with the Final Letter "o"

✓ **Lesson Check Point**

 Directions: Read each target word. Find the letter "o" and put a check (✓) in the column that identifies its position within the syllable.
지도: 각 대상 단어를 읽으십시오. 문자"o"를 찾아 체크 표시(✓)음절 내에서 위치를 식별하는 열에서.

Target Words	"o" is at the end of a one syllable word	"o" is at the end of the first syllable	"o" is at the end of a multi-syllable word
1. go			
2. ghetto			
3. bravo			
4. grocer			
5. hydro			

 Directions: Read each target word. Put a check (✓) under the correct column heading.
지도: 각 대상 단어를 읽으십시오. 올바른 열 제목 아래에 체크(✓)를 하십시오.

Target Words	"o" has the /ŏ/ sound as in the word <u>frog</u>	"o" has the /ō/ sound as in the word <u>go</u>	"o" has the /ə/ sound as in the word <u>carrot</u>	"o" is silent as in the word <u>people</u>
6. hotel				
7. pocket				
8. leopards				
9. complete				
10. wisdom				

Name: _____ Date: ___/___/_____ Score: _____

Lesson 15.6

Reading Letter "o" Words with the Schwa Vowel Sound

✓ **Lesson Check Point**

 Directions: Read each target word. Circle the word in the column that has the same "o" sound as the target word.
지도: 각 대상 단어를 읽으십시오. 대상 단어와 동일한 "o" 소리가 나는 열의 단어에 동그라미를 치십시오.

dozen	a. other
	b. opening

actor	a. parrot
	b. books

oppose	a. docks
	b. together

gallop	a. occur
	b. oceans

 Directions: Read each sentence and underline the letter "o" word that has the schwa vowel /ə/ sound or short vowel /ŭ/ sound. The anchor word for the letter "o" schwa vowel /ə/ sound is <u>carrot</u> and the letter "o" short vowel /ŭ/ sound is <u>dove</u>.
지도: 각 문장을 읽고 슈와 모음 /ə/ 소리 또는 단모음 /ŭ/ 소리가 있는 문자 "o" 단어에 밑줄을 긋습니다. 문자 "o" 슈와 모음 /ə/ 소리의 앵커 단어는 carrot이고 문자 "o" 단모음 /ŭ/ 소리는 dove입니다.

1. My brother opened two large, orange boxes.

2. Nothing was written in Oscar's new notebooks.

3. Mr. and Mrs. Lopez are going to the Ivory Coast.

4. In the afternoon, Orin drank cold coconut water.

5. My nephew is enrolled in an interesting history class.

6. Early in the morning, the pilot flew over South Africa.

Name: _____ Date:___/___/_____ Score:_____

Lesson 15.7

Reading Words with Vowel "o" Sounds: /ŏ/, /ō/ & /o͞o/

✓ Lesson Check Point

 Directions: Read each target word. Put a check (✓) under the correct column heading.
지도: 각 대상 단어를 읽으십시오. 올바른 열 제목 아래에 체크(✓)를 하십시오.

Target Words	"o" has the /ŏ/ sound as in the word <u>frog</u>	"o" has the /ō/ sound as in the word <u>go</u>	"o" has the /o͞o/ sound as in the word <u>to</u>
1. total			
2. doing			
3. proven			
4. holiday			
5. dollars			

 Directions: Read each sentence and underline the word that has a letter "o" that has the vowel /o͞o/ sound, as in the word <u>too</u>.
지도: 각 문장을 읽고 too라는 단어에서처럼 모음/o͞o/소리가 있는문자 "o"가 있는 단어에 밑줄을 긋습니다.

6. Do we have an appointment?

7. Don will return home at two o'clock.

8. Ron skillfully proved his answer was correct.

9. I did not lose any money in the stock market.

10. Mrs. Oscar said, "Everyone must move their books."

Name: _____ Date: ___/___/_____ Score: _____

Lesson 15.8

Reading Words with the "or" Letter Combination

✓ Lesson Check Point

 Directions: Read each target word. Circle the word in the column that has the same "o" + "r" sounds as the target word.

지도: 각 대상 단어를 읽으십시오. 가 있는 열에 있는 단어에 동그라미를 치십시오. 동일한"o" + "r"이 대상 단어로 들립니다.

core	a. corn
	b. corrupt

border	a. normal
	b. corral

memory	a. forest
	b. doctor

spectator	a. conductor
	b. boring

 Directions: Read each target word. Put a check (✓) under the correct column heading.

지도: 각 대상 단어를 읽으십시오. 올바른 열 제목 아래에 체크(✓)를 하십시오.

Target Words	"or" has the /ô/ + /r/ sounds as in the word <u>door</u>	"or" has the /ə/ + /r/ sounds as in the word <u>doctor</u>
1. core		
2. border		
3. memory		
4. spectator		

Name: _____ Date:___/___/_____ Score:_____

Lesson 15.8

Reading Words with the "or" Letter Combination

Dictionary Skills/ Vocabulary

✓ **Lesson Check Point**

Directions: Read each target word and its definition. Write the target word on the line in front of its meaning. Use a dictionary or the Internet to check your answers.

지도: 각 대상 단어와 그 정의를 읽으십시오. 의미 앞 줄에 대상단어를쓰십시오. 사전이나 인터넷을 사용하여 답을 확인하십시오.

Target Word Box				
shortest	corn	horse	poor	sport

1. _____ yellow or white grain
2. _____ a large four-legged animal
3. _____ measurement that is least in a series
4. _____ a physical activity and/or game
5. _____ a state of not having money for basic

Directions: Read each sentence and write the target word that correctly completes the sentence.

지도: 각 문장을읽고 다음과 같은 목표 단어를 쓰십시오. 장을올바르게 완성합니다.

6. Tom's favorite _____ is baseball.

7. The _____ woman is applying for a job.

8. The _____ is eating a pile of hay by the barn.

9. Horace is the _____ boy in Mr. James' class.

10. The farmer has healthy stalks of _____ on his farm.

Name: _____   Date: ___/___/_____   Score: _____

Lesson 15.9

Reading Words with a Silent Letter "o"

✓ **Lesson Check Point**

Directions: Read the target words in the word box. Write the words that have a silent letter "o" in the first column. Write the words that do not have a silent letter "o" in the second column.

지도: 단어 상자에 있는 대상 단어를 읽으십시오. 첫 번째 열에 묵음 문자"o"가 있는 단어를 쓰십시오. 두 번째 열에 묵음 문자"o"가 없는 단어를 쓰십시오.

Target Word Box				
total	rocks	orders	leopard	zero
leopards	Leonard	mouse	popular	people
subpoena	opening	Phoenix	brother	hoping
Phoenician	jeopardy	subpoenas	someone	jeopardize

Letter "o" is silent	Letter "o" has a letter "o" sound

Name: _____ Date:___/___/_____ Score:_____

Unit Review - O/o

Reading Words with Vowel "o" Sounds: /ŏ/, /ō/, /ə/ & Silent

✓ **Lesson Check Point**

 Directions: Read each target word. Circle the word in the column that has the same "o" sound as the target word.

지도: 각 대상 단어를 읽으십시오. 대상 단어와 동일한 "o" 소리가 나는 열의 단어에 동그라미를 치십시오.

motel	a. poster
	b. monkey

optical	a. rocking
	b. doing

observe	a. retrospect
	b. opening

subpoena	a. marigold
	b. leopard

 Directions: Read each target word. Put a check (✓) under the correct column heading.

지도: 각 대상 단어를 읽으십시오. 올바른 열 제목 아래에 체크(✓)를 하십시오.

Target Words	"o" has the /ŏ/ sound as in the word <u>frog</u>	"o" has the /ō/ sound as in the word <u>go</u>	"o" has the /ə/ sound as in the word <u>carrot</u>	"o" is silent as in the word <u>people</u>
1. motel				
2. optical				
3. observe				
4. subpoena				

Name: _____ Date: ___/___/_____ Score: _____

The Reading Challenge

Lesson 15.10

Reading Multisyllable Words

✓ **Lesson Check Point**

Directions: Read and divide each target word into syllables. Write each word and place a hyphen (-) between the syllables in the second column. Write the number of syllables in the third column. Use a dictionary or the Internet to check your answers.

지도: 각 대상 단어를 읽고 음절로 나눕니다. 각 단어를 쓰고 두 번째 열의 음절 사이에 하이픈(-)을 넣습니다. 세 번째 열에 음절 수를 쓰십시오. 사전이나 인터넷을 사용하여 답을 확인하십시오.

Target Words	Words Divided into Syllables	Number of Syllables
1. localize	_____	_____
2. total	_____	_____
3. remote	_____	_____
4. poetry	_____	_____
5. noble	_____	_____
6. devoting	_____	_____
7. pony	_____	_____
8. morning	_____	_____
9. moisture	_____	_____
10. pointless	_____	_____

Name: _____ Date: ___/___/_____ Score: _____

The Reading Challenge

Lesson 15.10

Reading Multisyllable Words

✓ Lesson Check Point

 Directions: Read each target word. Circle the word in the row that is divided correctly into syllables. Use a dictionary or the Internet to check your answers.

지도: 각 대상 단어를 읽으십시오. 음절로 올바르게 나누어진 행에 있는 단어에 동그라미를 치십시오. 사전이나 인터넷을 사용하여 답을 확인하십시오.

Model

| proposal | a. prop-o-sal | b. pro-po-sal | c. pro-pos-al (circled) |

| 1. calculator | a. cal-cul-ator | b. calc-ul-ator | c. cal-cu-la-tor |

| 2. Yoruba | a. Yo-ru-ba | b. Yor-u-ba | c. Yor-ub-a |

| 3. reservoir | a. re-ser-voir | b. res-er-voir | c. res-e-rvoir |

| 4. monitor | a. mon-it-or | b. mon-i-tor | c. mo-nit-or |

| 5. avocado | a. av-o-ca-do | b. av-oca-do | c. a-voc-a-do |

| 6. creditor | a. cre-dit-or | b. cred-it-or | c. cred-i-tor |

| 7. diploma | a. dip-lo-ma | b. di-plo-ma | c. di-plom-a |

| 8. marigold | a. ma-ri-gold | b. mar-i-gold | c. ma-rig-old |

Name: _____   Date:___/___/_____   Score:_____

Lesson 15.11

Reading and Writing

Proper and Common Nouns and Adjectives

Directions: Read the words in the word box. Put an (X) on the line next to each word that is written incorrectly. Remember that all proper nouns and proper adjectives are capitalized. Use a dictionary or the Internet to check your answers.

지도: 단어 상자에 있는 단어를 읽으십시오. 잘못 쓰여진 각 단어 옆의 줄에 (X)를 표시하십시오. 모든 고유 명사와 고유 형용사는 대문자임을 기억하십시오. 사전이나 인터넷을 사용하여 답을 확인하십시오.

Word Box		
___ orion	___ Ohio	___ optical
___ Oxford	___ occupant	___ Omnivore
___ october	___ Octopus	___ Ornament
___ observable	___ oval Office	___ Ottoman Empire

Directions: Read each unedited sentence and underline the word that is written incorrectly. Write each sentence correctly on the line.

지도: 편집되지 않은 각 문장을 읽고 잘못 쓰여진 단어에 밑줄을굿습 니다. 각 문장을 줄에 올바르게 쓰십시오.

Model
At <u>One</u> o'clock, the Owens family went to Onega Bay.
<u>At one o'clock, the Owens family went to Onega Bay.</u>

1. Mr. and Mrs. Oscar bought a house by the Ocean.
_____

2. Odessa is reading about the origin of the olympics.
_____

3. The professors at oxford are studying the ozone layer.
_____

4. our cruise ship, Odyssey, sailed across the Atlantic Ocean.
_____

Name: _____ Date:___/___/_____ Score:_____

Lesson 16.1

Reading Words with the Letter P/p

✓ Lesson Check Point

Directions: Read each target word. Find the letter "p" and put a check (✓) in the column that identifies its position: beginning, within or end.
지도: 각 대상 단어를 읽으십시오. 문자"p"를 찾아 체크 표시(✓)위치를 식별하는 열에서 시작, 내부 또는 끝.

Target Words	Beginning (First Letter)	Within	End (Last Letter)
1. grip			
2. pilot			
3. plain			
4. octopus			
5. complain			

Directions: Read each sentence and underline the words that begin with the letter "p." Write all the underlined words in alphabetical order on the lines below.
지도: 각 문장을 읽고"p"로 시작하는 단어에 밑줄을 긋습니다. 아래 줄에 밑줄 친 단어를 알파벳 순서로 모두 쓰십시오.

6. The Perez family is from Peru.

7. I work part-time at a perfume company.

8. The pharmacy is located in Houston Plaza.

9. Jenny has a pencil and five pens in her bag.

10. Dr. Andrew gave me a private physical examination.

_____   _____   _____
_____   _____   _____
_____   _____   _____
              _____

Name: _____ Date: ___/___/_____ Score: _____

Lesson 16.2

Reading Words with the "ph" Letter Combination

✓ Lesson Check Point

Directions: Read each target word. Circle the word in the column that has the same "ph" sound(s) as the target word.

지도: 각 대상 단어를 읽으십시오. 대상 단어와 동일한 "ph" 소리를 가진 열의 단어에 동그라미를 치십시오.

dolphin	a. physical
	b. shepherd

esophagus	a. photography
	b. upheaval

haphazard	a. physics
	b. upholster

physician	a. phrase
	b. uphold

Directions: Read each target word. Put a check (✓) under the correct column heading.

지도: 각 대상 단어를 읽으십시오. 올바른 열 제목 아래에 체크(✓)를 하십시오.

Target Words	"ph" has the /f/ sound as in the word <u>phone</u>	"ph" has the /p/ +/h/ sounds as in the word <u>uphill</u>
1. dolphin		
2. esophagus		
3. haphazard		
4. physician		

Name: _____ Date:___/___/_____ Score: _____

Lesson 16.3

Reading Words with the "pr" Letter Combination

Dictionary Skills/ Vocabulary

✓ Lesson Check Point

Directions: Read each target word and its definition. Write the letter of the definition on the line of each target word. Use a dictionary or the Internet to check your answers.
지도: 각 대상 단어와 그 정의를 읽으십시오. 각 대상 단어의 행에 정의의 문자를 씁니다. 사전이나 인터넷을 사용하여 답을 확인하십시오.

Target Words	Definitions
1. __ print	a. the son of a king
2. __ profit	b. money earned from the sale of products
3. __ prince	c. to do something repeatedly in order to improve
4. __ practice	d. state of a woman carrying a baby within her womb
5. __ pregnant	e. to produce an image or text on a surface

Directions: Read each sentence and write the target word that correctly completes the sentence.
지도: 각 문장을 읽고 다음과 같은 목표 단어를 쓰십시오. 장을 올바르게 완성합니다.

6. Alex has to _____ his violin every day.

7. My teacher, Mrs. Primis, is six months _____.

8. I will _____ a picture of an artist on my cover page.

9. The king is preparing the _____ to become a great ruler.

10. The business owner is planning to make a _____ this year.

Name: _____ Date:___/___/_____ Score: _____

Lesson 16.4

Reading Words with the "pl" Letter Combination

Dictionary Skills/ Vocabulary

✓ **Lesson Check Point**

 Directions: Read each target word and its definition. Write the target word on the line in front of its meaning. Use a dictionary or the Internet to check your answers.

지도: 각 대상 단어와 그 정의를 읽으십시오. 의미 앞 줄에 대상 단어 를 쓰십시오. 사전이나 인터넷을 사용하여 답을 확인하십시오.

Target Word Box				
planet	play	pliers	plaza	pleaded

1. _____ a metal or durable plastic tool
2. _____ the act of doing something fun
3. _____ to have appealed earnestly
4. _____ a small shopping center within a community
5. _____ sphere shaped, celestial object within the solar

 Directions: Read each sentence. Underline the word in the parentheses that correctly completes each sentence. Then, write the underlined word on the line.

지도: 각 문장을 읽으십시오. 각 문장을 올바르게 완성하는 괄호 안에 있는 단어에 밑줄을 긋습니다. 그런 다음 밑줄 친 단어를 줄에 쓰십시오.

6. Earth is the third _____ from the sun. (planet, pleaded)

7. The children will _____ baseball on Saturday. (plaza, play)

8. Paul needs a pair of _____ to fix the bench. (planet, pliers)

9. Peter's pastry shop is in the new shopping _____. (plaza, play)

10. At court, the plaintiff _____ with the judge. (pleaded, pliers)

Name: _____ Date:___/___/_____ Score: _____

Lesson 16.4

Reading Words with the "ple" Letter Combination

✓ Lesson Check Point

 Directions: Read each target word. Find the "ple" letter combination and put a check (✓) in the column that identifies its position: beginning, within or end.

지도: 각 대상 단어를 읽으십시오. "ple"문자 조합을 찾고위치를 식별하는 열에 체크(✓)를 하십시오: 시작, 내또는 끝.

Target Words	Beginning (First 3 Letters)	Within	End (Last 3 Letters)
1. dimple			
2. example			
3. pleasant			
4. principle			
5. incomplete			

 Directions: Read each target word. Put a check (✓) in the "yes" column if the "ple" letter combination has the /p/ + /ə/ + /l/ sounds. Put a check (✓) in the "no" column if the "ple" letter combination does not have the /p/ + /ə/ + /l/ sounds.

지도: 각 대상 단어를 읽으십시오. "ple" 문자 조합에/p/ + /ə/ + /l/ 소리가 있는 경우"yes" 열에 체크(✓)를 하십시오. "ple" 문자 조합에p/ + /ə/ + /l/ 소리가 없으면"no" 열에 체크(✓)를 하십시오.

Target Words	Yes	No
6. dimple		
7. example		
8. pleasant		
9. principle		
10. incomplete		

Name: _____ Date:___/___/_____ Score:_____

Lesson 17.1

Reading Words with the Letter Q/q

✓ **Lesson Check Point**

Directions: Read each target word. Find the letter "q" and put a check (✓) in the column that identifies its position: beginning, within or end.
지도: 각 대상 단어를 읽으십시오. 문자"q"를 찾아 체크 표시(✓)위치를 식별하는 열에서 시작, 내부 또는 끝.

Target Words	Beginning (First Letter)	Within	End (Last Letter)
1. conquer			
2. question			
3. quadruplet			
4. disqualified			
5. consequence			

Directions: Read each sentence and underline the words that begin with the letter "q." Write all the underlined words in alphabetical order on the lines below.
지도: 각 문장을 읽고"q"로 시작하는 단어에 밑줄을 긋습니다. 아래 줄에 밑줄 친 단어를 알파벳 순서로 모두 쓰십시오.

6. Janice plans to quit her job at the quilting mill.

7. Queenisha and Christopher quibbled over an issue.

8. Recently, the profits at Quantum Inc. have quadrupled.

9. Quincy is a quarterback on the high school's football team.

10. My mother made a beautiful queen-size quilt for her bed.

_____   _____   _____
_____   _____   _____
_____   _____   _____
               _____

Name: _____ Date: ___/___/_____ Score: _____

Lesson 17.2

Reading Words with the Letter "q" and "qu" Letter Combination

✓ Lesson Check Point

 Directions: Read each target word. Circle the word in the column that has the same "q" or "qu" sound(s) as the target word.
지도: 각 대상 단어를 읽으십시오. 대상 단어와 동일한 "q" 또는 "qu" 소리가 있는 열의 단어에 동그라미를 치십시오.

antique	a. quietly
	b. Albuquerque

quicken	a. acquire
	b. conquer

quarters	a. equator
	b. qindarka

boutique	a. question
	b. mosque

 Directions: Read each target word. Put a check (✓) under the correct column heading.
지도: 각 대상 단어를 읽으십시오. 올바른 열 제목 아래에 체크(✓)를 하십시오.

Target Words	"qu" has the /k/ sound as in the word <u>plaque</u>	"qu" has the /k/ + /w/ sounds as in the word <u>queen</u>
1. antique		
2. quicken		
3. quarters		
4. boutique		

Name: _____ Date:___/___/_____ Score:_____

Lesson 17.2

Reading Words with the "qu" Letter Combination

✓ Lesson Check Point

 Directions: Read each target word. Circle the word in the column that has the same "qu" sound(s) as the target word.
지도: 각 대상 단어를 읽으십시오. 대상 단어와 동일한 "qu" 소리가 있는 열의 단어에 동그라미를 치십시오.

lacquer	a. requirement
	b. racquet

squirrel	a. inquisitive
	b. boutique

inquiring	a. lacquer
	b. requests

consequence	a. opaque
	b. squarely

 Directions: Read each target word. Put a check (✓) under the correct column heading.
지도: 각 대상 단어를 읽으십시오. 올바른 열 제목 아래에 체크(✓)를 하십시오.

Target Words	"qu" has the /k/ + /w/ sounds as in the word <u>queen</u>	"qu" has the /k/ sound as in the word <u>plaque</u>	"qu" is silent as in the word <u>racquet</u>
1. lacquer			
2. squirrel			
3. inquiring			
4. consequence			

Name: _____ Date: ___/___/_____ Score: _____

The Reading Challenge

Lesson 17.3

Reading Multisyllable Words

✓ **Lesson Check Point**

Directions: Read and divide each target word into syllables. Write each word and place a hyphen (-) between the syllables in the second column. Write the number of syllables in the third column. Use a dictionary or the Internet to check your answers.

지도: 각 대상 단어를 읽고 음절로 나눕니다. 각 단어를 쓰고 두 번째 열의 음절 사이에 하이픈(-)을 넣습니다. 세 번째 열에 음절 수를 쓰십시오. 사전이나 인터넷을 사용하여 답을 확인하십시오.

Target Words	Words Divided into Syllables	Number of Syllables
1. quirky	_____	_____
2. quicksand	_____	_____
3. quilted	_____	_____
4. questioning	_____	_____
5. queasy	_____	_____
6. quality	_____	_____
7. qualitative	_____	_____
8. quarterly	_____	_____
9. qualification	_____	_____
10. quickening	_____	_____

Name: _____ Date: ___/___/_____ Score: _____

The Reading Challenge

Lesson 17.3

Reading Multisyllable Words

✓ **Lesson Check Point**

Directions: Read each target word. Circle the word in the row that is divided correctly into syllables. Use a dictionary or the Internet to check your answers.

지도: 각 대상 단어를 읽으십시오. 음절로 올바르게 나누어진 행에 있는 단어에 동그라미를 치십시오. 사전이나 인터넷을 사용하여 답을 확인하십시오.

Model

| quarter | a. quart-er | b. quar-ter | c. qu-arter |

1. quarantine	a. quar-an-tine	b. qua-rant-ine	c. qua-ran-tine
2. quadruplet	a. qua-drup-let	b. quad-rup-let	c. quad-rupl-et
3. qualified	a. qua-lif-ied	b. qua-li-fied	c. qual-i-fied
4. quicken	a. quick-en	b. qui-cken	c. quic-ken
5. quivering	a. qui-veri-ng	b. quiv-er-ing	c. qui-ver-ing
6. quotation	a. quot-a-tion	b. quo-ta-tion	c. quot-at-ion
7. quotient	a. quo-tient	b. quot-ient	c. qu-otient
8. quotable	a. quo-tab-le	b. quo-ta-ble	c. quot-a-ble

Name: _____   Date: ___/___/_____   Score: _____

Lesson 17.4

Reading and Writing

Proper and Common Nouns and Adjectives

Directions: Read the words in the word box. Put an (X) on the line next to each word that is written incorrectly. Remember that all proper nouns and proper adjectives are capitalized. Use a dictionary or the Internet to check your answers.

지도: 단어 상자에 있는 단어를 읽으십시오. 잘못 쓰여진 각 단어 옆의 줄에 (X)를 표시하십시오. 모든 고유 명사와 고유 형용사는 대문자임을 기억하십시오. 사전이나 인터넷을 사용하여 답을 확인하십시오.

Word Box		
___ quarterly	___ Quaker	___ qatar
___ Quotient	___ Questions	___ queen
___ quarantine	___ Mrs. quincy	___ quickly
___ Mr. Quinn	___ queen's Park	___ Quiver

Directions: Read each unedited sentence and underline the word that is written incorrectly. Write each sentence correctly on the line.

지도: 편집되지 않은 각 문장을 읽고 잘못 쓰여진 단어에 밑줄을긋습 니다. 각 문장을 줄에 올바르게 쓰십시오.

Model
The <u>queen</u> of England was very quiet.
<u>The Queen of England was very quiet.</u>

1. Quinn said, "Yemen and qatar are located on the Arabian Peninsula."
   _____

2. Dr. quinta practices medicine at Queens General Hospital.
   _____

3. Mr. Q is qualified for the position at quantum Incorporated.
   _____

4. Pam's Quadruplets are named Queen, Queenie, Quincy and Quinsy.
   _____

Name: _____ Date: ___/___/_____ Score: _____

Lesson 18.1

Reading Words with the Letter R/r

✓ Lesson Check Point

Directions: Read each target word. Find the letter "r" and put a check (✓) in the column that identifies its position: beginning, within or end.
지도: 각 대상 단어를 읽으십시오. 문자"r"을 찾아 체크 표시(✓)위치를 식별하는 열에서 시작, 내부 또는 끝.

Target Words	Beginning (First Letter)	Within	End (Last Letter)
1. finger			
2. radius			
3. carpet			
4. dollar			
5. graduation			

Directions: Read each sentence and underline the words that begin with the letter "r." Write all the underlined words in alphabetical order on the lines below.
지도: 각 문장을 읽고 문자"r"로 시작하는 단어에 밑줄을 긋습니다. 아래 줄에 밑줄 친 단어를 알파벳 순서로 모두 쓰십시오.

6. The runners are training for the Riverside Marathon.

7. Gary received a green rocket ship from his favorite aunt.

8. We are returning from a revitalizing tour of the Amazon.

9. Lily and her friends ate chicken and rice at the restaurant.

10. Molly read four nonfiction books about dogs and raccoons.

_____   _____   _____
_____   _____   _____
_____   _____   _____
                _____

Name: _____ Date: ___/___/_____ Score: _____

Lesson 18.2

Reading Words with the Letter "r" Combinations:
"br," "cr," "dr," "fr," "gr," "pr" and "tr"

✓ Lesson Check Point

Directions: Read the target words in the word box. Identify the words with the following letter combinations: "br," "cr," "dr," "fr," "gr," "pr" and "tr." Write the target word on the line that correctly completes each sentence.

지도: 단어 상자에 있는 대상 단어를 읽으십시오. "br," "cr," "dr," "fr," "gr," "pr" 및 "tr" 문자 조합으로 단어를 식별합니다. 각 문장을 올바르게 완성하는 행에 목표 단어를 쓰십시오.

Target Word Box			
groom	brown	truck	dress
cream	frozen		president
train	cross-examined		cry

1. Francis is eating fresh fruit with vanilla _____.

2. The bride and _____ are standing on a bridge.

3. Frank said, "The block of ice is _____ solid."

4. The _____ driver is driving along the highway.

5. Brenda is wearing a pretty _____ to the prom.

6. Yesterday, Brad was elected senior class _____.

7. The colors of the crayons are red, blue and _____.

8. The lawyer effectively _____ the character witness.

9. All babies _____ when they experience hunger.

10. Gare du Lyon is a magnificent _____ station in France.

Name: _____ Date:___/___/_____ Score:_____

The Reading Challenge

Lesson 18.3

Reading Multisyllable Words

✓ **Lesson Check Point**

Directions: Read and divide each target word into syllables. Write each word and place a hyphen (-) between the syllables in the second column. Write the number of syllables in the third column. Use a dictionary or the Internet to check your answers.

지도: 각 대상 단어를 읽고 음절로 나눕니다. 각 단어를 쓰고 두 번째 열의 음절 사이에 하이픈(-)을 넣습니다. 세 번째 열에 음절 수를 쓰십시오. 사전이나 인터넷을 사용하여 답을 확인하십시오.

Target Words	Words Divided into Syllables	Number of Syllables
1. rocket	_____	_____
2. rarely	_____	_____
3. recalling	_____	_____
4. ratify	_____	_____
5. recap	_____	_____
6. ravine	_____	_____
7. receiver	_____	_____
8. redeeming	_____	_____
9. raisin	_____	_____
10. robotics	_____	_____

Name: _____ Date: ___/___/_____ Score: _____

The Reading Challenge

Lesson 18.3

Reading Multisyllable Words

✓ Lesson Check Point

Directions: Read each target word. Circle the word in the row that is divided correctly into syllables. Use a dictionary or the Internet to check your answers.

지도: 각 대상 단어를 읽으십시오. 음절로 올바르게 나누어진 행에 있는 단어에 동그라미를 치십시오. 사전이나 인터넷을 사용하여 답을 확인하십시오.

Model

| runaway | a. ru-na-way | b. run-a-way (circled) | c. run-aw-ay |

| 1. recapture | a. re-cap-ture | b. re-capt-ure | c. rec-ap-ture |

| 2. romantic | a. rom-an-tic | b. ro-mant-ic | c. ro-man-tic |

| 3. rigorous | a. rig-o-rous | b. ri-gor-ous | c. rig-or-ous |

| 4. refugee | a. re-fu-gee | b. ref-u-gee | c. ref-ug-ee |

| 5. ridicule | a. rid-i-cule | b. ri-dic-ule | c. ri-di-cule |

| 6. royalty | a. ro-yal-ty | b. roy-al-ty | c. roy-a-lty |

| 7. reversal | a. re-ver-sal | b. rev-er-sal | c. re-vers-al |

| 8. recliner | a. recl-i-ner | b. re-clin-er | c. rec-li-ner |

Name: _____   Date: ___/___/_____   Score: _____

Lesson 18.4

Reading and Writing

Proper and Common Nouns and Adjectives

Directions: Read the words in the word box. Put an (X) on the line next to each word that is written incorrectly. Remember that all proper nouns and proper adjectives are capitalized. Use a dictionary or the Internet to check your answers.

지도: 단어 상자에 있는 단어를 읽으십시오. 잘못 쓰여진 각 단어 옆의 줄에 (X)를 표시하십시오. 모든 고유 명사와 고유 형용사는 대문자임을 기억하십시오. 사전이나 인터넷을 사용하여 답을 확인하십시오.

Word Box		
__ Ranger	__ RSVP	__ Raffle
__ reunion	__ royalty	__ realtor
__ Raccoon	__ roman Empire	__ ruthenia
__ rio Grande	__ Rhodes scholar	__ riverside

Directions: Read each unedited sentence and underline the word that is written incorrectly. Write each sentence correctly on the line.

지도: 편집되지 않은 각 문장을 읽고 잘못 쓰여진 단어에 밑줄을긋습 니다. 각 문장을 줄에 올바르게 쓰십시오.

Model
We saw two <u>Retired</u> racehorses at Richardson Ranch.
We saw two retired racehorses at Richardson Ranch.

1. Roya is Reading her favorite play, "Romeo and Juliet!"
   _____

2. My friend, Rose, bought a nice ring in rio de Janeiro, Brazil.
   _____

3. Mr. Raymond is studying russian at Russia's best university.
   _____

4. rita learned that the Nile River provides rich soil for agriculture.
   _____

Name: _____ Date: ___/___/_____ Score: _____

Lesson 19.1

Reading Words with the Letter S/s

✓ **Lesson Check Point**

Directions: Read each target word. Find the letter "s" and put a check (✓) in the column that identifies its position: beginning, within or end.
지도: 각 대상 단어를 읽으십시오. 문자"s"를 찾아 체크 표시(✓)위치를 식별하는 열에서 시작, 내부 또는 끝.

Target Words	Beginning (First Letter)	Within	End (Last Letter)
1. single			
2. seminar			
3. constant			
4. brothers			
5. cheeseburger			

Directions: Read each sentence and underline the words that begin with the letter "s." Write all the underlined words in alphabetical order on the lines below.
지도: 각 문장을 읽고"s"로 시작하는 단어에 밑줄을 긋습니다. 아래 줄에 밑줄 친 단어를 알파벳 순서로 모두 쓰십시오.

6. You cannot cut a sandwich with scissors.

7. Joy wrote four sentences about sailboats.

8. At college, I am studying computer science.

9. Everyone is saving money for the school trip.

10. We are scheduled to go shopping at one o'clock.

_____   _____   _____
_____   _____   _____
_____   _____   _____

Name: _____ Date: ___/___/_____ Score: _____

Lesson 19.1

Reading Words with the Letter S/s

✓ **Lesson Check Point**

 Directions: Read each target word. Circle the word in the column that has the same "s" sound as the target word.
지도: 각 대상 단어를 읽으십시오. 대상 단어와 동일한 "s" 소리가 나는 열의 단어에 동그라미를 치십시오.

| daisy | a. twins |
| | b. sauce |

| tissue | a. wins |
| | b. sugary |

| version | a. leisure |
| | b. impose |

| sandwich | a. classmate |
| | b. divisible |

 Directions: Read each target word. Put a check (✓) under the correct column heading.
지도: 각 대상 단어를 읽으십시오. 올바른 열 제목 아래에 체크(✓)를 하십시오.

Target Words	"s" has the /s/ sound as in the word <u>sun</u>	"s" has the /sh/ sound as in the word <u>sugar</u>	"s" has the /z/ sound as in the word <u>his</u>	"s" has the /zh/ sound as in the word <u>vision</u>
1. daisy				
2. tissue				
3. version				
4. sandwich				

Name: _____   Date: ___/___/_____   Score: _____

Lesson 19.2

Reading Words with the "sion," "sial" & "scious" Suffixes

✓ Lesson Check Point

 Directions: Read each target word. Circle the word in the column that has the same "sion," "sial" or "scious" sound as the target word.
지도: 각 대상 단어를 읽으십시오. 대상 단어와 동일한 "sion," "sial" 또는 "scious" 소리가 나는 열의 단어에 동그라미를 치십시오.

decision	a. version
	b. controversial

discussion	a. collision
	b. expression

submission	a. division
	b. compassion

unconscious	a. consensus
	b. preconscious

 Directions: Read each target word. Put a check (✓) under the correct column heading.
지도: 각 대상 단어를 읽으십시오. 올바른 열 제목 아래에 체크(✓)를 하십시오.

Target Words	"sion" has the /sh/ +/ə/+/n/ sounds as in the word <u>passion</u>	"sion" has the /zh/ +/ə/+/n/ sounds as in the word <u>vision</u>	"scious" has the /sh/ +/ə/+/s/ sounds as in the word <u>conscious</u>
1. decision			
2. discussion			
3. submission			
4. unconscious			

Name: _____ Date: ___/___/_____ Score: _____

Lesson 19.3

Reading Words with the "sch" Letter Combination

✓ Lesson Check Point

 Directions: Read each target word. Circle the word in the column that has the same "sch" sound(s) as the target word.
지도: 각 대상 단어를 읽으십시오. 대상 단어와 같은 "sch" 소리가 나는 열의 단어에 동그라미를 치십시오

schlep	a. school
	b. schmear

schism	a. schlep
	b. schema

scholar	a. schilling
	b. school

schooner	a. schmooze
	b. schematic

 Directions: Read each target word. Put a check (✓) under the correct column heading.
지도: 각 대상 단어를 읽으십시오. 올바른 열 제목 아래에 체크(✓)를 하십시오.

Target Words	"sch" has the /s/ + /k/ sounds as in the word school	"sch" has the /sh/ sound as in the word schilling
1. schlep		
2. schism		
3. scholar		
4. schooner		

Name: _____ Date:___/___/_____ Score:_____

Lesson 19.4

Reading Words with the "scr," "shr," "spr" & "str" Letter Combinations

Dictionary Skills/ Vocabulary

✓ Lesson Check Point

Directions: Read each target word and its definition. Write the letter of the definition on the line of each target word. Use a dictionary or the Internet to check your answers.
지도: 각 대상 단어와 그 정의를 읽으십시오. 각 대상 단어의 행에 정의의 문자를 씁니다. 사전이나 인터넷을 사용하여 답을 확인하십시오.

Target Words	Definitions
1. __ script	a. written words of a play
2. __ sprained	b. an emotional state of being worried
3. __ stressed	c. to have raised shoulders up and down
4. __ shrugged	d. to have used a small amount of something
5. __ scrimped	e. to have had a physical injury to a body part

Directions: Read each sentence. Underline the word in the parentheses that correctly completes each sentence. Then, write the underlined word on the line.
지도: 각 문장을 읽으십시오. 각 문장을 올바르게 완성하는 괄호 안에 있는 단어에 밑줄을 긋습니다. 그런 다음 밑줄 친 단어를 줄에 쓰십시오.

6. I _____ and saved money to buy supplies. (scrimped, shrugged)

7. I am learning to write a _____ in my English class. (shrugged, script)

8. Jamal is _____ about taking his examinations. (stressed, script)

9. I _____ my ankle during the ball game. (sprained, stressed)

10. He _____ his shoulders in response to the questions. (scrimped, shrugged)

Name: _____ Date: ___/___/_____ Score: _____

Lesson 19.5

Reading Words with the "sl" & "sle" Letter Combinations

Dictionary Skills/ Vocabulary

✓ **Lesson Check Point**

Directions: Read each target word and its definition. Write the target word on the line in front of its meaning. Use a dictionary or the Internet to check your answers.

지도: 각 대상 단어와 그 정의를 읽으십시오. 의미 앞 줄에 대상단어를 쓰십시오. 사전이나 인터넷을 사용하여 답을 확인하십시오.

Target Word Box				
slanting	slimy	slippers	slow	slurps

1. _____ backless footwear
2. _____ not moving quickly
3. _____ something that feels sticky or slippery
4. _____ making noise while drinking a beverage
5. _____ the position of an object leaning in one

Directions: Read each sentence. Underline the word in the parentheses that correctly completes each sentence. Then, write the underlined word on the line.

지도: 각 문장을 읽으십시오. 각 문장을 올바르게 완성하는 괄호 안에 있는 단어에 밑줄을 긋습니다. 그런 다음 밑줄 친 단어를 줄에 쓰십시오.

6. The new driver drove in the _____ lane. (slow, slimy)

7. Samantha _____ her soda loudly. (slurps, slippers)

8. The _____ fish slipped out of my hands. (slanting, slimy)

9. Mrs. Smith wears her _____ in the kitchen. (slurps, slippers)

10. The people in the painting are _____ to the right. (slanting, slow)

Name: _____ Date:___/___/_____ Score:_____

Lesson 19.5

Reading Words with the "sle" Letter Combination

✓ **Lesson Check Point**

 Directions: Read each target word. Find the "sle" letter combination and put a check (✓) in the column that identifies its position: beginning, within or end.

지도: 각 대상 단어를 읽으십시오. "sle" 문자 조합을 찾고위치를 식별하는 열에 체크(✓)를 하십시오: 시작, 내또는 끝.

Target Words	Beginning (First 3 Letters)	Within	End (Last 3 Letters)
1. sled			
2. hassle			
3. slender			
4. measles			
5. sleeping			

 Directions: Read each target word. Put a check (✓) in the "yes" column if the "sle" letter combination has the /s/ + /ə/ + /l/ or /z/ + /ə/ + /l/ sounds. Put a check (✓) in the "no" column if the "sle" letter combination does not have the /s/ + /ə/ + /l/ or /z/ + /ə/ + /l/ sounds.

지도: 각 대상 단어를 읽으십시오. "sle" 문자 조합에/s/ + /ə/ + /l/또는 /z/ + /ə/ + /l/소리 가 있으면"yes" 열에 체크(✓)를 하십시오. "sle" 문자 조합에/s/ + /ə/ + /l/또는 /z/ + /ə/ + /l/소리가 없으면"no" 열에 체크(✓)를 하십시오.

Target Words	Yes	No
6. sled		
7. hassle		
8. slender		
9. measles		
10. sleeping		

Name: _____ Date: ___/___/_____ Score: _____

Lesson 19.6

Reading Words with the "sm" Letter Combination

✓ Lesson Check Point

Directions: Read each target word. Circle the word in the column that has the same "sm" sounds as the target word.
지도: 각 대상 단어를 읽으십시오. 대상 단어와 동일한 "sm" 소리가 나는 열의 단어에 동그라미를 치십시오.

activism	a. cosmopolitan
	b. capitalism

cytoplasm	a. absenteeism
	b. cosmonauts

bridesmaid	a. vandalism
	b. newsman

newsmonger	a. extremism
	b. mesmerized

Directions: Read each target word. Put a check (✓) under the correct column heading.
지도: 각 대상 단어를 읽으십시오. 올바른 열 제목 아래에 체크(✓)를 하십시오.

Target Words	"sm" has the /s/ + /m/ sounds as in the word <u>smell</u>	"sm" has the /z/ + /m/ sounds as in the word <u>cosmic</u>	"sm" has the /z/ + /ə/ + /m/ sounds as in the word <u>autism</u>
1. activism			
2. cytoplasm			
3. bridesmaid			
4. newsmonger			

Name: _____ Date: ___/___/_____ Score: _____

Lesson 19.7

Reading Words with the "ss" Letter Combination

✓ Lesson Check Point

 Directions: Read each target word. Circle the word in the column that has the same "ss" sound(s) as the target word.
지도: 각 대상 단어를 읽으십시오. 대상 단어와 동일한 "ss" 소리가 나는 열의 단어에 동그라미를 치십시오.

| Missouri | a. misstep |
| | b. dissolve |

| misstated | a. misspelled |
| | b. mission |

| aggression | a. concussion |
| | b. disservice |

| mission | a. tissues |
| | b. dissatisfy |

 Directions: Read each target word. Put a check (✓) under the correct column heading.
지도: 각 대상 단어를 읽으십시오. 올바른 열 제목 아래에 체크(✓)를 하십시오.

Target Words	"ss" has the /sh/ sound as in the word tissue	"ss" has the /s/ + /s/ sounds as in the word misspell	"ss" has the /z/ sound as in the word dissolve
1. Missouri			
2. misstated			
3. aggression			
4. mission			

Name: _____ Date: ___/___/_____ Score: _____

Lesson 19.8

Reading Words with a Silent Letter "s"

✓ Lesson Check Point

Directions: Read the target words in the word box. Write the words that have a silent letter "s" in the first column. Write the words that do not have a silent letter "s" in the second column.

지도: 단어 상자에 있는 대상 단어를 읽으십시오. 첫 번째 열에 묵음문자 "s"가 있는 단어를 씁니다. 두 번째 열에 묵음 문자"s"가 없는 단어를 쓰십시오.

Target Word Box				
obese	isles	mass	aisle	guess
results	nests	assist	pupils	lesson
island	screen	debris	forsake	stories
Arkansas	humans	exposes	coconuts	blossom

Letter "s" is silent	Letter "s" has the /s/, /z/ or /sh/ sound

Name: _____ Date: ___/___/_____ Score: _____

The Reading Challenge

Lesson 19.9

Reading Multisyllable Words

✓ **Lesson Check Point**

Directions: Read and divide each target word into syllables. Write each word and place a hyphen (-) between the syllables in the second column. Write the number of syllables in the third column. Use a dictionary or the Internet to check your answers.

지도: 각 대상 단어를 읽고 음절로 나눕니다. 각 단어를 쓰고 두 번째 열의 음절 사이에 하이픈(-)을 넣습니다. 세 번째 열에 음절 수를 쓰십시오. 사전이나 인터넷을 사용하여 답을 확인하십시오.

Target Words	Words Divided into Syllables	Number of Syllables
1. sentiment		
2. silver		
3. shipment		
4. seventh		
5. soda		
6. sneaker		
7. shamrock		
8. secondly		
9. scheduling		
10. sewing		

Name: _____ Date: ___/___/_____ Score: _____

The Reading Challenge

Lesson 19.9

Reading Multisyllable Words

✓ **Lesson Check Point**

Directions: Read each target word. Circle the word in the row that is divided correctly into syllables. Use a dictionary or the Internet to check your answers.

지도: 각 대상 단어를 읽으십시오. 음절로 올바르게 나누어진 행에 있는 단어에 동그라미를 치십시오. 사전이나 인터넷을 사용하여 답을 확인하십시오.

Model

| Saturday | a. Sa-tur-day | b. Sat-ur-day ⭕ | c. Sa-turd-ay |

| 1. sectional | a. sec-tion-al | b. sect-ion-al | c. se-ction-al |

| 2. solution | a. so-lut-ion | b. sol-ut-ion | c. so-lu-tion |

| 3. situate | a. si-tuat-e | b. sit-ua-te | c. sit-u-ate |

| 4. slavery | a. sla-ver-y | b. slav-er-y | c. sla-ve-ry |

| 5. sisterhood | a. sis-ter-hood | b. si-ster-hood | c. sis-terh-ood |

| 6. sodium | a. sod-i-um | b. so-diu-m | c. so-di-um |

| 7. scorpion | a. scor-p-ion | b. scor-pi-on | c. sco-rpi-on |

| 8. survival | a. sur-viv-al | b. sur-vi-val | c. surv-i-val |

Name: _____ Date:___/___/_____ Score:_____

Lesson 19.10

Reading and Writing

Proper and Common Nouns and Adjectives

Directions: Read the words in the word box. Put an (X) on the line next to each word that is written incorrectly. Remember that all proper nouns and proper adjectives are capitalized. Use a dictionary or the Internet to check your answers.

지도: 단어 상자에 있는 단어를 읽으십시오. 잘못 쓰여진 각 단어 옆의 줄에 (X)를 표시하십시오. 모든 고유 명사와 고유 형용사는 대문자임을 기억하십시오. 사전이나 인터넷을 사용하여 답을 확인하십시오.

Word Box		
___ Senegal	___ senior	___ sidney
___ seaweed	___ Shelter	___ Seminar
___ Shipyard	___ Saturday	___ saudi Arabia
___ Shepherd	___ Sahara Desert	___ Sierra Leone

Directions: Read each unedited sentence and underline the word that is written incorrectly. Write each sentence correctly on the line.

지도: 편집되지 않은 각 문장을 읽고 잘못 쓰여진 단어에 밑줄을긋습 니다. 각 문장을 줄에 올바르게 쓰십시오.。

Model
<u>sandy</u> is going to Salt Lake City on Sunday.
Sandy is going to Salt Lake City on Sunday.

1. The students cannot sit in silence for Six minutes.
   _____

2. On saturday, Senator Smith made a sensational speech.
   _____

3. The short story entitled, "Seven siblings" has a shocking plot.
   _____

4. Sidney Elementary School is scheduled to open in september.
   _____

Name: _____ Date:___/___/_____ Score:_____

Lesson 20.1

Reading Words with the Letter T/t

Directions: Read each target word. Find the letter "t" and put a check (✓) in the column that identifies its position: beginning, within or end.
지도: 각 대상 단어를 읽으십시오. 문자"t"를 찾아 체크 표시(✓)위치를 식별하는 열에서 시작, 내부 또는 끝.

Target Words	Beginning (First Letter)	Within	End (Last Letter)
1. poet			
2. rocket			
3. liberty			
4. thunder			
5. mustard			

Directions: Read each sentence and underline the words that begin with the letter "t." Write all the underlined words in alphabetical order on the lines below.
지도: 각 문장을 읽고 문자"t"로 시작하는 단어에 밑줄을 긋습니다. 아래 줄에 밑줄 친 단어를 알파벳 순서로 모두 쓰십시오.

6. I taped four pages in my textbook.

7. Patrick said, "Tortillas are very tasty."

8. Gina's telephone is tan and dark brown.

9. On Saturday, we will watch television together.

10. My second grade teacher read a book about tigers.

_____   _____   _____
_____   _____   _____
_____   _____   _____
                   _____

Name: _____ Date: ___/___/_____ Score: _____

Lesson 20.2

Reading Words with the "thm" Letter Combination

✓ Lesson Check Point

Directions: Read each target word. Circle the word in the column that has the same "thm" sound(s) as the target word.

지도: 각 대상 단어를 읽으십시오. 대상 단어와 동일한 "thm" 소리가 있는 열의 단어에 동그라미를 치십시오.

birthmark	a. asthmatic
	b. bathmat

isthmian	a. asthma
	b. Pathmark

algorithm	a. rhythm
	b. isthmus

biorhythm	a. birthmarks
	b. antilogarithm

Directions: Read each target word. Put a check (✓) under the correct column heading.

지도: 각 대상 단어를 읽으십시오. 올바른 열 제목 아래에 체크(✓)를 하십시오.

Target Words	"thm" has the /th/ + /ə/ + /m/ sounds as in the word <u>rhythm</u>	"thm" has the /th/ + /m/ sounds as in the word <u>bathmat</u>	"thm" silent "th" + /m/ sound as in the word <u>asthma</u>
1. birthmark			
2. isthmian			
3. algorithm			
4. biorhythm			

Name: _____ Date: ___/___/_____ Score: _____

Lesson 20.3

Reading Words with the "tion," "tial" & "tious" Suffixes

✓ Lesson Check Point

 Directions: Read each target word. Circle the word in the column that has the same "tion," "tial" or "tious" sound as the target word.
지도: 각 대상 단어를 읽으십시오. 대상 단어와 같은 "tion," "tial" 또는 "tious" 소리가 나는 열의 단어에 동그라미를 치십시오.

| sequential | a. deferential |
| | b. traditional |

| fractional | a. partial |
| | b. attention |

| additional | a. extinction |
| | b. cautiously |

| bumptious | a. federation |
| | b. conscientious |

 Directions: Read each target word. Put a check (✓) under the correct column heading.
지도: 각 대상 단어를 읽으십시오. 올바른 열 제목 아래에 체크(✓)를 하십시오.

Target Words	"tion" has the /sh/ + /ə/ + /n/ sounds as in the word <u>education</u>	"tial" has the /sh/ + /ə/ + /l/ sounds as in the word <u>partial</u>	"tious" has the /sh/ + /ə/ + /s/ sounds as in the word <u>ambitious</u>
1. sequential			
2. fractional			
3. additional			
4. bumptious			

Name: _____ Date:___/___/_____ Score:_____

Lesson 20.4

Reading Words with the "tr" Letter Combination

Dictionary Skills/ Vocabulary

✓ Lesson Check Point

Directions: Read each target word and its definition. Write the letter of the definition on the line of each target word. Use a dictionary or the Internet to check your answers.
지도: 각 대상 단어와 그 정의를 읽으십시오. 각 대상 단어의 행에 정의의 문자를 씁니다. 사전이나 인터넷을 사용하여 답을 확인하십시오.

Target Words	Definitions
1. __ tree	a. a path in a wooden area
2. __ trap	b. a device used to catch things
3. __ trail	c. to take a trip from one place to another
4. __ travel	d. the betrayal of one's country by helping its enemies
5. __ treason	e. woody plant with a thick trunk

Directions: Read each sentence. Underline the word in the parentheses that correctly completes each sentence. Then, write the underlined word on the line.
지도: 각 문장을 읽으십시오. 각 문장을 올바르게 완성하는 괄호 안에 있는 단어에 밑줄을 긋습니다. 그런 다음 밑줄 친 단어를 줄에 쓰십시오.

6. The mouse was caught in the _____. (trap, travel)

7. I sat under a shady _____ in the park. (tree, treason)

8. The traitor was arrested for high _____. (treason, trap)

9. The toddlers are riding their tricycles along the _____. (tree, trail)

10. Today, Troy is scheduled to _____ to Tennessee. (trail, travel)

Name: _____ Date:___/___/_____ Score:_____

Lesson 20.5

Reading Words with the "tle" Letter Combination

✓ Lesson Check Point

 Directions: Read each target word. Find the "tle" letter combination and put a check (✓) in the column that identifies its position: beginning, within or end.
지도: 각 대상 단어를 읽으십시오. "tle" 문자 조합을 찾고위치를 식별하는 열에 체크(✓)를 하십시오: 시작, 내또는 끝.

Target Words	Beginning (First 3 Letters)	Within	End (Last 3 Letters)
1. beetle			
2. rattle			
3. bootleg			
4. limitless			
5. effortless			

 Directions: Read each target word. Put a check (✓) in the "yes" column if the "tle" letter combination has the /t/ + /ə/ + /l/ sounds. Put a check (✓) in the "no" column if the "tle" letter combination does not have the /t/ + /ə/ + /l/ sounds.
지도: 각 대상 단어를 읽으십시오. "tle" 문자 조합에/t/ + /ə/ + /l/ 소리가 있으면 "yes" 열에 체크(✓)를 하십시오. "tle" 문자 조합에/t/ + /ə/ + /l/ 소리가 없으면 "no" 열에 체크(✓)를 하십시오.

Target Words	Yes	No
6. beetle		
7. rattle		
8. bootleg		
9. limitless		
10. effortless		

Name: _____   Date: ___/___/_____   Score: _____

Lesson 20.6

Reading Words with the Letter "t" Sounds

✓ Lesson Check Point

 Directions: Read each target word. Circle the word in the column that has the same "t" sound as the target word.

지도: 각 대상 단어를 읽으십시오. 대상 단어와 "t" 소리가 같은 열의 단어에 동그라미를 치십시오.

actor	a. fracture
	b. connective

fixture	a. expect
	b. feature

indicted	a. factor
	b. actuary

righteous	a. thunder
	b. obituary

 Directions: Read each target word. Put a check (✓) under the correct column heading.

지도: 각 대상 단어를 읽으십시오. 올바른 열 제목 아래에 체크(✓)를 하십시오.

Target Words	"t" has the /t/ sound as in the word <u>multiply</u>	"t" has the /ch/ sound as in the word <u>picture</u>	"t" has the /sh/ sound as in the word <u>position</u>
1. actor			
2. fixture			
3. indicted			
4. righteous			

Name: _____ Date: ___/___/_____ Score: _____

Lesson 20.7

Reading Words with a Silent Letter "t"

✓ **Lesson Check Point**

Directions: Read the target words in the word box. Write the words that have a silent letter "t" in the first column. Write the words that do not have a silent letter "t" in the second column.

지도: 단어 상자에 있는 대상 단어를 읽으십시오. 첫 번째 열에 묵음문자 "t"가 있는 단어를 쓰십시오. 두 번째 열에 묵음 문자"t"가 없는 단어를 쓰십시오.

Target Word Box				
hasten	fault	contract	ballet	digit
educate	debut	buffet	soften	litter
chapter	fainting	fasten	trouble	timely
rapport	tsunami	attach	generate	dustpan

Letter "t" is silent

Letter "t" has the /t/ sound

Name: _____ Date:___/___/_____ Score:_____

The Reading Challenge

Lesson 20.8

Reading Multisyllable Words

 Lesson Check Point

 Directions: Read and divide each target word into syllables. Write each word and place a hyphen (-) between the syllables in the second column. Write the number of syllables in the third column. Use a dictionary or the Internet to check your answers.

지도: 각 대상 단어를 읽고 음절로 나눕니다. 각 단어를 쓰고 두 번째 열의 음절 사이에 하이픈(-)을 넣습니다. 세 번째 열에 음절 수를 쓰십시오. 사전이나 인터넷을 사용하여 답을 확인하십시오.

Target Words	Words Divided into Syllables	Number of Syllables
1. treatment	_____	_____
2. tutorial	_____	_____
3. tenderly	_____	_____
4. today	_____	_____
5. tiger	_____	_____
6. thicken	_____	_____
7. treadmill	_____	_____
8. twentieth	_____	_____
9. themselves	_____	_____
10. transported	_____	_____

Name: _____ Date: ___/___/_____ Score: _____

The Reading Challenge

Lesson 20.8

Reading Multisyllable Words

✓ **Lesson Check Point**

 Directions: Read each target word. Circle the word in the row that is divided correctly into syllables. Use a dictionary or the Internet to check your answers.

지도: 각 대상 단어를 읽으십시오. 음절로 올바르게 나누어진 행에 있는 단어에 동그라미를 치십시오. 사전이나 인터넷을 사용하여 답을 확인하십시오.

Model

| telephone | a. te-lep-hone | b. tel-e-phone | c. te-le-phone |

| 1. typify | a. typ-i-fy | b. ty-pi-fy | c. typ-if-y |

| 2. tropical | a. tro-pi-cal | b. tro-pic-al | c. trop-i-cal |

| 3. thematic | a. them-at-ic | b. the-m-atic | c. the-mat-ic |

| 4. tendency | a. ten-denc-y | b. ten-den-cy | c. tend-en-cy |

| 5. treasury | a. treas-u-ry | b. treas-ur-y | c. trea-sur-y |

| 6. tragedy | a. trag-e-dy | b. tra-ged-y | c. trag-ed-y |

| 7. together | a. tog-et-her | b. to-geth-er | c. to-get-her |

| 8. tricycle | a. tri-cy-cle | b. tri-cyc-le | c. tric-yc-le |

Name: _____ Date: ___/___/_____ Score: _____

Lesson 20.9

Reading and Writing

Proper and Common Nouns and Adjectives

Directions: Read the words in the word box. Put an (X) on the line next to each word that is written incorrectly. Remember that all proper nouns and proper adjectives are capitalized. Use a dictionary or the Internet to check your answers.

지도: 단어 상자에 있는 단어를 읽으십시오. 잘못 쓰여진 각 단어 옆의 줄에 (X)를 표시하십시오. 모든 고유 명사와 고유 형용사는 대문자임을 기억하십시오. 사전이나 인터넷을 사용하여 답을 확인하십시오.

Word Box					
__	thirst	__	Tibet	__	teapot
__	Tutor	__	triplet	__	Tornado
__	tampa	__	texture	__	Trickster
__	tuesday	__	Tomorrow	__	Tennessee

Directions: Read each unedited sentence and underline the word that is written incorrectly. Write each sentence correctly on the line.

지도: 편집되지 않은 각 문장을 읽고 잘못 쓰여진 단어에 밑줄을긋습 니다. 각 문장을 줄에 올바르게 쓰십시오.

Model
On <u>thursday</u>, a tornado destroyed my hometown.
<u>On Thursday, a tornado destroyed my hometown.</u>

1. The Taxicab driver drives all over Trenton, Tennessee.
_____

2. the Texas tourism office is located in Town Hall.
_____

3. I quenched my thirst with green tea from thailand.
_____

4. My English Textbook has a passage about the City of Troy.
_____

Name: _____ Date: ___/___/_____ Score: _____

Lesson 21.1

Reading Words with the Letter U/u

✓ Lesson Check Point

 Directions: Read each target word. Find the letter "u" and put a check (✓) in the column that identifies its position: beginning, within or end.
지도: 각 대상 단어를 읽으십시오. 문자"u"를 찾아 체크 표시(✓)위치를 식별하는 열에서 시작, 내부 또는 끝.

Target Words	Beginning (First Letter)	Within	End (Last Letter)
1. Peru			
2. south			
3. refuge			
4. umbrella			
5. university			

 Directions: Read each target word. Read the words in the row and circle the word that has a different vowel "u" sound.
지도: 각 대상 단어를 읽으십시오. 줄에 있는 단어를 읽고 모음"u" 소리가 다른 단어에 동그라미를 치세요.다른 단어에 동그라미를 치세요.

Target Words				
6. glum	bug	pub	dual	rug
7. dunk	sup	hug	puff	fluke
8. lung	puck	rule	jug	dug
9. hunch	hub	plug	flume	mug
10. umbrella	club	buns	hunting	quiet

Name: _____ Date:___/___/_____ Score: _____

Lesson 21.2

Reading Words with the Short Vowel "u" Sound

✓ Lesson Check Point

 Directions: Read the words in the four boxes. Circle two words with the short vowel /ŭ/ sound. The anchor word for the short vowel /ŭ/ sound is up.
지도: 네 개의 상자에 있는 단어를 읽으십시오. 짧은 모음 /ŭ/ 소리로 두 단어에 동그라미를 치십시오. 단모음 /ŭ/ 소리의 기준어는 up입니다.

gulp	duke		skull	chunk		munch	tofu
huge	stump		mule	brute		blush	cube

flush	tube		hung	fuss		guard	true
skunk	fluke		blue	rude		slush	hump

 Directions: Read the words in the four boxes. Circle two words that rhyme. Rhyming words have the same ending sound, such as just and must.
지도: 네 개의 상자에 있는 단어를 읽으십시오. 해당하는 두 단어에동그라미 표시운. 운율이 있는 단어는 just 및 must와 같이 끝 소리가 같습니다.

rub	tub		dusk	quite		jump	muse
guess	guide		tusk	duo		buy	pump

cue	gruel		run	bruise		hutch	Dutch
rung	sung		burn	sun		prune	hue

Name: _____ Date: ___/___/_____ Score: _____

Lesson 21.2

Reading & Writing Words with the Short Vowel "u" Sound

✓ Lesson Check Point

Directions: Read each sentence and underline three words with the short vowel /ŭ/ sound. Then, write the underlined words on the lines below. The anchor word for the short vowel /ŭ/ sound is <u>up</u>.

지도: 각 문장을 읽고 세 단어에 짧은 모음 /ŭ/ 소리에 밑줄을 긋습니다. 그런 다음 밑줄 친 단어를 아래 줄에 쓰십시오. 단모음 /ŭ/ 소리의 기준 어는 up입니다.

Model

Ulysses, the <u>drummer</u>, <u>jumps</u> when he plays the <u>drums</u>.

    drummer   jumps   drums

1. At lunchtime, Sue said, "Do not run in the hut!"

   _____ _____ _____

2. The baby cubs used to jump on the tree stumps.

   _____ _____ _____

3. The truck driver had a huge lunch at the clubhouse.

   _____ _____ _____

4. The cute bugs look like they are having fun in the mud.

   _____ _____ _____

5. Bruce's new album is entitled, "Running in the Hot Summer Sun."

   _____ _____ _____

Name: _____ Date: ___/___/_____ Score: _____

Lesson 21.3

Reading Words with the Long Vowel "u" Sound

✓ Lesson Check Point

 Directions: Read the words in the four boxes. Circle two words with the long vowel /yoo/ or /oo/ sound. The anchor word for the long vowel /yoo/ and /oo/ sounds is <u>tube</u>.

지도: 네 개의 상자에 있는 단어를 읽으십시오. 장모음 /yoo/ 또는 /oo/ 소리 로 두 단어에 동그라미를 치십시오. 장모음의 앵커 단어 /yoo/ 및 /oo/ 소리는 tube입니다.

tribute	dune	much	used	produce	nullify
hump	puff	rusty	defuse	hunch	exclude

intrude	rung	pollute	jaguar	liquid	guess
huge	plumber	guitar	spruce	dual	visual

 Directions: Read the words in the four boxes. Circle two words that rhyme. Rhyming words have the same ending sound, such as <u>rule</u> and <u>mule</u>.

지도: 네 개의 상자에 있는 단어를 읽으십시오. 해당하는 두 단어에 동그라미 표시운. 운율이 있는 단어는 rule 및 mule과 같이 끝 소리가 같습니다.

rung	tube	hung	true	hunter	truck
cube	hush	issue	blushing	tissue	argue

husky	duke	dusty	lunch	slum	blue
bumper	fluke	cute	brute	brush	cue

Name: _____ Date: ___/___/_____ Score: _____

Lesson 21.3

Reading & Writing Words with the Long Vowel "u" Sound

✓ **Lesson Check Point**

Directions: Read each sentence and underline three words with the long vowel /y$\overline{oo}$/ or /$\overline{oo}$/ sound. Then, write the underlined words on the lines below. The anchor word for the long vowel /y$\overline{oo}$/ and /$\overline{oo}$/ sounds is <u>tube</u>.

지도: 각 문장을 읽고 긴 단어로 세 단어에 밑줄을 긋습니다. 모음 /y$\overline{oo}$/ 또는 /$\overline{oo}$/ 소리. 그런 다음 밑줄 친 단어를 아래 줄에 쓰십시오. 장모음 /y$\overline{oo}$/ 및 /$\overline{oo}$/ 소리의 앵커 워드는 tube입니다.

Model

<u>Bruce</u> is going to play the <u>tuba</u> and drums in <u>Uganda</u>.

    Bruce   tuba   Uganda
   _____   _____   _____

1. The students are studying about producers and consumers.

   _____   _____   _____

2. The truants did not graduate because of their acts of truancy.

   _____   _____   _____

3. The students living on Hunter Avenue will graduate in August.

   _____   _____   _____

4. In June, I will take a fun-filled vacation to Peru and Yugoslavia.

   _____   _____   _____

5. In July, the drummer argued about his contractual agreement.

   _____   _____   _____

Name: _____ Date: ___/___/_____ Score: _____

Review Lessons 21.2 & 21.3

Reading Short Vowel and Long Vowel Words

Directions: Read the target words in the word box. In the first column, write the words that have the short vowel /ŭ/ sound, as in the word <u>up</u>. In the second column, write the words that have the long vowel /yo͞o/ or /o͞o/ sound, as in the word <u>tube</u>.

지도: 단어 상자에 있는 대상 단어를 읽으십시오. 첫 번째 열에는 up 단어와 같이 단모음 /ŭ/ 소리가 나는 단어를 씁니다. 두 번째 칸에는 장모음 /yo͞o/ 또는 /o͞o/ 소리, 단어 tube에서와 같이.

Target Word Box				
husky	true	lunch	argue	salute
Dutch	rusty	visual	drunk	chunky
confuse	reduce	flushing	strung	annual
pollute	execute	blushing	graduate	brushing

Letter "u" has the /ŭ/ sound as in the word <u>up</u>

Letter "u" has the /yo͞o/ or /o͞o/ sound as in the word <u>tube</u>

Name: _____ Date:___/___/_____ Score: _____

Lesson 21.4

Reading Words with Letter "u" Vowel Pairs

✓ Lesson Check Point

Directions: Read each target word. Circle the word in the column that has the same vowel "ua," "ue" or "ui" sound(s) as the target word.
지도: 각 대상 단어를 읽으십시오. 대상 단어와 동일한 모음"ua," "ue" 또는 "ui" 소리를 갖는 열의 단어에 동그라미를 치십시오.

venue	a. Joshua
	b. argue

clues	a. juicer
	b. conceptual

nuisance	a. bruise
	b. perpetual

visual	a. blue
	b. usual

Directions: Read each target word. Put a check (✓) under the correct column heading.
지도: 각 대상 단어를 읽으십시오. 올바른 열 제목 아래에 체크(✓)를 하십시오.

Target Words	Words have the long "u" sound as in the word <u>blue</u>	Words do not have the long "u" sound
1. due		
2. suite		
3. factual		
4. continue		

Name: _____ Date: ___/___/_____ Score: _____

Lesson 21.5

Reading Words with the Final Letter "u"

✓ Lesson Check Point

 Directions: Read each target word. Find the letter "u" and put a check (✓) in the column that identifies its position within the syllable.
지도: 각 대상 단어를 읽으십시오. 대상 단어와 "u" 소리가 같은 열의 단어에 동그라미를 치십시오.

Target Words	"u" is at the end of a one syllable word	"u" is at the end of the first syllable	"u" is at the end of a multi-syllable word
1. flu			
2. Peru			
3. menu			
4. humor			
5. tubercle			

 Directions: Read each target word. Put a check (✓) under the correct column heading.
지도: 각 대상 단어를 읽으십시오. 올바른 열 제목 아래에 체크(✓)를 하십시오.

Target Words	"u" has the /ŭ/ sound as in the word <u>tub</u>	"u" has the /yōō/ sound as in the word <u>tube</u>	"u" has the /ə/ sound as in the word <u>circus</u>	"u" is silent as in the word <u>build</u>
6. argue				
7. built				
8. sunny				
9. particular				
10. vaguely				

Name: _____ Date: ___/___/_____ Score: _____

Lesson 21.6

Reading Letter "u" Words with the Schwa Vowel Sound

✓ **Lesson Check Point**

 Directions: Read each target word. Circle the word in the column that has the same "u" sound as the target word.
지도: 각 대상 단어를 읽으십시오. 대상 단어와 "u" 소리가 같은 열의 단어에 동그라미를 치십시오.

Saturday	a. campus
	b. upstairs

aut<u>u</u>mn	a. pitiful
	b. umbrella

focus	a. curve
	b. litmus

support	a. busted
	b. circus

 Directions: Read each sentence and underline the letter "u" word that has the schwa vowel /ə/ sound. The anchor word for the letter "u" schwa vowel sound is <u>campus</u>.
지도: 각 문장을 읽고 슈와 모음 /ə/ 소리가 있는 문자 "u" 단어에 밑줄을 긋습니다. 문자 "u" 슈와 모음 소리의 앵커 단어는 campus입니다.

1. Porcupines are mammals with a coat of sharp quills.

2. Eugene is having difficulty completing his assignment.

3. My students are learning to subtract two-digit numbers.

4. Today, the faculty members received their course outline.

5. On Sunday, my uncle drank a medium glass of plum juice.

6. At the circus, the students looked up and saw the acrobats.

Name: _____ Date:___/___/_____ Score:_____

Lesson 21.7

Reading Words with the "ur" Letter Combination

Dictionary Skills/ Vocabulary

✓ Lesson Check Point

Directions: Read each target word and its definition. Write the letter of the definition on the line of each target word. Use a dictionary or the Internet to check your answers.
지도: 각 대상 단어와 그 정의를 읽으십시오. 각 대상 단어의 행에 정의의 문자를 씁니다. 사전이나 인터넷을 사용하여 답을 확인하십시오.

Target Words	Definitions
1. __ curly	a. someone who steals things
2. __ curtain	b. description of something twisted into coils
3. __ burglar	c. fabric that hangs by a window
4. __ hurricane	d. to have designed a place with furniture
5. __ furnished	e. a cyclone with strong winds and heavy rain

Directions: Read each sentence and write the target word on the line that correctly completes the sentence.
지도: 각 문장을읽고 다음과 같은 목표 단어를 쓰십시오. 장을올바르게 완성합니다.

6. Susan tied the gifts with red _____ ribbons.

7. The tropical storm was upgraded to a _____.

8. The living room _____ is designed to block the sun.

9. The _____ was arrested for robbing the jewelry store.

10. David _____ his apartment with expensive antiques.

Name: _____ Date: ___/___/_____ Score: _____

Lesson 21.8

Reading Words with a Silent Letter "u"

✓ **Lesson Check Point**

Directions: Read the target words in the word box. Write the words that have a silent letter "u" in the first column. Write the words that do not have a silent letter "u" in the second column.

지도: 단어 상자에 있는 대상 단어를 읽으십시오. 첫 번째 열에 묵음문자 "u"가 있는 단어를 쓰십시오. 두 번째 열에 묵음 문자"u"가 없는 단어를 쓰십시오.

Target Word Box				
Peru	buildings	butcher	disguise	league
guilty	numerous	laughter	rubbing	intrigue
biscuits	pudding	puppy	perfume	musical
salute	vogue	summer	guess	Guinea

Letter "u" is silent	Letter "u" has a letter "u" sound

Name: _____ Date: ___/___/_____ Score: _____

Unit Review - U/u

Reading Words with Vowel "u" Sounds: /ŭ/, /o͞o/, /ə/ & Silent

✓ **Lesson Check Point**

Directions: Read each target word. Circle the word in the column that has the same "u" sound as the target word.

지도: 각 대상 단어를 읽으십시오. 대상 단어와 "u" 소리가 같은 열의 단어에 동그라미를 치십시오.

ruler	a. frugal
	b. struck

laugh	a. shoulder
	b. argument

support	a. crumble
	b. industry

drummer	a. clubs
	b. beauty

Directions: Read each target word. Put a check (✓) under the correct column heading.

지도: 각 대상 단어를 읽으십시오. 올바른 열 제목 아래에 체크(✓)를 하십시오.

Target Words	"u" has the /ŭ/ sound as in the word <u>tub</u>	"u" has the /o͞o/ sound as in the word <u>tube</u>	"u" has the /ə/ sound as in the word <u>circus</u>	"u" is silent as in the word <u>build</u>
1. ruler				
2. laugh				
3. support				
4. drummer				

Name: _____ Date: ___/___/_____ Score: _____

The Reading Challenge

Lesson 21.9

Reading Multisyllable Words

✓ **Lesson Check Point**

Directions: Read and divide each target word into syllables. Write each word and place a hyphen (-) between the syllables in the second column. Write the number of syllables in the third column. Use a dictionary or the Internet to check your answers.

지도: 각 대상 단어를 읽고 음절로 나눕니다. 각 단어를 쓰고 두 번째 열의 음절 사이에 하이픈(-)을 넣습니다. 세 번째 열에 음절 수를 쓰십시오. 사전이나 인터넷을 사용하여 답을 확인하십시오.

Target Words	Words Divided into Syllables	Number of Syllables
1. jumpers	_____	_____
2. cushion	_____	_____
3. brushing	_____	_____
4. fullest	_____	_____
5. eluding	_____	_____
6. butcher	_____	_____
7. volume	_____	_____
8. defusing	_____	_____
9. customer	_____	_____
10. arguing	_____	_____

Unit U Lesson 21.9

Name: _____ Date: ___/___/_____ Score: _____

The Reading Challenge

Lesson 21.9

Reading Multisyllable Words

✓ **Lesson Check Point**

Directions: Read each target word. Circle the word in the row that is divided correctly into syllables. Use a dictionary or the Internet to check your answers.

지도: 각 대상 단어를 읽으십시오. 음절로 올바르게 나누어진 행에 있는 단어에 동그라미를 치십시오. 사전이나 인터넷을 사용하여 답을 확인하십시오.

Model

| visualize | a. vis-ua-lize | b. vi-su-al-ize (circled) | c. vis-u-a-lize |

1. execute	a. ex-e-cute	b. ex-ec-ute	c. e-xec-ute
2. absolute	a. ab-so-lute	b. abs-o-lute	c. ab-sol-ute
3. punctual	a. pun-ctu-al	b. punc-tu-al	c. pu-nctu-al
4. resuming	a. res-u-ming	b. re-sum-ing	c. re-sumi-ng
5. included	a. incl-u-ded	b. in-clud-ed	c. inc-lud-ed
6. refusing	a. ref-u-sing	b. re-fus-ing	c. ref-us-ing
7. gradual	a. grad-ual	b. gra-du-al	c. grad-u-al
8. consuming	a. con-sum-ing	b. cons-u-ming	c. con-su-ming

Name: _____ Date: ___/___/_____ Score: _____

Lesson 21.10

Reading and Writing

Proper and Common Nouns and Adjectives

Directions: Read the words in the word box. Put an (X) on the line next to each word that is written incorrectly. Remember that all proper nouns and proper adjectives are capitalized. Use a dictionary or the Internet to check your answers.

지도: 단어 상자에 있는 단어를 읽으십시오. 잘못 쓰여진 각 단어 옆의 줄에 (X)를 표시하십시오. 모든 고유 명사와 고유 형용사는 대문자임을 기억하십시오. 사전이나 인터넷을 사용하여 답을 확인하십시오.

Word Box		
___ utah	___ usually	___ USA
___ Uproar	___ ural River	___ Ugliest
___ UNICEF	___ ursa Minor	___ upgrade
___ United Kingdom	___ Uzbekistan	___ Utterance

Directions: Read each unedited sentence and underline the word that is written incorrectly. Write each sentence correctly on the line.

지도: 편집되지 않은 각 문장을 읽고 잘못 쓰여진 단어에 밑줄을 긋습 니다. 각 문장을 줄에 올바르게 쓰십시오.

Model
Mrs. Ubangi usually has union meetings at a local <u>University</u>.
<u>Mrs. Ubangi usually has union meetings at a local university.</u>

1. Last year, university students hiked Up the Ural Mountains.
   _____

2. The UNICEF volunteers are helping Underprivileged children.
   _____

3. Mr. Udell enjoys reading Unusual books about UFO sightings.
   _____

4. The students from uzbekistan are on our university's honor roll.
   _____

Name: _____ Date: ___/___/_____ Score: _____

Lesson 22.1

Reading Words with the Letter V/v

✓ **Lesson Check Point**

Directions: Read each target word. Find the letter "v" and put a check (✓) in the column that identifies its position: beginning, within or end.
지도: 각 대상 단어를 읽으십시오. 문자"v"를 찾아 체크 표시(✓)위치를 식별하는 열에서 시작, 내부 또는 끝.

Target Words	Beginning (First Letter)	Within	End (Last Letter)
1. travail			
2. savings			
3. Vikings			
4. volcanic			
5. Yugoslav			

Directions: Read each sentence and underline the words that begin with the letter "v." Write all the underlined words in alphabetical order on the lines below.
지도: 각 문장을 읽고"v"로 시작하는 단어에 밑줄을 긋습니다. 아래 줄에 밑줄 친 단어를 알파벳 순서로 모두 쓰십시오.

6. My visor blocks the vivid rays of the sun.

7. Our new vitamins taste like vanilla cream.

8. I used the computer to enter a virtual volcano.

9. During the tour, I had a clear view of Victoria Falls.

10. The villagers voted for an entirely new government.

_____ _____ _____
_____ _____ _____
_____ _____ _____
                _____

Name: _____ Date: ___/___/_____ Score: _____

The Reading Challenge

Lesson 22.2

Reading Multisyllable Words

✓ **Lesson Check Point**

Directions: Read and divide each target word into syllables. Write each word and place a hyphen (-) between the syllables in the second column. Write the number of syllables in the third column. Use a dictionary or the Internet to check your answers.

지도: 각 대상 단어를 읽고 음절로 나눕니다. 각 단어를 쓰고 두 번째 열의 음절 사이에 하이픈(-)을 넣습니다. 세 번째 열에 음절 수를 쓰십시오. 사전이나 인터넷을 사용하여 답을 확인하십시오.

Target Words	Words Divided into Syllables	Number of Syllables
1. veto		
2. voiceless		
3. vaulting		
4. version		
5. video		
6. vascular		
7. vividly		
8. versus		
9. viruses		
10. vigorous		

Name: _____ Date: ___/___/_____ Score: _____

The Reading Challenge

Lesson 22.2

Reading Multisyllable Words

✓ **Lesson Check Point**

Directions: Read each target word. Circle the word in the row that is divided correctly into syllables. Use a dictionary or the Internet to check your answers.

지도: 각 대상 단어를 읽으십시오. 음절로 올바르게 나누어진 행에 있는 단어에 동그라미를 치십시오. 사전이나 인터넷을 사용하여 답을 확인하십시오.

Model

| volcano | a. vo-lcan-o | b. vol-can-o | c. vol-ca-no (circled) |

| 1. violin | a. vi-ol-in | b. vi-o-lin | c. vio-li-n |

| 2. verbalize | a. ver-bali-ze | b. verb-al-ize | c. ver-bal-ize |

| 3. vanity | a. van-i-ty | b. va-ni-ty | c. van-it-y |

| 4. vocable | a. vo-cab-le | b. vo-c-able | c. vo-ca-ble |

| 5. virtual | a. virt-u-al | b. vir-tu-al | c. vir-tua-l |

| 6. venison | a. ve-nis-on | b. ven-i-son | c. ven-is-on |

| 7. Vietnam | a. Vi-et-nam | b. Vie-t-nam | c. Vi-etna-m |

| 8. vestibule | a. ves-ti-bule | b. ves-tib-ule | c. vest-i-bule |

Learn To Read English With Directions In Korean   Copyrighted Material

Name: _____ Date: ___/___/_____ Score: _____

Lesson 22.3

Reading and Writing

Proper and Common Nouns and Adjectives

Directions: Read the words in the word box. Put an (X) on the line next to each word that is written incorrectly. Remember that all proper nouns and proper adjectives are capitalized. Use a dictionary or the Internet to check your answers.

지도: 단어 상자에 있는 단어를 읽으십시오. 잘못 쓰여진 각 단어 옆의 줄에 (X)를 표시하십시오. 모든 고유 명사와 고유 형용사는 대문자임을 기억하십시오. 사전이나 인터넷을 사용하여 답을 확인하십시오.

Word Box		
__ version	__ venus	__ vertex
__ vocal cord	__ venice	__ Vessel
__ victoria Falls	__ virginia	__ vocabulary
__ Volcano Island	__ Vanessa	__ valentine's Day

Directions: Read each unedited sentence and underline the word that is written incorrectly. Write each sentence correctly on the line.

지도: 편집되지 않은 각 문장을 읽고 잘못 쓰여진 단어에 밑줄을긋습 니다. 각 문장을 줄에 올바르게 쓰십시오.

Model
In the fall, the leaves in <u>vermont</u> have vibrant colors.
In the fall, the leaves in Vermont have vibrant colors.

1. The vikings made many treacherous ocean voyages.
_____

2. vinny received five African violet plants on Valentine's Day.
_____

3. We are scheduled to play four Volleyball games in Virginia.
_____

4. In November, I plan to Vacation in the British Virgin Islands.
_____

Name: _____ Date: ___/___/_____ Score: _____

Lesson 23.1

Reading Words with the Letter W/w

✓ **Lesson Check Point**

Directions: Read each target word. Find the letter "w" and put a check (✓) in the column that identifies its position: beginning, within or end.
지도: 각 대상 단어를 읽으십시오. 문자"w"를 찾아 체크 표시(✓)위치를 식별하는 열에서 시작, 내부 또는 끝.

Target Words	Beginning (First Letter)	Within	End (Last Letter)
1. answer			
2. washing			
3. somehow			
4. tomorrow			
5. crossword			

Directions: Read each sentence and underline the words that begin with the letter "w." Write all the underlined words in alphabetical order on the lines below.
지도: 각 문장을 읽고"w"로 시작하는 단어에 밑줄을 긋습니다. 아래 줄에 밑줄 친 단어를 알파벳 순서로 모두 쓰십시오.

6. I ate white fish and rice at Adrienne's wedding.

7. The man in the wheelchair is a wealthy businessman.

8. My college professor is writing a wonderful new book.

9. Joanne bought her hair extensions at Western Wig Store.

10. During the summer, Brenda likes to walk in the wilderness.

_____   _____   _____

_____   _____   _____

_____   _____   _____

_____

Name: _____ Date:___/___/_____ Score:_____

Lesson 23.2

Reading Words with a Vowel before the Letter "w"

✓ Lesson Check Point

 Directions: Read each target word. Circle the word in the column that has the same "aw," "ew" or "ow" sound as the target word.
지도: 각 대상 단어를 읽으십시오. 대상 단어와 같은 "aw," "ew" 또는 "ow" 소리가 나는 열의 단어에 동그라미를 치십시오.

nephew	a. sewn
	b. renewal

flawless	a. awareness
	b. pawn

plowing	a. widow
	b. crowds

tomorrow	a. sew
	b. crew

 Directions: Read each target word. Put a check (✓) under the correct column heading.
지도: 각 대상 단어를 읽으십시오. 올바른 열 제목 아래에 체크(✓)를 하십시오.

Target Words	Underlined letters have /o͞o/ sound as in the word <u>few</u>	Underlined letters have /ô/ sound as in the word <u>law</u>	Underlined letters have /ō/ sound as in the word <u>sew</u>	Underlined letters have /ou/ sound as in the word <u>cow</u>
1. neph<u>ew</u>				
2. fl<u>aw</u>less				
3. pl<u>ow</u>ing				
4. tomorr<u>ow</u>				

Name: _____ Date:___/___/_____ Score:_____

Lesson 23.3

Reading Words with a Silent "w" and "wr" Letter Combination

Dictionary Skills/ Vocabulary

✓ **Lesson Check Point**

Directions: Read each target word and its definition. Write the letter of the definition on the line of each target word. Use a dictionary or the Internet to check your answers.
지도: 각 대상 단어와 그 정의를 읽으십시오. 각 대상 단어의 행에 정의의 문자를 씁니다. 사전이나 인터넷을 사용하여 답을 확인하십시오.

Target Words	Definitions
1. _ wrote	a. in an incorrect manner
2. _ wreck	b. to destroy or damage something
3. _ wrench	c. a tool used to tighten or loosen an object
4. _ wrongly	d. a material used to wrap something
5. _ wrapping	e. to have communicated by forming letters on paper

Directions: Read each sentence. Underline the word in the parentheses that correctly completes each sentence. Then, write the underlined word on the line.
지도: 각 문장을 읽으십시오. 각 문장을 올바르게 완성하는 괄호 안에 있는 단어에 밑줄을 긋습니다. 그런 다음 밑줄 친 단어를 줄에 쓰십시오.

6. Wanda _____ a long business letter. (wrecked, wrote)

7. The storm _____ the fishing fleet. (wrecked, wrongly)

8. Wendell was _____ accused of a crime. (wrapping, wrongly)

9. I used a hammer and a _____ to fix the chair. (wrote, wrench)

10. Remove the plastic _____ before eating the sandwich. (wrapping, wrench)

Name: _____   Date: ___/___/_____   Score: _____

Lesson 23.3

Reading Words with a Silent Letter "w"

✓ **Lesson Check Point**

Directions: Read the target words in the word box. Write the words that have a silent letter "w" in the first column. Write the words that do not have a silent letter "w" in the second column.

지도: 단어 상자에 있는 대상 단어를 읽으십시오. 첫 번째 열에 묵음문자 "w"가 있는 단어를 쓰십시오. 두 번째 열에 묵음 문자"w"가 없는 단어를 쓰십시오.

Target Word Box				
wrong	two	pillow	writes	wrap
answer	wrench	earwax	writings	widow
backward	wrinkle	freeway	earthworm	winter
driftwood	doorway	dwindle	Wednesday	firewood

Letter "w" is silent   **Letter "w" has the /w/ sound**

_____   _____
_____   _____
_____   _____
_____   _____
_____   _____
_____   _____
_____   _____
_____   _____
_____   _____
_____   _____

Name: _____ Date:___/___/_____ Score:_____

The Reading Challenge

Lesson 23.4

Reading Multisyllable Words

✓ **Lesson Check Point**

Directions: Read and divide each target word into syllables. Write each word and place a hyphen (-) between the syllables in the second column. Write the number of syllables in the third column. Use a dictionary or the Internet to check your answers.

지도: 각 대상 단어를 읽고 음절로 나눕니다. 각 단어를 쓰고 두 번째 열의 음절 사이에 하이픈(-)을 넣습니다. 세 번째 열에 음절 수를 쓰십시오. 사전이나 인터넷을 사용하여 답을 확인하십시오.

Target Words	Words Divided into Syllables	Number of Syllables
1. winterize	_____	_____
2. worldly	_____	_____
3. windy	_____	_____
4. weather	_____	_____
5. watchman	_____	_____
6. wetland	_____	_____
7. walnut	_____	_____
8. wrinkle	_____	_____
9. welcoming	_____	_____
10. window	_____	_____

Name: _____ Date:___/___/_____ Score:_____

The Reading Challenge

Lesson 23.4

Reading Multisyllable Words

✓ **Lesson Check Point**

 Directions: Read each target word. Circle the word in the row that is divided correctly into syllables. Use a dictionary or the Internet to check your answers.
지도: 각 대상 단어를 읽으십시오. 음절로 올바르게 나누어진 행에 있는 단어에 동그라미를 치십시오. 사전이나 인터넷을 사용하여 답을 확인하십시오.

Model

| wonderful | a. wo-nder-ful | (b. won-der-ful) | c. won-derf-ul |

1. waterfall	a. wa-ter-fall	b. wat-er-fall	c. wa-terf-all
2. weathering	a. wea-ther-ing	b. weath-e-ring	c. weath-er-ing
3. wolverine	a. wol-ver-ine	b. wol-ve-rine	c. wolv-er-ine
4. westernize	a. we-stern-ize	b. west-ern-ize	c. west-er-nize
5. whatever	a. wha-tev-er	b. whate-v-er	c. what-ev-er
6. webpage	a. web-page	b. web-pa-ge	c. we-bpa-ge
7. washable	a. wa-sha-ble	b. wa-shab-le	c. wash-a-ble
8. westerly	a. wes-ter-ly	b. west-er-ly	c. we-ster-ly

Unit W
Lesson 23.4

Name: _____ Date: ___/___/_____ Score: _____

Lesson 23.5

Reading and Writing

Proper and Common Nouns and Adjectives

Directions: Read the words in the word box. Put an (X) on the line next to each word that is written incorrectly. Remember that all proper nouns and proper adjectives are capitalized. Use a dictionary or the Internet to check your answers.

지도: 단어 상자에 있는 단어를 읽으십시오. 잘못 쓰여진 각 단어 옆의 줄에 (X)를 표시하십시오. 모든 고유 명사와 고유 형용사는 대문자임을 기억하십시오. 사전이나 인터넷을 사용하여 답을 확인하십시오.

Word Box					
___	witness	___	woman	___	Weasel
___	Wetland	___	wakayama	___	wellness
___	Workout	___	wednesday	___	Waterbury
___	woodcutter	___	West Indian	___	Waterfront

Directions: Read each unedited sentence and underline the word that is written incorrectly. Write each sentence correctly on the line.

지도: 편집되지 않은 각 문장을 읽고 잘못 쓰여진 단어에 밑줄을 긋습 니다. 각 문장을 줄에 올바르게 쓰십시오.

Model

We walked along the winding path that led to the <u>Waterfalls</u>.
<u>We walked along the winding path that led to the waterfalls.</u>

1. A factory in wisconsin made Wendell's wristwatch.

   _____

2. In the West Indies, I ate delicious fish with White sauce.

   _____

3. wendy said, "South America is in the Western Hemisphere."

   _____

4. In my opinion, Woody woodpecker is a wonderful character.

   _____

Name: _____ Date: ___/___/_____ Score: _____

Lesson 24.1

Reading Words with the Letter X/x

✓ **Lesson Check Point**

Directions: Read each target word. Find the letter "x" and put a check (✓) in the column that identifies its position: beginning, within or end.
지도: 각 대상 단어를 읽으십시오. 문자 "x"를 찾아 체크 표시(✓)위치를 식별하는 열에서 시작, 내부 또는 끝.

Target Words	Beginning (First Letter)	Within	End (Last Letter)
1. annex			
2. fixate			
3. explore			
4. complex			
5. xylophone			

Directions: Read each sentence and underline the words that begin with the letter "x." Write all the underlined words in alphabetical order on the lines below.
지도: 각 문장을 읽고 문자 "x"로 시작하는 단어에 밑줄을 긋습니다. 아래 줄에 밑줄 친 단어를 알파벳 순서로 모두 쓰십시오.

6. Xander attends xylophone lessons every Tuesday.

7. During my vacation to China, I will visit Xian and Xining.

8. I am reading the biographies of Malcolm X and Francis Xavier.

9. Dr. Xerxes used the surgical instrument, xyster, to scrape bones.

10. X-linked refers to a trait controlled by genes on the X-chromosome.

_____   _____   _____
_____   _____   _____
_____   _____   _____
             _____

Name: _____ Date: ___/___/_____ Score: _____

Lesson 24.1

Reading Words with the Letter X/x

✓ Lesson Check Point

Directions: Read each target word. Circle the word in the column that has the same "x" sound(s) as the target word.
지도: 각 대상 단어를 읽으십시오. 대상 단어와 동일한"x" 소리가 있는 열의 단어에 동그라미를 치십시오.

xylem	a. exhaustive
	b. xeric

Xerxes	a. anxious
	b. Xerox

excellent	a. galaxy
	b. exact

exhilarate	a. existence
	b. explicit

Directions: Read each target word. Put a check (✓) under the correct column heading.
지도: 각 대상 단어를 읽으십시오. 올바른 열 제목 아래에 체크(✓)를하십시오.

Target Words	"x" has the /k/ + /s/ sounds as in the word <u>box</u>	"x" has the /z/ sound as in the word <u>xylophone</u>	"x" has the /g/ + /z/ sounds as in the word <u>exhibit</u>	"x" has the /k/ + /sh/ sounds as in the word <u>anxious</u>
1. xylem				
2. Xerxes I				
3. excellent				
4. exhilarate				

The Reading Challenge

Lesson 24.2

Reading Multisyllable Words

✓ Lesson Check Point

Directions: Read and divide each target word into syllables. Write each word and place a hyphen (-) between the syllables in the second column. Write the number of syllables in the third column. Use a dictionary or the Internet to check your answers.

지도: 각 대상 단어를 읽고 음절로 나눕니다. 각 단어를 쓰고 두 번째 열의 음절 사이에 하이픈(-)을 넣습니다. 세 번째 열에 음절 수를 쓰십시오. 사전이나 인터넷을 사용하여 답을 확인하십시오.

Target Words	Words Divided into Syllables	Number of Syllables
1. xylophone		
2. oxide		
3. fixture		
4. extracting		
5. example		
6. oxygen		
7. textile		
8. waxing		
9. taxation		
10. exercise		

Name: _____ Date: ___/___/_____ Score: _____

The Reading Challenge

Lesson 24.2

Reading Multisyllable Words

✓ Lesson Check Point

Directions: Read each target word. Circle the word in the row that is divided correctly into syllables. Use a dictionary or the Internet to check your answers.
지도: 각 대상 단어를 읽으십시오. 음절로 올바르게 나누어진 행에 있는 단어에 동그라미를 치십시오. 사전이나 인터넷을 사용하여 답을 확인하십시오.

Model

| oxidized | a. ox-i-dized (circled) | b. oxi-d-ized | c. o-xi-dized |

1. extremely	a. ex-tremel-y	b. ex-tre-mely	c. ex-treme-ly
2. deoxidize	a. de-oxi-dize	b. de-ox-i-dize	c. deo-xi-dize
3. exactly	a. ex-act-ly	b. e-xact-ly	c. ex-a-ctly
4. xenoliths	a. xen-o-liths	b. xe-noli-ths	c. xe-nolit-hs
5. expanding	a. exp-an-ding	b. ex-pand-ing	c. exp-and-ing
6. vexation	a. vex-at-ion	b. vex-a-tion	c. ve-xat-ion
7. xerophytes	a. xer-o-phytes	b. xe-rophy-tes	c. xero-phytes
8. oxygen	a. oxy-g-en	b. o-xyg-en	c. ox-y-gen

Name: _____ Date: ___/___/_____ Score: _____

Lesson 24.3

Reading and Writing

Proper and Common Nouns and Adjectives

Directions: Read the words in the word box. Put an (X) on the line next to each word that is written incorrectly. Remember that all proper nouns and proper adjectives are capitalized. Use a dictionary or the Internet to check your answers.

지도: 단어 상자에 있는 단어를 읽으십시오. 잘못 쓰여진 각 단어 옆의 줄에 (X)를 표시하십시오. 모든 고유 명사와 고유 형용사는 대문자임을 기억하십시오. 사전이나 인터넷을 사용하여 답을 확인하십시오.

Word Box		
__ xuzhou	__ xebec	__ Xenon
__ xylocaine	__ xylems	__ Xavier
__ xylophone	__ xanthus	__ xerxes I
__ Xylography	__ Xenophobia	__ xenophobes

Directions: Read each unedited sentence and underline the word that is written incorrectly. Write each sentence correctly on the line.

지도: 편집되지 않은 각 문장을 읽고 잘못 쓰여진 단어에 밑줄을 긋습 니다. 각 문장을 줄에 올바르게 쓰십시오.

Model
Xia said, "The population of xankandi is 33,000 people."
Xia said, "The population of Xankandi is 33,000 people."

1. xian's mother bought her a new xylophone.
   _____

2. The greatest King of Persia was King xerxes I.
   _____

3. I am convinced that Xylocaine numbs the pain.
   _____

4. Dr. Xavier was gentle as he scraped his patient's bones with a Xyster.
   _____

Name: _____ Date:___/___/_____ Score: _____

Lesson 25.1

Reading Words with the Letter Y/y

✓ **Lesson Check Point**

Directions: Read each target word. Find the letter "y" and put a check (✓) in the column that identifies its position: beginning, within or end.
지도: 각 대상 단어를 읽으십시오. 문자"y"를 찾아 체크 표시(✓)위치를 식별하는 열에서 시작, 내부 또는 끝.

Target Words	Beginning (First Letter)	Within	End (Last Letter)
1. yogurt			
2. money			
3. slippery			
4. keyboard			
5. yearning			

Directions: Read each sentence and underline the words that begin with the letter "y." Write all the underlined words in alphabetical order on the lines below.
지도: 각 대상 단어를 읽으십시오. 문자"y를 찾아 체크 표시(✓)위치를식별하는 열에서 시작, 내부 또는 끝.

6. The yellow yogurt has an artificial lemon flavor.

7. Our yogi practices yoga at least three times a day.

8. The young people are staying at the local youth hostel.

9. Kathy bought a bright orange yo-yo for her younger sister.

10. Yesterday, I drew the y-axis and the x-axis on graph paper.

_____   _____   _____

_____   _____   _____

_____   _____   _____

_____

Name: _____ Date:___/___/_____ Score:_____

Lesson 25.1

Reading Words with the Letter Y/y

✓ Lesson Check Point

 Directions: Read each target word. Circle the word in the row that has a different "y" sound than the target word.
지도: 각 대상 단어를 읽으십시오. 목표 단어와 다른 "y" 소리가 나는 행의 단어에 동그라미를 치십시오.

Target Words				
1. yahoo	you'll	youth	baby	yours
2. Egypt	typical	symbol	hymn	yesterday
3. magnify	typing	money	goodbye	styling
4. analysis	catalyst	rhyming	calypso	bicycle
5. Wednesday	younger	prayer	honey	highway

 Directions: Read the words in the four boxes. Circle two words that have the same "y" sound.
지도: 네 개의 상자에 있는 단어를 읽으십시오. "y" 소리가 같은 두 단어에 동그라미를 치십시오.

baby	style
yours	eyeballs

type	thyme
today	mystery

Kenya	May
yield	typing

candy	gym
analyze	rhyme

symptom	paralyze
yucky	hypnosis

young	yogurt
goodbye	bicycles

Name: _____ Date: ___/___/_____ Score: _____

Lesson 25.2

Reading Words with a Vowel before the Letter "y"

✓ Lesson Check Point

 Directions: Read each target word. Circle the word in the column that has the same "y" sound as the target word.
지도: 각 대상 단어를 읽으십시오. 목표 단어와 같은 "y" 소리가 나는 열의 단어에 동그라미를 치십시오.

oyster	a. voyagers
	b. money

buyers	a. guys
	b. soliloquy

papaya	a. today
	b. yielding

monkey	a. youngest
	b. playing

 Directions: Read each target word. Put a check (✓) under the correct column heading.
지도: 각 대상 단어를 읽으십시오. 올바른 열 제목 아래에 체크(✓)를 하십시오.

Target Words	"y" has the /y/ sound as in the word <u>yes</u>	"oy" has the /oi/ sound as in the word <u>boy</u>	"y" has the /ī/ sound as in the word <u>by</u>	"y" is silent as in the word <u>day</u>
1. oyster				
2. buyers				
3. papaya				
4. monkey				

Name: _____ Date:___/___/_____ Score: _____

Lesson 25.3

Reading Words with the "cy" Letter Combination

✓ **Lesson Check Point**

 Directions: Read each target word. Find the "cy" letter combination and put a check (✓) in the column to identify its position in the word: beginning, within or end.
지도: 각 대상 단어를 읽으십시오. "cy" 문자 조합을 찾고 열에 체크(✓)를 넣어 단어에서 시작, 안에 또는 끝의 위치를 식별합니다.

Target Words	Beginning (First 2 Letters)	Within	End (Last 2 Letters)
1. cycling			
2. cynical			
3. regency			
4. democracy			
5. encyclopedia			

 Directions: Read each target word. Put a check (✓) under the correct column heading.
지도: 각 대상 단어를 읽으십시오. 올바른 열 제목 아래에 체크(✓)를 하십시오.

Target Words	"cy" has the /s/ + /ĭ/ sounds as in the word <u>cylinder</u>	"cy" has the /s/ + /ī/ sounds as in the word <u>cycle</u>	"cy" has the /s/ + /ē/ sounds as in the word <u>agency</u>
6. cycling			
7. cynical			
8. regency			
9. democracy			
10. encyclopedia			

Name: _____ Date: ___/___/_____ Score: _____

Lesson 25.4

Reading Words with the Final Letter "y"

✓ **Lesson Check Point**

 Directions: Read each target word. Find the letter "y" and put a check (✓) in the column that identifies its position within the word.
지도: 각 대상 단어를 읽으십시오. 문자"y"를 찾아 체크 표시(✓)단어내에서의 위치를 식별하는 열에서.

Target Words	"y" is at the end of a one syllable word	"y" is at the end of the first syllable	"y" is at the end of a multi-syllable word
1. guy			
2. testify			
3. hybrid			
4. comply			
5. mommy			

 Directions: Read each target word. Put a check (✓) under the correct column heading.
지도: 각 대상 단어를 읽으십시오. 올바른 열 제목 아래에 체크(✓)를하십시오.

Target Words	"y" has the /ē/ sound as in the word <u>agency</u>	"y" has the /ī/ sound as in the word <u>flying</u>
6. guy		
7. testify		
8. hybrid		
9. comply		
10. mommy		

Name: _____ Date:___/___/_____ Score: _____

Lesson 25.5

Reading Words with the "yr" Letter Combination

✓ Lesson Check Point

 Directions: Read each target word. Circle the word in the column that has the same "yr" sounds as the target word.
지도: 각 대상 단어를 읽으십시오. 목표 단어와 같은"yr" 소리가 나는 열의 단어에 동그라미를 치십시오.

Tyrol	a. myrtle
	b. syringe

papyrus	a. playroom
	b. Byron

pyramidal	a. lyrical
	b. lyre

pyrotechnics	a. gyrate
	b. tyrannous

 Directions: Read each target word. Put a check (✓) under the correct column heading.
지도: 각 대상 단어를 읽으십시오. 올바른 열 제목 아래에 체크(✓)를하십시오.

Target Words	"yr" has the /û/ + /r/ sounds as in the word myrtle	"yr" has the /ĭ/ + /r/ sounds as in the word pyramid	"yr" has the /ī/ + /r/ sounds as in the word gyro	"yr" has the /ə/ + /r/ sounds as in the word martyr
1. Tyrol				
2. papyrus				
3. pyramidal				
4. pyrotechnics				

Name: _____ Date: ___/___/_____ Score: _____

Lesson 25.6

Reading Letter "y" Words with the Schwa Vowel Sound

 Lesson Check Point

 Directions: Read each target word. Circle the word in the column that has the same "y" sound as the target word.
지도: 각 대상 단어를 읽으십시오. 대상 단어와 "y" 소리가 같은 열의 단어에 동그라미를 치십시오.

vinyl	a. briefly
	b. polymer

beryl	a. mandatory
	b. Pennsylvania

polyvinyl	a. Polynesia
	b. instantly

Tyrrhenian Sea	a. Polynesian
	b. pyrometer

 Directions: Read each target word. Put a check (✓) under the correct column heading.
지도: 각 대상 단어를 읽으십시오. 올바른 열 제목 아래에 체크(✓)를 하십시오.

Target Words	"y" has the /ə/ sound as in the word <u>syringe</u>	"y" does not have the /ə/ sound
1. vinyl		
2. beryl		
3. polyvinyl		
4. Tyrrhenian Sea		

Name: _____   Date: ___/___/_____   Score: _____

Lesson 25.7

Reading Words with a Silent Letter "y"

✓ **Lesson Check Point**

Directions: Read the target words in the word box. Write the words that have a silent letter "y" in the first column. Write the words that do not have a silent letter "y" in the second column.

지도: 단어 상자에 있는 대상 단어를 읽으십시오. 첫 번째 열에 묵음문자 "y"가 있는 단어를 쓰십시오. 두 번째 열에 묵음 문자"y"가 없는 단어를 쓰십시오.

Target Word Box				
gray	day	yes	sway	essay
yellow	steady	clay	young	Yankee
yardage	needy	prey	journey	academy
Tuesday	honey	yearbook	yardstick	Thursday

Letter "y" is silent

Letter "y" has the /y/ or /ē/ sound

Name: _____ Date: ___/___/_____ Score: _____

The Reading Challenge

Lesson 25.8

Reading Multisyllable Words

 Lesson Check Point

 Directions: Read and divide each target word into syllables. Write each word and place a hyphen (-) between the syllables in the second column. Write the number of syllables in the third column. Use a dictionary or the Internet to check your answers.

지도: 각 대상 단어를 읽고 음절로 나눕니다. 각 단어를 쓰고 두 번째 열의 음절 사이에 하이픈(-)을 넣습니다. 세 번째 열에 음절 수를 쓰십시오. 사전이나 인터넷을 사용하여 답을 확인하십시오.

Target Words	Words Divided into Syllables	Number of Syllables
1. yachting	_____	_____
2. youngsters	_____	_____
3. Yuletide	_____	_____
4. yahoo	_____	_____
5. yielding	_____	_____
6. youthful	_____	_____
7. yardstick	_____	_____
8. yelping	_____	_____
9. yearly	_____	_____
10. yardage	_____	_____

Name: _____ Date: ___/___/_____ Score: _____

The Reading Challenge

Lesson 25.8

Reading Multisyllable Words

✓ **Lesson Check Point**

 Directions: Read each target word. Circle the word in the row that is divided correctly into syllables. Use a dictionary or the Internet to check your answers.
지도: 각 대상 단어를 읽으십시오. 음절로 올바르게 나누어진 행에 있는 단어에 동그라미를 치십시오. 사전이나 인터넷을 사용하여 답을 확인하십시오.

Model

| yesterday | a. ye-ster-day | b. yest-er-day | c. yes-ter-day (circled) |

| 1. Yoruba | a. Yor-u-ba | b. Yo-ru-ba | c. Yo-rub-a |

| 2. Yugoslav | a. Yug-o-slav | b. Yu-go-slav | c. Yu-gos-lav |

| 3. yearly | a. year-ly | b. ye-ar-ly | c. yearl-y |

| 4. yodeler | a. yo-del-er | b. yod-e-ler | c. yod-el-er |

| 5. yielding | a. yie-ldi-ng | b. yield-ing | c. yie-lding |

| 6. yonder | a. yond-er | b. yon-der | c. yo-nder |

| 7. yourself | a. yo-ur-self | b. your-self | c. you-rse-lf |

| 8. yoking | a. yo-king | b. yok-ing | c. yoki-ng |

Name: _____ Date:___/___/_____ Score: _____

Lesson 25.9

Reading and Writing

Proper and Common Nouns and Adjectives

Directions: Read the words in the word box. Put an (X) on the line next to each word that is written incorrectly. Remember that all proper nouns and proper adjectives are capitalized. Use a dictionary or the Internet to check your answers.

지도: 단어 상자에 있는 단어를 읽으십시오. 잘못 쓰여진 각 단어 옆의 줄에 (X)를 표시하십시오. 모든 고유 명사와 고유 형용사는 대문자임을 기억하십시오. 사전이나 인터넷을 사용하여 답을 확인하십시오.

Word Box		
___ Yeast	___ Yoga	___ yeshiva
___ Youth	___ yugoslavia	___ yucatan
___ Yiddish	___ Yokohama	___ Yearbook
___ Yellow River	___ Yogyakarta	___ Yinchuan

Directions: Read each unedited sentence and underline the word that is written incorrectly. Write each sentence correctly on the line.

지도: 편집되지 않은 각 문장을 읽고 잘못 쓰여진 단어에 밑줄을긋습 니다. 각 문장을 줄에 올바르게 쓰십시오.

Model
Is the New York <u>yankees</u> your favorite baseball team?
<u>Is the New York Yankees your favorite baseball team?</u>

1. I scheduled two Yoga classes at Yorktown Gym.
   _____

2. Mr. yelp painted his house in Yorktown sunshine yellow.
   _____

3. The Yearbook pictures were taken at Yosemite National Park.
   _____

4. All the young people in my class have new, brightly colored Yo-yos.

Name: _____ Date: ___/___/_____ Score: _____

Lesson 26.1

Reading Words with the Letter Z/z

✓ Lesson Check Point

Directions: Read each target word. Find the letter "z" and put a check (✓) in the column that identifies its position: beginning, within or end.
지도: 각 대상 단어를 읽으십시오. 문자"z"를 찾아 체크 표시(✓)위치를 식별하는 열에서 시작, 내부 또는 끝.

Target Words	Beginning (First Letter)	Within	End (Last Letter)
1. waltz			
2. quartz			
3. Zambia			
4. realized			
5. organized			

Directions: Read each sentence and underline the words that begin with the letter "z." Write all the underlined words in alphabetical order on the lines below.
지도: 각 문장을 읽고"z"로 시작하는 단어에 밑줄을 긋습니다. 아래 줄에 밑줄 친 단어를 알파벳 순서로 모두 쓰십시오.

6. The zookeeper's car is in the no parking zone.

7. The zipper on Jenny's zebra print coat is broken.

8. One day, Mr. and Mrs. Zangara will visit Zambia.

9. The interns at the zoo are enrolled in the zoology program.

10. Zeezee said, "Zululand is steeped in ancient history and tradition."

_____   _____   _____

_____   _____   _____

_____   _____   _____

_____

Name: _____ Date: ___/___/_____ Score: _____

Lesson 26.1

Reading Words with the Letter Z/z

✓ Lesson Check Point

Directions: Read each target word. Circle the word in the column that has the same "z" sound as the target word.
지도: 각 대상 단어를 읽으십시오. 대상 단어와 "z" 소리가 같은 열의 단어에 동그라미를 치십시오.

ritzy	a. lizard
	b. Biarritz

zebras	a. chutzpah
	b. capitalizes

zippers	a. squeezes
	b. quetzal

influenza	a. freezes
	b. Lutz

Directions: Read each target word. Put a check (✓) under the correct column heading.
지도: 각 대상 단어를 읽으십시오. 올바른 열 제목 아래에 체크(✓)를 하십시오.

Target Words	"z" has the /z/ sound as in the word <u>zipper</u>	"z" has the /s/ sound as in the word <u>quartz</u>
1. ritzy		
2. zebras		
3. zippers		
4. influenza		

Name: _____ Date: ___/___/_____   Score: _____

Lesson 26.2

Reading Words with a Silent Letter "z"

✓ **Lesson Check Point**

 Directions: Read the target words in the word box. Write the words that have a silent letter "z" in the first column. Write the words that do not have a silent letter "z" in the second column.

지도: 단어 상자에 있는 대상 단어를 읽으십시오. 첫 번째 열에 묵음 문자 "z"가 있는 단어를 쓰십시오. 두 번째 열에 묵음 문자"z"가 없는 단어를 쓰십시오.

Target Word Box				
lazy	sizzle	grizzly	fizzled	blazed
drizzle	dazzle	hazel	puzzles	sizzling
buzzing	emphasize	lizard	influenza	magnetize
amazement	burglarize	nuzzle	computerize	intermezzo

Letter "z" is silent   **Letter "z" has the /z/ or /s/ sound**

Name: _____ Date:___/___/_____ Score:_____

The Reading Challenge

Lesson 26.3

Reading Multisyllable Words

✓ **Lesson Check Point**

 Directions: Read and divide each target word into syllables. Write each word and place a hyphen (-) between the syllables in the second column. Write the number of syllables in the third column. Use a dictionary or the Internet to check your answers.

지도: 각 대상 단어를 읽고 음절로 나눕니다. 각 단어를 쓰고 두 번째 열의 음절 사이에 하이픈(-)을 넣습니다. 세 번째 열에 음절 수를 쓰십시오. 사전이나 인터넷을 사용하여 답을 확인하십시오.

Target Words	Words Divided into Syllables	Number of Syllables
1. zygote	_____	_____
2. zealots	_____	_____
3. zirconium	_____	_____
4. zenith	_____	_____
5. zero	_____	_____
6. zestful	_____	_____
7. Zambia	_____	_____
8. Zanzibar	_____	_____
9. zinger	_____	_____
10. zodiac	_____	_____

Learn To Read English With Directions In Korean

Name: _____ Date:___/___/_____ Score: _____

The Reading Challenge

Lesson 26.3

Reading Multisyllable Words

✓ **Lesson Check Point**

 Directions: Read each target word. Circle the word in the row that is divided correctly into syllables. Use a dictionary or the Internet to check your answers.
지도: 각 대상 단어를 읽으십시오. 음절로 올바르게 나누어진 행에 있는 단어에 동그라미를 치십시오. 사전이나 인터넷을 사용하여 답을 확인하십시오.

Model

| zoology | a. zo-ol-o-gy (circled) | b. zoo-lo-gy | c. zool-o-gy |

1. zestful	a. ze-stful	b. zes-tful	c. zest-ful
2. Zambian	a. Zam-bi-an	b. Zam-b-ian	c. Zamb-ian
3. Zanzibar	a. Za-nzib-ar	b. Zan-zi-bar	c. Zanz-i-bar
4. Zealand	a. Ze-aland	b. Zeal-and	c. Zea-land
5. zealous	a. zeal-ous	b. zea-lous	c. zeal-ou-s
6. zebra	a. ze-bra	b. zeb-ra	c. ze-br-a
7. zygote	a. zygo-te	b. zyg-ote	c. zy-gote
8. zymurgy	a. zy-mur-gy	b. zym-u-rgy	c. zy-mu-rgy

Name: _____ Date: ___/___/_____ Score: _____

Lesson 26.4

Reading and Writing

Proper and Common Nouns and Adjectives

Directions: Read the words in the word box. Put an (X) on the line next to each word that is written incorrectly. Remember that all proper nouns and proper adjectives are capitalized. Use a dictionary or the Internet to check your answers.

지도: 단어 상자에 있는 단어를 읽으십시오. 잘못 쓰여진 각 단어 옆의 줄에 (X)를 표시하십시오. 모든 고유 명사와 고유 형용사는 대문자임을 기억하십시오. 사전이나 인터넷을 사용하여 답을 확인하십시오.

Word Box		
__ zenith	__ zonal	__ Zealot
__ zucchini	__ Zoology	__ zealous
__ zambezi	__ zululand	__ Zippers
__ Zaragoza	__ zero hour	__ Zebra

Directions: Read each unedited sentence and underline the word that is written incorrectly. Write each sentence correctly on the line.

지도: 편집되지 않은 각 문장을 읽고 잘못 쓰여진 단어에 밑줄을긋습 니다. 각 문장을 줄에 올바르게 쓰십시오.

Model

The steep path zigzags through the <u>zagros</u> Mountains.
<u>The steep path zigzags through the Zagros Mountains.</u>

1. Yesterday, I saw three large Zebras at the San Diego Zoo.
   _____

2. On Friday, the bright sun in zimbabwe rose towards its zenith.
   _____

3. Zola said, "zanzibar is located off the east coast of Africa."
   _____

4. The zambezi River flows from Zambia into the Mozambique Channel.
   _____

Name: _____ Date: ___/___/_____ Score: _____

Appendix 1.0

Introduction of the Letter A/a

✓ **Lesson Check Point**

 Directions: Circle the correct letter "a" pair: uppercase and lowercase letters.
지도: 올바른 문자"a" 쌍에 동그라미를 치십시오: 대문자와 소문자.

    Ea   Ae   Ao   Aa   aZ

 Directions: The uppercase letter "A" is in the first column. Look at the four letters in the row and circle the lowercase letter that matches the uppercase letter "A."
지도: 대문자"A"는 첫 번째 열에 있습니다. 행의 네 글자를 보고 대문자 "A"와 일치하는 소문자에 동그라미를 치십시오.

A	g	a	e	o
A	u	e	i	a
A	a	o	y	e
A	e	c	a	q

 Directions: The lowercase letter "a" is in the first column. Look at the four letters in the row and circle the uppercase letter that matches the lowercase letter "a."
지도: 소문자"a"는 첫 번째 열에 있습니다. 행의 네 글자를 보고 소문자 "a"와 일치하는 대문자에 동그라미를 치세요.

a	C	A	E	R
a	X	D	G	A
a	A	G	D	S
a	O	C	A	W

Name: _____ Date: ___/___/_____ Score: _____

Appendix 2.0

Introduction of the Letter B/b

✓ Lesson Check Point

 Directions: Circle the correct letter "b" pair: uppercase and lowercase letters.
지도: 올바른 문자"b" 쌍에 동그라미를 치십시오: 대문자와 소문자.

fB   Bq   bB   bD   Pb

 Directions: The uppercase letter "B" is in the first column. Look at the four letters in the row and circle the lowercase letter that matches the uppercase letter "B."
지도: 대문자"B"는 첫 번째 열에 있습니다. 행의 네 글자를 보고 대문자 "B"와 일치하는 소문자에 동그라미를 치십시오.

B	p	q	b	d
B	f	d	h	b
B	m	b	f	h
B	k	d	b	l

 Directions: The lowercase letter "b" is in the first column. Look at the four letters in the row and circle the uppercase letter that matches the lowercase letter "b."
지도: 소문자"b"는 첫 번째 열에 있습니다. 행의 네 글자를 보고 소문자 "b"와 일치하는 대문자에 동그라미를 치세요.

b	B	M	F	H
b	P	H	B	G
b	M	B	V	N
b	X	T	B	J

Name: _____ Date: ___/___/_____ Score: _____

Appendix 2.0

Letter Recognition B/b

Uppercase and Lowercase Letter

✓ Lesson Check Point

 Directions: Read each target word. Read the words in the row and circle the word that begins with a different letter.

지도: 각 대상 단어를 읽으십시오. 행에 있는 단어를 읽고 다른 문자로시작하는 단어에 동그라미를 치십시오.

Target Words				
1. buffet	boss	danger	bottle	biscuit
2. brain	basket	blank	pads	bride
3. brick	behave	beef	big	demand
4. butter	dent	bank	black	bill
5. brass	blade	bin	bell	queen

 Directions: Read the words in the four boxes. Circle two words that start with the uppercase and lowercase letter "b."

지도: 네 개의 상자에 있는 단어를 읽으십시오. 대문자와 소문자"b"로 시작하는 두 단어에 동그라미를 치십시오.

Boy	Toy
boy	Soy

Ball	hall
Hall	ball

Book	Hook
book	Took

Had	had
bad	Bad

Bank	Tank
bank	tank

Bread	head
bread	Head

Name: _____ Date: ___/___/_____ Score: _____

Appendix 3.0

Introduction of the Letter C/c

✓ Lesson Check Point

 Directions: Circle the correct letter "c" pair: uppercase and lowercase letters.
지도: 올바른 문자"c" 쌍에 동그라미를 치십시오: 대문자와 소문자.

      Cf   Cc   Kc   cD   Co

 Directions: The uppercase letter "C" is in the first column. Look at the four letters in the row and circle the lowercase letter that matches the uppercase letter "C."
지도: 대문자"C"는 첫 번째 열에 있습니다. 행의 네 글자를 보고대문자 "C"와 일치하는 소문자에 동그라미를 치십시오.

C	c	g	h	k
C	s	c	u	j
C	n	p	d	c
C	c	v	s	o

 Directions: The lowercase letter "c" is in the first column. Look at the four letters in the row and circle the uppercase letter that matches the lowercase letter "c."
지도: 소문자"c"는 첫 번째 열에 있습니다. 행의 네 글자를 보고소문자 "c"와 일치하는 대문자에 동그라미를 치세요.

c	K	G	C	O
c	H	J	D	C
c	Q	G	C	V
c	C	B	Q	G

Name: _____ Date: ___/___/_____ Score: _____

Appendix 3.0

Letter Recognition C/c

Uppercase and Lowercase Letter

✓ Lesson Check Point

 Directions: Read each target word. Read the words in the row and circle the word that begins with a different letter.
지도: 각 대상 단어를 읽으십시오. 행에 있는 단어를 읽고 다른 문자로시작하는 단어에 동그라미를 치십시오.

Target Words				
1. cart	cry	oblong	curtain	city
2. choice	calculate	queen	cutter	cycle
3. cherish	ankle	chill	comb	cup
4. calcium	Goat	circle	choke	caption
5. convert	cherish	career	cell	boss

 Directions: Read the words in the four boxes. Circle two words that start with the uppercase and lowercase letter "c."
지도: 네 개의 상자에 있는 단어를 읽으십시오. 대문자와 소문자 "c"로 시작하는 두 단어에 동그라미를 치십시오.

Case	base
Quiet	camp

Open	Cream
cargo	pool

Castle	vase
keep	coat

cream	Chase
box	grapes

jump	cash
Child	food

old	orange
cold	Crib

Name: _____ Date: ___/___/_____ Score: _____

Appendix 4.0

Introduction of the Letter D/d

✓ **Lesson Check Point**

 Directions: Circle the correct letter "d" pair: uppercase and lowercase letters.
지도: 올바른 문자"d" 쌍에 동그라미를 치십시오: 대문자와 소문자.

    Db   Fd   Dd   Od   Gd

 Directions: The uppercase letter "D" is in the first column. Look at the four letters in the row and circle the lowercase letter that matches the uppercase letter "D."
지도: 대문자"D"는 첫 번째 열에 있습니다. 행의 네 글자를 보고대문자 "D"와 일치하는 소문자에 동그라미를 치십시오.

D	b	f	h	d
D	j	d	p	t
D	h	n	d	b
D	p	b	d	k

 Directions: The lowercase letter "d" is in the first column. Look at the four letters in the row and circle the uppercase letter that matches the lowercase letter "d."
지도: 소문자"d"는 첫 번째 열에 있습니다. 행의 네 글자를 보고소문자 "d"와 일치하는 대문자에 동그라미를 치세요.

d	H	D	B	K
d	P	J	D	B
d	D	B	E	R
d	S	K	B	D

Name: _____ Date: ___/___/_____ Score: _____

Appendix 4.0

Letter Recognition D/d

Uppercase and Lowercase Letter

✓ **Lesson Check Point**

 Directions: Read each target word. Read the words in the row and circle the word that begins with a different letter.
지도: 각 대상 단어를 읽으십시오. 행에 있는 단어를 읽고 다른 문자로 시작하는 단어에 동그라미를 치십시오.

Target Words				
1. dog	dive	dress	dew	both
2. due	deal	place	date	draw
3. dole	ditch	dome	bread	dwarf
4. depth	drop	dish	prize	deck
5. drain	quite	doze	dream	dodge

 Directions: Read the words in the four boxes. Circle two words that start with the uppercase and lowercase letter "d."
지도: 네 개의 상자에 있는 단어를 읽으십시오. 대문자와 소문자 "d"로 시작하는 두 단어에 동그라미를 치십시오.

top	Dance
dear	ball

drum	Open
Pop	Deck

dry	Queen
Deer	Prince

friend	Due
Ox	drink

Box	Dress
dodge	boat

Old	Pie
Dad	doubt

Name: _____ Date: ___/___/_____ Score: _____

Appendix 5.0

Introduction of the Letter E/e

✓ **Lesson Check Point**

 Directions: Circle the correct letter "e" pair: uppercase and lowercase letters.
지도: 올바른 문자"e" 쌍에 동그라미를 치십시오: 대문자와 소문자.

      eF   Ee   Ec   eC   Qe

 Directions: The uppercase letter "E" is in the first column. Look at the four letters in the row and circle the lowercase letter that matches the uppercase letter "E."
지도: 대문자"E"는 첫 번째 열에 있습니다. 행의 네 글자를 보고 대문자 "E"와 일치하는 소문자에 동그라미를 치십시오.

E	c	e	s	x
E	a	c	d	e
E	e	s	c	w
E	v	g	e	o

 Directions: The lowercase letter "e" is in the first column. Look at the four letters in the row and circle the uppercase letter that matches the lowercase letter "e."
지도: 소문자"e"는 첫 번째 열에 있습니다. 행의 네 글자를 보고 소문자 "e"와 일치하는 대문자에 동그라미를 치세요.

e	F	E	H	T
e	D	T	E	Y
e	E	D	R	N
e	X	S	F	E

Name: _____ Date: ___/___/_____ Score: _____

Appendix 6.0

Introduction of the Letter F/f

✓ **Lesson Check Point**

 Directions: Circle the correct letter "f" pair: uppercase and lowercase letters.
지도: 올바른 문자"f" 쌍에 동그라미를 치십시오: 대문자와 소문자.

    Fd   fF   Yf   Ef   Bf

 Directions: The uppercase letter "F" is in the first column. Look at the four letters in the row and circle the lowercase letter that matches the uppercase letter "F."
지도: 대문자"F"는 첫 번째 열에 있습니다. 행의 네 글자를 보고대문자 "F"와 일치하는 소문자에 동그라미를 치십시오.

F	k	f	h	t
F	h	t	p	f
F	f	l	d	h
F	b	k	f	t

 Directions: The lowercase letter "f" is in the first column. Look at the four letters in the row and circle the uppercase letter that matches the lowercase letter "f."
지도: 소문자"f"는 첫 번째 열에 있습니다. 행의 네 글자를 보고소문자 "f"와 일치하는 대문자에 동그라미를 치세요.

f	B	F	E	H
f	E	K	L	F
f	F	H	M	E
f	J	F	E	P

Name: _____ Date: ___/___/_____ Score: _____

Appendix 6.0

Letter Recognition F/f

Uppercase and Lowercase Letter

✓ **Lesson Check Point**

Directions: Read each target word. Read the words in the row and circle the word that begins with a different letter.

지도: 각 대상 단어를 읽으십시오. 행에 있는 단어를 읽고 다른 문자로시작하는 단어에 동그라미를 치십시오.

Target Words				
1. fry	try	fact	foal	fuse
2. flag	folk	fly	house	foam
3. fail	farm	keep	flee	five
4. feed	flame	head	fish	flew
5. flour	love	fox	flesh	fax

Directions: Read the words in the four boxes. Circle two words that start with the uppercase and lowercase letter "f."

지도: 네 개의 상자에 있는 단어를 읽으십시오. 대문자와 소문자"f"로 시작하는 두 단어에 동그라미를 치십시오.

World	feel
Fawn	drive

boats	Books
Flea	fit

Fit	breeze
Houses	flush

Fetch	fill
Eggs	dove

fret	Keeps
Film	depth

ghost	Flair
draw	flow

Name: _____ Date:___/___/_____ Score: _____

Appendix 7.0

Introduction of the Letter G/g

✓ **Lesson Check Point**

 Directions: Circle the correct letter "g" pair: uppercase and lowercase letters.
지도: 올바른 문자"g" 쌍에 동그라미를 치십시오: 대문자와 소문자.

    Gj   qG   Gg   Jg   Gp

 Directions: The uppercase letter "G" is in the first column. Look at the four letters in the row and circle the lowercase letter that matches the uppercase letter "G."
지도: 대문자"G"는 첫 번째 열에 있습니다. 행의 네 글자를 보고대문자 "G"와 일치하는 소문자에 동그라미를 치십시오.

G	j	o	g	l
G	g	y	j	p
G	q	g	z	y
G	y	p	q	g

 Directions: The lowercase letter "g" is in the first column. Look at the four letters in the row and circle the uppercase letter that matches the lowercase letter "g."
지도: 소문자"g"는 첫 번째 열에 있습니다. 행의 네 글자를 보고소문자 "g"와 일치하는 대문자에 동그라미를 치세요.

g	O	G	J	L
g	G	Q	O	J
g	O	P	Q	G
g	Q	F	G	O

Name: _____ Date: ___/___/_____ Score: _____

Appendix 7.0

Letter Recognition G/g

Uppercase and Lowercase Letter

✓ **Lesson Check Point**

 Directions: Read each target word. Read the words in the row and circle the word that begins with a different letter.

지도: 각 대상 단어를 읽으십시오. 행에 있는 단어를 읽고 다른 문자로 시작하는 단어에 동그라미를 치십시오.

Target Words				
1. greet	judge	grill	gear	glow
2. good	group	glimpse	paint	gain
3. gang	give	boat	growth	gulf
4. guess	grace	job	get	gill
5. grade	gem	grow	girl	pool

 Directions: Read the words in the four boxes. Circle two words that start with the uppercase and lowercase letter "g."

지도: 네 개의 상자에 있는 단어를 읽으십시오. 대문자와 소문자"g"로 시작하는 두 단어에 동그라미를 치십시오.

get	jet
Peach	Goat

Pen	boat
Greek	give

ball	Gain
grow	jeans

golf	Gray
plant	deep

place	good
jump	Grant

Gift	pie
gum	Ox

Name: _____ Date: ___/___/_____ Score: _____

Appendix 8.0

Introduction of the Letter H/h

✓ Lesson Check Point

 Directions: Circle the correct letter "h" pair: uppercase and lowercase letters.
지도: 올바른 문자"h" 쌍에 동그라미를 치십시오: 대문자와 소문자.

    Hh   bH   Bh   hF   Hk

 Directions: The uppercase letter "H" is in the first column. Look at the four letters in the row and circle the lowercase letter that matches the uppercase letter "H."
지도: 대문자"H"는 첫 번째 열에 있습니다. 행의 네 글자를 보고 대문자 "H"와 일치하는 소문자에 동그라미를 치십시오.

H	l	h	g	t
H	h	v	l	q
H	t	b	h	f
H	f	p	t	h

 Directions: The lowercase letter "h" is in the first column. Look at the four letters in the row and circle the uppercase letter that matches the lowercase letter "h."
지도: 소문자"h"는 첫 번째 열에 있습니다. 행의 네 글자를 보고 소문자 "h"와 일치하는 대문자에 동그라미를 치세요.

h	F	H	T	S
h	G	T	H	R
h	H	D	J	T
h	B	H	U	L

Name: _____ Date: ___/___/_____ Score: _____

Appendix 8.0

Letter Recognition H/h

Uppercase and Lowercase Letter

✓ Lesson Check Point

 Directions: Read each target word. Read the words in the row and circle the word that begins with a different letter.
지도: 각 대상 단어를 읽으십시오. 행에 있는 단어를 읽고 다른 문자로시작하는 단어에 동그라미를 치십시오.

Target Words				
1. hit	hive	hood	like	hub
2. hike	tape	health	hall	hook
3. heal	hair	horn	leaves	he
4. hard	hole	bath	heap	hand
5. hose	jump	hang	hence	haul

 Directions: Read the words in the four boxes. Circle two words that start with the uppercase and lowercase letter "h."
지도: 네 개의 상자에 있는 단어를 읽으십시오. 대문자와 소문자 "h"로 시작하는 두 단어에 동그라미를 치십시오.

herb	tree
brown	Hoard

pink	teeth
home	Heed

light	Hand
bath	hop

hair	Heal
keep	true

look	Horse
hemp	found

Half	hot
dress	top

Learn To Read English With Directions In Korean

Name: _____ Date: ___/___/_____ Score: _____

Appendix 9.0

Introduction of the Letter I/i

✓ **Lesson Check Point**

 Directions: Circle the correct letter "i" pair: uppercase and lowercase letters.
지도: 올바른 문자"i" 쌍에 동그라미를 치십시오: 대문자와 소문자.

    Ii   Ij   iJ   Im   Ti

 Directions: The uppercase letter "I" is in the first column. Look at the four letters in the row and circle the lowercase letter that matches the uppercase letter "I."
지도: 대문자"I"는 첫 번째 열에 있습니다. 행의 네 글자를 보고 대문자 "I"와 일치하는 소문자에 동그라미를 치십시오.

I	j	i	l	y
I	f	j	x	i
I	i	h	t	v
I	t	d	h	i

 Directions: The lowercase letter "i" is in the first column. Look at the four letters in the row and circle the uppercase letter that matches the lowercase letter "i."
지도: 소문자"i"는 첫 번째 열에 있습니다. 행의 네 글자를 보고 소문자 "i"와 일치하는 대문자에 동그라미를 치세요.

i	K	I	T	J
i	I	L	H	K
i	D	Y	I	L
i	J	G	K	I

Name: _____ Date: ___/___/_____ Score: _____

Appendix 10.0

Introduction of the Letter J/j

✓ **Lesson Check Point**

 Directions: Circle the correct letter "j" pair: uppercase and lowercase letters.
지도: 올바른 문자"j" 쌍에 동그라미를 치십시오: 대문자와 소문자.

jY　　　　　yJ　　　　　Gj　　　　　Jj　　　　　jL

 Directions: The uppercase letter "J" is in the first column. Look at the four letters in the row and circle the lowercase letter that matches the uppercase letter "J."
지도: 대문자"J"는 첫 번째 열에 있습니다. 행의 네 글자를 보고 대문자 "J"와 일치하는 소문자에 동그라미를 치십시오.

J	y	g	j	l
J	j	v	y	q
J	p	j	g	b
J	g	y	j	p

 Directions: The lowercase letter "j" is in the first column. Look at the four letters in the row and circle the uppercase letter that matches the lowercase letter "j."
지도: 소문자"j"는 첫 번째 열에 있습니다. 행의 네 글자를 보고 소문자 "j"와 일치하는 대문자에 동그라미를 치세요.

j	K	J	C	L
j	J	O	G	U
j	Q	C	J	O
j	G	V	U	J

Name: _____ Date: ___/___/_____ Score: _____

Appendix 10.0

Letter Recognition J/j

Uppercase and Lowercase Letter

✓ **Lesson Check Point**

 Directions: Read each target word. Read the words in the row and circle the word that begins with a different letter.
지도: 각 대상 단어를 읽으십시오. 행에 있는 단어를 읽고 다른 문자로시작하는 단어에 동그라미를 치십시오.

Target Words				
1. jaw	jet	jay	yes	joint
2. join	pie	jean	junk	jade
3. jump	jazz	guess	jar	jog
4. jungle	job	gem	judge	jeep
5. January	jail	jug	joke	years

 Directions: Read the words in the four boxes. Circle two words that start with the uppercase and lowercase letter "j."
지도: 네 개의 상자에 있는 단어를 읽으십시오. 대문자와 소문자"h"로 시작하는 두 단어에 동그라미를 치십시오.

Joke	Goat
yes	juice

just	Jolt
prince	your

youth	June
jock	queen

quest	price
jog	Jam

young	Jail
jot	golf

grand	jump
press	Juicy

Name: _____ Date:___/___/_____ Score:_____

Appendix 11.0

Introduction of the Letter K/k

✓ **Lesson Check Point**

 Directions: Circle the correct letter "k" pair: uppercase and lowercase letters.
지도: 올바른 문자"k" 쌍에 동그라미를 치십시오: 대문자와 소문자.

    kB   Kl   kt   kY   Kk

 Directions: The uppercase letter "K" is in the first column. Look at the four letters in the row and circle the lowercase letter that matches the uppercase letter "K."
지도: 대문자"K"는 첫 번째 열에 있습니다. 행의 네 글자를 보고대문자 "K"와 일치하는 소문자에 동그라미를 치십시오.

K	l	k	y	p
K	b	f	k	l
K	p	h	d	k
K	k	j	l	p

 Directions: The lowercase letter "k" is in the first column. Look at the four letters in the row and circle the uppercase letter that matches the lowercase letter "k."
지도: 소문자"k"는 첫 번째 열에 있습니다. 행의 네 글자를 보고소문자 "k"와 일치하는 대문자에 동그라미를 치세요.

k	K	L	M	Y
k	M	N	K	L
k	J	K	H	B
k	V	N	K	T

Name: _____ Date: ___/___/_____ Score: _____

Appendix 11.0

Letter Recognition K/k

Uppercase and Lowercase Letter

✓ **Lesson Check Point**

Directions: Read each target word. Read the words in the row and circle the word that begins with a different letter.
지도: 각 대상 단어를 읽으십시오. 행에 있는 단어를 읽고 다른 문자로 시작하는 단어에 동그라미를 치십시오.

Target Words				
1. kid	kin	house	keel	know
2. knit	keen	knight	king	lace
3. kind	kale	body	key	keep
4. krill	hatch	keg	knock	kick
5. kept	drop	karts	knot	kelp

Directions: Read the words in the four boxes. Circle two words that start with the uppercase and lowercase letter "k."
지도: 네 개의 상자에 있는 단어를 읽으십시오. 대문자와 소문자 "k" 로 시작하는 두 단어에 동그라미를 치십시오.

keep	house
Kiss	Eats

dreams	Know
kind	friends

jumps	home
Knock	kick

laughs	knight
bounce	Keys

Knit	kept
free	tree

Knob	trips
hope	kale

Name: _____ Date: ___/___/_____ Score: _____

Appendix 12.0

Introduction of the Letter L/l

✓ Lesson Check Point

 Directions: Circle the correct letter "l" pair: uppercase and lowercase letters.
지도: 올바른 문자"l" 쌍에 동그라미를 치십시오: 대문자와 소문자.

    hL   Lk   lT   Ll   lJ

 Directions: The uppercase letter "L" is in the first column. Look at the four letters in the row and circle the lowercase letter that matches the uppercase letter "L."
지도: 대문자"L"는 첫 번째 열에 있습니다. 행의 네 글자를 보고 대문자 "L"와 일치하는 소문자에 동그라미를 치십시오.

L	k	l	f	h
L	j	f	l	b
L	l	h	j	x
L	b	y	k	l

 Directions: The lowercase letter "l" is in the first column. Look at the four letters in the row and circle the uppercase letter that matches the lowercase letter "l."
지도: 소문자"l"는 첫 번째 열에 있습니다. 행의 네 글자를 보고 소문자 "l"와 일치하는 대문자에 동그라미를 치세요.

l	L	K	H	V
l	E	F	L	K
l	M	V	T	L
l	L	H	V	E

Name: _____ Date: ___/___/_____ Score: _____

Appendix 12.0

Letter Recognition L/l

Uppercase and Lowercase Letter

✓ **Lesson Check Point**

 Directions: Read each target word. Read the words in the row and circle the word that begins with a different letter.
지도: 각 대상 단어를 읽으십시오. 행에 있는 단어를 읽고 다른 문자로 시작하는 단어에 동그라미를 치십시오.

Target Words				
1. leaf	lack	lush	town	land
2. link	jump	like	lard	left
3. lead	lift	lance	brown	leg
4. late	lunch	friends	leek	latch
5. lick	dreams	limp	lank	live

 Directions: Read the words in the four boxes. Circle two words that start with the uppercase and lowercase letter "l."
지도: 네 개의 상자에 있는 단어를 읽으십시오. 대문자와 소문자 "l"로 시작하는 두 단어에 동그라미를 치십시오.

trees	Lend		boats	Drops		house	Law
fruits	lane		Line	lash		list	drips

Less	lynch		Lots	home		Leak	drive
front	dress		bumps	lump		launch	found

Name: _____ Date:___/___/_____ Score:_____

Appendix 13.0

Introduction of the Letter M/m

✓ **Lesson Check Point**

 Directions: Circle the correct letter "m" pair: uppercase and lowercase letters.
지도: 올바른 문자"m" 쌍에 동그라미를 치십시오: 대문자와 소문자.

    Um   Nm   Mw   Mn   Mm

 Directions: The uppercase letter "M" is in the first column. Look at the four letters in the row and circle the lowercase letter that matches the uppercase letter "M."
지도: 대문자"M"는 첫 번째 열에 있습니다. 행의 네 글자를 보고 대문자 "M"와 일치하는 소문자에 동그라미를 치십시오.

M	n	m	n	h
M	w	n	u	m
M	u	v	m	n
M	m	u	n	o

 Directions: The lowercase letter "m" is in the first column. Look at the four letters in the row and circle the uppercase letter that matches the lowercase letter "m."
지도: 소문자"m"는 첫 번째 열에 있습니다. 행의 네 글자를 보고 소문자 "m"와 일치하는 대문자에 동그라미를 치세요.

m	N	U	M	W
m	M	V	X	J
m	V	W	Z	M
m	X	M	U	N

Name: _____ Date: ___/___/_____ Score: _____

Appendix 13.0

Letter Recognition M/m

Uppercase and Lowercase Letter

✓ Lesson Check Point

Directions: Read each target word. Read the words in the row and circle the word that begins with a different letter.
지도: 각 대상 단어를 읽으십시오. 행에 있는 단어를 읽고 다른 문자로 시작하는 단어에 동그라미를 치십시오.

Target Words				
1. meat	mood	mixed	were	might
2. mind	nail	mince	much	mean
3. moist	mug	meal	vote	miss
4. made	mumps	mouth	mist	nest
5. musk	world	mall	mock	mint

Directions: Read the words in the four boxes. Circle two words that start with the uppercase and lowercase letter "m."
지도: 네 개의 상자에 있는 단어를 읽으십시오. 대문자와 소문자 "m"로 시작하는 두 단어에 동그라미를 치십시오.

noise	moon
vest	Main

write	noon
most	Maid

Make	news
vowel	mouse

used	mane
Move	numb

Mold	milk
nerve	wrote

mourn	nine
Mail	cause

Name: _____ Date: ___/___/_____ Score: _____

Appendix 14.0

Introduction of the Letter N/n

✓ **Lesson Check Point**

 Directions: Circle the correct letter "n" pair: uppercase and lowercase letters.
지도: 올바른 문자"n" 쌍에 동그라미를 치십시오: 대문자와 소문자.

    Nm   Vn   nW   Nn   Mn

 Directions: The uppercase letter "N" is in the first column. Look at the four letters in the row and circle the lowercase letter that matches the uppercase letter "N."
지도: 대문자"N"는 첫 번째 열에 있습니다. 행의 네 글자를 보고 대문자 "N"와 일치하는 소문자에 동그라미를 치십시오.

N	v	n	u	o
N	y	u	w	n
N	n	j	m	f
N	u	b	n	v

 Directions: The lowercase letter "n" is in the first column. Look at the four letters in the row and circle the uppercase letter that matches the lowercase letter "n."
지도: 소문자"n"는 첫 번째 열에 있습니다. 행의 네 글자를 보고 소문자 "n"와 일치하는 대문자에 동그라미를 치세요.

n	M	W	N	V
n	N	C	W	X
n	U	H	X	N
n	T	N	Z	U

Name: _____ Date: ___/___/_____ Score: _____

Appendix 14.0

Letter Recognition N/n

Uppercase and Lowercase Letter

✓ Lesson Check Point

 Directions: Read each target word. Read the words in the row and circle the word that begins with a different letter.
지도: 각 대상 단어를 읽으십시오. 행에 있는 단어를 읽고 다른 문자로 시작하는 단어에 동그라미를 치십시오.

Target Words				
1. nerve	noon	right	news	noun
2. noise	make	near	night	need
3. neck	nail	nose	nice	rope
4. nine	name	none	moist	next
5. name	numb	note	nest	use

 Directions: Read the words in the four boxes. Circle two words that start with the uppercase and lowercase letter "n."
지도: 네 개의 상자에 있는 단어를 읽으십시오. 대문자와 소문자 "n"로 시작하는 두 단어에 동그라미를 치십시오.

mall	you
numb	New

unto	Name
house	nerve

much	Near
need	good

Nap	mops
ran	norm

Null	mock
neat	vote

neck	Nest
race	mom

Name: _____ Date: ___/___/_____ Score: _____

Appendix 15.0

Introduction of the Letter O/o

✓ **Lesson Check Point**

 Directions: Circle the correct letter "o" pair: uppercase and lowercase letters.
지도: 올바른 문자"o" 쌍에 동그라미를 치십시오: 대문자와 소문자.

     Po   Qo   Oc   Oo   Co

 Directions: The uppercase letter "O" is in the first column. Look at the four letters in the row and circle the lowercase letter that matches the uppercase letter "O."
지도: 대문자"O"는 첫 번째 열에 있습니다. 행의 네 글자를 보고 대문자 "O"와 일치하는 소문자에 동그라미를 치십시오.

O	o	d	g	s
O	c	s	u	o
O	g	o	c	q
O	d	g	o	c

 Directions: The lowercase letter "o" is in the first column. Look at the four letters in the row and circle the uppercase letter that matches the lowercase letter "o."
지도: 소문자"o"는 첫 번째 열에 있습니다. 행의 네 글자를 보고 소문자 "o"와 일치하는 대문자에 동그라미를 치세요.

o	D	O	Q	G
o	C	Q	V	O
o	Q	C	O	S
o	O	H	Q	C

Name: _____ Date:___/___/_____ Score:_____

Appendix 16.0

Introduction of the Letter P/p

✓ Lesson Check Point

 Directions: Circle the correct letter "p" pair: uppercase and lowercase letters.
지도: 올바른 문자 "p" 쌍에 동그라미를 치십시오: 대문자와 소문자.

    Pd   bP   Dp   Pp   Bp

 Directions: The uppercase letter "P" is in the first column. Look at the four letters in the row and circle the lowercase letter that matches the uppercase letter "P."
지도: 대문자 "P"는 첫 번째 열에 있습니다. 행의 네 글자를 보고 대문자 "P"와 일치하는 소문자에 동그라미를 치십시오.

P	q	b	d	p
P	p	d	g	j
P	g	p	h	f
P	d	g	p	b

 Directions: The lowercase letter "p" is in the first column. Look at the four letters in the row and circle the uppercase letter that matches the lowercase letter "p."
지도: 소문자 "p"는 첫 번째 열에 있습니다. 행의 네 글자를 보고 소문자 "p"와 일치하는 대문자에 동그라미를 치세요.

p	R	P	Q	B
p	P	D	F	D
p	F	K	P	Q
p	B	S	G	P

Name: _____ Date: ___/___/_____ Score: _____

Appendix 16.0

Letter Recognition P/p

Uppercase and Lowercase Letter

✓ Lesson Check Point

Directions: Read each target word. Read the words in the row and circle the word that begins with a different letter.
지도: 각 대상 단어를 읽으십시오. 행에 있는 단어를 읽고 다른 문자로시 작하는 단어에 동그라미를 치십시오.

Target Words				
1. pen	pledge	quote	prince	porch
2. play	years	plug	park	pear
3. pitch	peer	pinch	quartz	pop
4. patch	poise	prompt	place	bond
5. praise	queen	pain	pile	proof

Directions: Read the words in the four boxes. Circle two words that start with the uppercase and lowercase letter "p."
지도: 네 개의 상자에 있는 단어를 읽으십시오. 대문자와 소문자 "p"로 시작하는 두 단어에 동그라미를 치십시오.

beach	Peach
teach	patch

fast	past
last	Pearl

Pad	push
Bad	Dad

Say	Day
pay	Path

Pave	Dave
pop	Have

Deal	meal
peel	Pets

Name: _____ Date: ___/___/_____ Score: _____

Appendix 17.0

Introduction of the Letter Q/q

✓ **Lesson Check Point**

 Directions: Circle the correct letter "q" pair: uppercase and lowercase letters.
지도: 올바른 문자"q" 쌍에 동그라미를 치십시오: 대문자와 소문자.

    Pq   Bq   Qq   Oq   pQ

 Directions: The uppercase letter "Q" is in the first column. Look at the four letters in the row and circle the lowercase letter that matches the uppercase letter "Q."
지도: 대문자"Q"는 첫 번째 열에 있습니다. 행의 네 글자를 보고 대문자 "Q"와 일치하는 소문자에 동그라미를 치십시오.

Q	p	d	q	d
Q	g	q	j	b
Q	q	f	g	j
Q	j	y	p	q

 Directions: The lowercase letter "q" is in the first column. Look at the four letters in the row and circle the uppercase letter that matches the lowercase letter "q."
지도: 소문자"q"는 첫 번째 열에 있습니다. 행의 네 글자를 보고 소문자 "q"와 일치하는 대문자에 동그라미를 치세요.

q	D	Q	S	H
q	O	S	R	Q
q	Q	D	C	O
q	C	Z	Q	S

Name: _____ Date: ___/___/_____ Score: _____

Appendix 17.0

Letter Recognition Q/q

Uppercase and Lowercase Letter

✓ **Lesson Check Point**

Directions: Read each target word. Read the words in the row and circle the word that begins with a different letter.

지도: 각 대상 단어를 읽으십시오. 행에 있는 단어를 읽고 다른 문자로시작하는 단어에 동그라미를 치십시오.

Target Words				
1. quiz	jumps	quota	quire	quaint
2. quince	quack	quench	quarrel	guest
3. queen	quick	young	quartz	quit
4. quirk	quote	quest	puppy	quack
5. quench	paints	queen	quartz	quicken

Directions: Read the words in the four boxes. Circle two words that start with the uppercase and lowercase letter "q."

지도: 네 개의 상자에 있는 단어를 읽으십시오. 대문자와 소문자 "q"로 시작하는 두 단어에 동그라미를 치십시오.

quite	peace	qualm	Quality	puppy	Quiver
Jupiter	Quiet	Opens	jumps	quarter	Cover

Opera	Quiche	qualify	Over	people	jelly
dance	quibble	Quacks	person	Quicken	query

Name: _____ Date:___/___/_____ Score:_____

Appendix 18.0

Introduction of the Letter R/r

✓ Lesson Check Point

 Directions: Circle the correct letter "r" pair: uppercase and lowercase letters.
지도: 올바른 문자"r" 쌍에 동그라미를 치십시오: 대문자와 소문자.

    rR   Rv   rX   kR   rP

 Directions: The uppercase letter "R" is in the first column. Look at the four letters in the row and circle the lowercase letter that matches the uppercase letter "R."
지도: 대문자"R"는 첫 번째 열에 있습니다. 행의 네 글자를 보고 대문자 "R"와 일치하는 소문자에 동그라미를 치십시오.

R	x	r	f	h
R	g	v	s	r
R	r	x	z	v
R	j	r	a	c

 Directions: The lowercase letter "r" is in the first column. Look at the four letters in the row and circle the uppercase letter that matches the lowercase letter "r."
지도: 소문자"r"는 첫 번째 열에 있습니다. 행의 네 글자를 보고 소문자 "r"와 일치하는 대문자에 동그라미를 치세요.

r	F	S	T	R
r	R	F	W	E
r	F	C	A	R
r	X	R	H	D

Name: _____ Date: ___/___/_____ Score: _____

Appendix 18.0

Letter Recognition R/r

Uppercase and Lowercase Letter

✓ Lesson Check Point

 Directions: Read each target word. Read the words in the row and circle the word that begins with a different letter.
지도: 각 대상 단어를 읽으십시오. 행에 있는 단어를 읽고 다른 문자로시 작하는 단어에 동그라미를 치십시오.

Target Words				
1. role	ride	nine	ranch	rope
2. ring	music	rose	right	raise
3. rail	ripe	rough	real	closed
4. rose	rank	cream	rinse	roof
5. run	rhyme	root	noon	read

 Directions: Read the words in the four boxes. Circle two words that start with the uppercase and lowercase letter "r."
지도: 네 개의 상자에 있는 단어를 읽으십시오. 대문자와 소문자"r"로 시작하는 두 단어에 동그라미를 치십시오.

Roach	games
numb	rub

march	rake
cave	Round

ring	Road
need	Peek

Pain	mouth
Roast	race

citizen	rink
Rent	Person

Rode	peer
rice	part

Name: _____ Date:___/___/_____ Score:_____

Appendix 19.0

Introduction of the Letter S/s

✓ **Lesson Check Point**

 Directions: Circle the correct letter "s" pair: uppercase and lowercase letters.
지도: 올바른 문자"s" 쌍에 동그라미를 치십시오: 대문자와 소문자.

    Sc   sZ   cS   sX   sS

 Directions: The uppercase letter "S" is in the first column. Look at the four letters in the row and circle the lowercase letter that matches the uppercase letter "S."
지도: 대문자"S"는 첫 번째 열에 있습니다. 행의 네 글자를 보고 대문자 "S"와 일치하는 소문자에 동그라미를 치십시오.

S	c	s	x	z
S	z	o	c	s
S	s	j	z	t
S	g	c	s	k

 Directions: The lowercase letter "s" is in the first column. Look at the four letters in the row and circle the uppercase letter that matches the lowercase letter "s."
지도: 소문자"s"는 첫 번째 열에 있습니다. 행의 네 글자를 보고 소문자 "s"와 일치하는 대문자에 동그라미를 치세요.

s	X	C	T	S
s	O	S	C	Z
s	G	C	S	X
s	S	G	O	U

Name: _____ Date: ___/___/_____ Score: _____

Appendix 19.0

Letter Recognition S/s

Uppercase and Lowercase Letter

✓ **Lesson Check Point**

Directions: Read each target word. Read the words in the row and circle the word that begins with a different letter.
지도: 각 대상 단어를 읽으십시오. 행에 있는 단어를 읽고 다른 문자로시 작하는 단어에 동그라미를 치십시오.

Target Words				
1. son	since	cash	skate	scale
2. snow	sketch	shell	seek	chick
3. shape	zoo	sell	shrub	soar
4. sheet	smile	save	slip	mother
5. search	seem	shade	corn	school

Directions: Read the words in the four boxes. Circle two words that start with the uppercase and lowercase letter "s."
지도: 네 개의 상자에 있는 단어를 읽으십시오. 대문자와 소문자"s"로 시작하는 두 단어에 동그라미를 치십시오.

court	Sharp
grows	sour

slash	Sale
zipper	Clash

Zoo	silk
Share	clock

house	clowns
Size	sew

shark	cord
Snow	zebra

show	vases
zero	Snore

Name: _____ Date: ___/___/_____ Score: _____

Appendix 20.0

Introduction of the Letter T/t

✓ **Lesson Check Point**

 Directions: Circle the correct letter "t" pair: uppercase and lowercase letters.
지도: 올바른 문자"t" 쌍에 동그라미를 치십시오: 대문자와 소문자.

| Tl | tZ | tJ | Tt | Tk |

 Directions: The uppercase letter "T" is in the first column. Look at the four letters in the row and circle the lowercase letter that matches the uppercase letter "T."
지도: 대문자"T"는 첫 번째 열에 있습니다. 행의 네 글자를 보고 대문자 "T"와 일치하는 소문자에 동그라미를 치십시오.

T	j	l	t	h
T	l	f	b	t
T	t	h	f	d
T	j	l	t	f

 Directions: The lowercase letter "t" is in the first column. Look at the four letters in the row and circle the uppercase letter that matches the lowercase letter "t."
지도: 소문자"t"는 첫 번째 열에 있습니다. 행의 네 글자를 보고 소문자 "t"와 일치하는 대문자에 동그라미를 치세요.

t	H	T	J	A
t	L	K	L	T
t	T	A	X	L
t	Y	F	T	H

Name: _____ Date: ___/___/_____ Score: _____

Appendix 20.0

Letter Recognition T/t

Uppercase and Lowercase Letter

✓ **Lesson Check Point**

Directions: Read each target word. Read the words in the row and circle the word that begins with a different letter.
지도: 각 대상 단어를 읽으십시오. 행에 있는 단어를 읽고 다른 문자로시작하는 단어에 동그라미를 치십시오.

Target Words				
1. turn	thirst	fool	train	thorn
2. tool	touch	trunk	love	tent
3. tank	than	tenth	tang	help
4. them	tap	tour	drip	thank
5. truck	hope	tray	third	tare

Directions: Read the words in the four boxes. Circle two words that start with the uppercase and lowercase letter "t."
지도: 네 개의 상자에 있는 단어를 읽으십시오. 대문자와 소문자"t"로 시작하는 두 단어에 동그라미를 치십시오.

Thanks	term
lick	Fine

Phone	trace
Toy	home

Left	Tart
boat	tint

Twirl	keen
Rain	tube

trail	leaf
Tone	fun

Kind	dock
Tub	take

Learn To Read English With Directions In Korean

Name: _____ Date: ___/___/_____ Score: _____

Appendix 21.0

Introduction of the Letter U/u

✓ **Lesson Check Point**

 Directions: Circle the correct letter "u" pair: uppercase and lowercase letters.
지도: 올바른 문자"u" 쌍에 동그라미를 치십시오: 대문자와 소문자.

    Yu   Uu   Vu   Ou   vU

 Directions: The uppercase letter "U" is in the first column. Look at the four letters in the row and circle the lowercase letter that matches the uppercase letter "U."
지도: 대문자"U"는 첫 번째 열에 있습니다. 행의 네 글자를 보고 대문자 "U"와 일치하는 소문자에 동그라미를 치십시오.

U	j	s	u	v
U	o	g	h	u
U	u	k	v	o
U	v	r	o	u

 Directions: The lowercase letter "u" is in the first column. Look at the four letters in the row and circle the uppercase letter that matches the lowercase letter "u."
지도: 소문자"u"는 첫 번째 열에 있습니다. 행의 네 글자를 보고 소문자 "u"와 일치하는 대문자에 동그라미를 치세요.

u	U	V	C	X
u	Z	C	U	V
u	Y	E	V	U
u	T	U	N	O

Name: _____ Date:___/___/_____ Score:_____

Appendix 22.0

Introduction of the Letter V/v

✓ **Lesson Check Point**

 Directions: Circle the correct letter "v" pair: uppercase and lowercase letters.
지도: 올바른 문자"v" 쌍에 동그라미를 치십시오: 대문자와 소문자.

    Cv   Uv   Vv   Xv   Vk

 Directions: The uppercase letter "V" is in the first column. Look at the four letters in the row and circle the lowercase letter that matches the uppercase letter "V."
지도: 대문자"V"는 첫 번째 열에 있습니다. 행의 네 글자를 보고 대문자 "V"와 일치하는 소문자에 동그라미를 치십시오.

V	u	v	x	y
V	v	u	n	s
V	c	b	v	x
V	m	v	u	z

 Directions: The lowercase letter "v" is in the first column. Look at the four letters in the row and circle the uppercase letter that matches the lowercase letter "v."
지도: 소문자"v"는 첫 번째 열에 있습니다. 행의 네 글자를 보고 소문자 "v"와 일치하는 대문자에 동그라미를 치세요.

v	X	Y	T	V
v	T	V	U	M
v	V	Y	X	S
v	J	F	V	Z

Name: _____ Date: ___/___/_____ Score: _____

Appendix 22.0

Letter Recognition V/v

Uppercase and Lowercase Letter

✓ **Lesson Check Point**

 Directions: Read each target word. Read the words in the row and circle the word that begins with a different letter.
지도: 각 대상 단어를 읽으십시오. 행에 있는 단어를 읽고 다른 문자로시 작하는 단어에 동그라미를 치십시오.

Target Words				
1. vine	went	view	vogue	verb
2. vault	vent	volt	March	vague
3. vow	keys	vein	vest	vane
4. vamp	valve	water	vote	versed
5. voiced	vile	void	vouch	walk

 Directions: Read the words in the four boxes. Circle two words that start with the uppercase and lowercase letter "v."
지도: 네 개의 상자에 있는 단어를 읽으십시오. 대문자와 소문자"v"로 시작하는 두 단어에 동그라미를 치십시오.

mean	van
worm	Verse

Vase	sour
root	veil

force	Voice
verge	Wept

Vain	apple
visit	cost

veto	Vice
wake	neck

white	raise
Vex	veer

Name: _____ Date: ___/___/_____ Score: _____

Appendix 23.0

Introduction of the Letter W/w

✓ Lesson Check Point

 Directions: Circle the correct letter "w" pair: uppercase and lowercase letters.
지도: 올바른 문자"w" 쌍에 동그라미를 치십시오: 대문자와 소문자.

wV   Ww   Uw   Wv   Yw

 Directions: The uppercase letter "W" is in the first column. Look at the four letters in the row and circle the lowercase letter that matches the uppercase letter "W."
지도: 대문자"W"는 첫 번째 열에 있습니다. 행의 네 글자를 보고 대문자 "W"와 일치하는 소문자에 동그라미를 치십시오.

W	v	w	x	y
W	u	t	c	w
W	w	u	v	m
W	n	y	w	f

 Directions: The lowercase letter "w" is in the first column. Look at the four letters in the row and circle the uppercase letter that matches the lowercase letter "w."
지도: 소문자"w"는 첫 번째 열에 있습니다. 행의 네 글자를 보고 소문자 "w"와 일치하는 대문자에 동그라미를 치세요.

w	V	M	W	N
w	U	W	V	A
w	W	X	C	M
w	X	V	Y	W

Name: _____ Date: ___/___/_____ Score: _____

Appendix 23.0

Letter Recognition W/w

Uppercase and Lowercase Letter

✓ Lesson Check Point

Directions: Read each target word. Read the words in the row and circle the word that begins with a different letter.
지도: 각 대상 단어를 읽으십시오. 행에 있는 단어를 읽고 다른 문자로 시작하는 단어에 동그라미를 치십시오.

Target Words				
1. what	wedge	wrist	mugs	write
2. wire	which	warm	wreck	voyage
3. wear	warn	noon	wound	went
4. wages	while	wise	weak	Mouse
5. wheeze	vowel	waist	wipe	wrest

Directions: Read the words in the four boxes. Circle two words that start with the uppercase and lowercase letter "w."
지도: 네 개의 상자에 있는 단어를 읽으십시오. 대문자와 소문자 "w"로 시작하는 두 단어에 동그라미를 치십시오.

want	Nail
Wig	video

Match	Where
wrong	None

With	whack
Merge	Vision

Mud	Verdict
whim	Wart

Nuts	wrung
volcano	White

Wool	Volume
Noise	wet

Name: _____ Date: ___/___/_____ Score: _____

Appendix 24.0

Introduction of the Letter X/x

✓ **Lesson Check Point**

 Directions: Circle the correct letter "x" pair: uppercase and lowercase letters.
지도: 올바른 문자"x" 쌍에 동그라미를 치십시오: 대문자와 소문자.

| Xz | Kx | Xx | xY | Xk |

 Directions: The uppercase letter "X" is in the first column. Look at the four letters in the row and circle the lowercase letter that matches the uppercase letter "X."
지도: 대문자"X"는 첫 번째 열에 있습니다. 행의 네 글자를 보고 대문자 "X"와 일치하는 소문자에 동그라미를 치십시오.

X	x	y	z	s
X	v	x	k	y
X	u	z	a	x
X	x	v	k	z

 Directions: The lowercase letter "x" is in the first column. Look at the four letters in the row and circle the uppercase letter that matches the lowercase letter "x."
지도: 소문자"x"는 첫 번째 열에 있습니다. 행의 네 글자를 보고 소문자 "x"와 일치하는 대문자에 동그라미를 치세요.

x	K	X	Z	V
x	B	K	V	X
x	X	V	U	Y
x	Y	X	K	F

Name: _____ Date:___/___/_____ Score:_____

Appendix 24.0

Letter Recognition X/x

Uppercase and Lowercase Letter

✓ Lesson Check Point

 Directions: Read each target word. Read the words in the row and circle the word that does not contain a letter "x."
지도: 각 대상 단어를 읽으십시오. 행에 있는 단어를 읽고 문자 "x"가 포함되지 않은 단어에 동그라미를 치십시오.

Target Words				
1. axed	vamp	ox	mixing	annex
2. tax	taxi	waxy	cooks	flex
3. max	exit	Texas	yes	reflex
4. mix	next	sixth	foxes	cents
5. extra	toxic	fax	boxes	goats

 Directions: Read the words in the four boxes. Circle two words that start with the uppercase and lowercase letter "x."
지도: 네 개의 상자에 있는 단어를 읽으십시오. 대문자와 소문자 "x"로 시작하는 두 단어에 동그라미를 치십시오.

extra	x-ray
Xylan	vote

cortex	excel
Xylene	xanthate

kind	xenon
vault	Xerox

xeric	Xanadu
kale	nail

x-axis	yours
Xylose	knit

Xiphoid	out
mean	xanthoma

Name: _____ Date: ___/___/_____ Score: _____

Appendix 25.0

Introduction of the Letter Y/y

✓ **Lesson Check Point**

 Directions: Circle the correct letter "y" pair: uppercase and lowercase letters.
지도: 올바른 문자"y" 쌍에 동그라미를 치십시오: 대문자와 소문자.

    Yg   Yy   Jy   Yj   Xy

 Directions: The uppercase letter "Y" is in the first column. Look at the four letters in the row and circle the lowercase letter that matches the uppercase letter "Y."
지도: 대문자"Y"는 첫 번째 열에 있습니다. 행의 네 글자를 보고 대문자 "Y"와 일치하는 소문자에 동그라미를 치십시오.

Y	j	y	x	p
Y	y	g	j	l
Y	g	q	y	j
Y	j	y	g	v

 Directions: The lowercase letter "y" is in the first column. Look at the four letters in the row and circle the uppercase letter that matches the lowercase letter "y."
지도: 소문자"y"는 첫 번째 열에 있습니다. 행의 네 글자를 보고 소문자 "y"와 일치하는 대문자에 동그라미를 치세요.

y	F	G	Y	X
y	Y	L	M	J
y	B	C	X	Y
y	Y	L	Z	G

Name: _____ Date:___/___/_____ Score:_____

Appendix 25.0

Letter Recognition Y/y

Uppercase and Lowercase Letter

✓ Lesson Check Point

Directions: Read each target word. Read the words in the row and circle the word that begins with a different letter.
지도: 각 대상 단어를 읽으십시오. 행에 있는 단어를 읽고 다른 문자로시작하는 단어에 동그라미를 치십시오.

Target Words				
1. yoke	yield	year	quick	y-axis
2. yeast	peace	yeast	yard	yes
3. yonder	yam	yonder	yak	great
4. Yankee	basket	yuppie	yolk	yo-yo
5. younger	yap	group	yogurt	yonder

Directions: Read the words in the four boxes. Circle two words that start with the uppercase and lowercase letter "y."
지도: 네 개의 상자에 있는 단어를 읽으십시오. 대문자와 소문자"y"로 시작하는 두 단어에 동그라미를 치십시오.

Yacht	paid		yield	good		jean	yoke
yes	glimpse		jog	Year		quit	Your

yeast	Yikes		purse	yoga		juice	glue
group	joke		Yard	joint		Yon	young

Learn To Read English With Directions In Korean

Name: _____ Date:___/___/_____ Score: _____

Appendix 26.0

Introduction of the Letter Z/z

✓ Lesson Check Point

 Directions: Circle the correct letter "z" pair: uppercase and lowercase letters.
지도: 올바른 문자"z" 쌍에 동그라미를 치십시오: 대문자와 소문자.

zX　　　　Zz　　　　Yz　　　　Zv　　　　zF

 Directions: The uppercase letter "Z" is in the first column. Look at the four letters in the row and circle the lowercase letter that matches the uppercase letter "Z."
지도: 대문자"Z"는 첫 번째 열에 있습니다. 행의 네 글자를 보고 대문자 "Z"와 일치하는 소문자에 동그라미를 치십시오.

Z	z	c	x	y
Z	x	t	z	g
Z	c	g	s	z
Z	y	h	z	a

 Directions: The lowercase letter "z" is in the first column. Look at the four letters in the row and circle the uppercase letter that matches the lowercase letter "z."
지도: 소문자"z"는 첫 번째 열에 있습니다. 행의 네 글자를 보고 소문자 "z"와 일치하는 대문자에 동그라미를 치세요.

z	D	Z	X	C
z	Z	C	V	N
z	M	G	B	Z
z	Z	N	W	X

Name: _____ Date: ___/___/_____ Score: _____

Appendix 26.0

Letter Recognition Z/z

Uppercase and Lowercase Letter

✓ Lesson Check Point

Directions: Read each target word. Read the words in the row and circle the word that begins with a different letter.
지도: 각 대상 단어를 읽으십시오. 행에 있는 단어를 읽고 다른 문자로시작하는 단어에 동그라미를 치십시오.

Target Words				
1. zero	zillion	zone	zeal	sold
2. zebras	zag	wear	zip	zygote
3. zinger	vase	zodiac	zoo	zipper
4. zenith	zinc	zonal	suit	zig
5. zoning	zoom	school	zany	zinc

Directions: Read the words in the four boxes. Circle two words that start with the uppercase and lowercase letter "z."
지도: 네 개의 상자에 있는 단어를 읽으십시오. 대문자와 소문자"z"로 시작하는 두 단어에 동그라미를 치십시오.

swing	Nose
Zillion	zero

sugar	zeal
wet	Zebra

zinger	Zoo
strive	water

zig	stream
Zebu	wing

sweet	Zone
zap	mouse

Never	swan
Ziti	zinc

Your Next Step:
Learn To Read English Vowels With Directions In Korean

www.ingramcontent.com/pod-product-compliance
Lightning Source LLC
Chambersburg PA
CBHW080800300426
44114CB00020B/2776